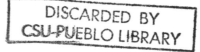

LATIN AMERICAN HISTORICAL DICTIONARIES SERIES
Edited by A. Curtis Wilgus

1. Moore, Richard E. *Guatemala*. rev. ed. 1973.

2. Hedrick, Basil C. & Anne K. *Panama*. 1970.

3. Rudolph, Donna Keyse & G. A. *Venezuela*. 1971.

4. Heath, Dwight B. *Bolivia*. 1972.

5. Flemion, Philip F. *El Salvador*. 1972.

6. Meyer, Harvey K. *Nicaragua*. 1972.

7. Bizzarro, Salvatore. *Chile*. 1972.

8. Kolinski, Charles J. *Paraguay*. 1973.

Historical Dictionary of Guatemala

Revised edition

by
RICHARD E. MOORE

Latin American Historical Dictionaries, No. 1

The Scarecrow Press, Inc.
Metuchen, N. J.   1973

R
F 1462
M 8
1973

Library of Congress Cataloging in Publication Data

Moore, Richard E   1932-
    Historical dictionary of Guatemala.

    (Latin American historical dictionaries, no. 1)
    Bibliography: p.
    1. Guatemala--History--Dictionaries. I. Title.
F1462.M6 1973   917.281'03'03   73-2828
ISBN 0-8108-0604-5

Dedicated to

Miguel Ángel Asturias

Editor's Foreword

The first edition of this Dictionary was a pioneering venture for librarians and students of Latin America and it supplemented other books about Guatemala including Who's Who compilations and encyclopedias. When Professor Moore suggested this book to Ralph Shaw, then president of Scarecrow Press, the proposal was readily accepted and the volume was soon published. The idea naturally followed of providing a series of such guides to individual Latin American countries, which Dr. Shaw then asked me to organize--to locate and invite compilers and to serve as General Editor. Shortly, efforts began to bear fruit and the Series was on its way.

Being a pioneer is not an entirely new role for Professor Moore, especially in the field of library administration and management. He was born in Abilene, Kansas in 1932. After completing high school he served in Korea (1951-54) in the United States Navy. In 1958 he obtained a B. A. degree at Ft. Hays (Kansas) State College with a major in history and literature. His interest in Latin American history led to a M. A. degree at the University of Kansas with a thesis concerned with Guatemala. This necessitated research in that country, and while there he studied anthropology at the University of San Carlos. Meanwhile, his desire to become a practicing librarian moved him to take another M. A. degree, this time in library science at the University of Oklahoma. Since then his library interests have been paramount. He has served as librarian at the University of Iowa (1962-64), at Portland State University (1964-65), at the University of California at Santa Cruz (1965-68), and at Southern Oregon College since 1968, where he has been technical services librarian, acting library director, and associate library director, which position he now holds.

Professor Moore has been a leading participant in a variety of local, state and regional library activities. He has served as treasurer of the Pacific Northwest Library Association and is now the editor of its Quarterly. He is president of the Southern Oregon Library Federation which publishes bibliographies and bibliographical guides. He has served on several committees of the Oregon Library Association and has been a member of the Oregon State Library Advisory Board and a member of the Oregon Book Society Advisory Board. His many activities have attracted the attention of the editors of the Biographical Dictionary of Librarians and the Directory of Latin Americanists in the United States, in both of which his biography appears.

Between these tasks Professor Moore still has time for research and publication. He collects books, especially on Guatemala, and when the opportunity affords he relaxes as a mountain climber. He is married and has two children.

In the first edition of his Dictionary Professor Moore set a pattern which has been largely followed by other contributors to the Series. With this revised and enlarged edition he has extended still further his contribution to the understanding of this small but important Latin American country.

A. Curtis Wilgus
Emiritus Director
School of Inter-American Studies
University of Florida

Introduction

The revised edition of the Historical Dictionary of Guatemala is an attempt at refining the earlier edition to make this a more useful basic guide to information about Guatemala. To do so, several of the categories of different types of information have been expanded--for example the biographical sketches now include more living Guatemalan newsmakers; geographical place names have been added, and more historical persons and events are included. Statistical information, e.g. population figures, has been up-dated. Beyond this, a second part consisting of a bibliographical essay on colonial resources and an annotated bibliography of material on present day and historical Guatemala has been substituted for the bibliography appearing in the earlier edition.

The basic arrangement of the Dictionary remains alphabetical with frequent cross references for variant spellings, initials, etc. Persons included are native Guatemalans with the exception of colonial leaders from the Spanish Empire. Also, there are included numerous persons from other parts of Central America who, frequently, consider themselves Guatemalan.

Whenever possible, birth and death dates have been included. Often one or both dates can not be confirmed and, in those cases, the date is left off. Important events for each person are included; for writers this includes a listing of their more important writings.

Place names have been taken from the Diccionario geográfico de Guatemala (1962/63). All population statistics have been taken from the 1964 census, second edition, published in 1969 under the title Algunos caracteristicas de la población de Guatemala, 1964, resultados de tabulación manual by the Dirección General de Estadística of Guatemala. Also added are population projections by department up to 1980 made by the Consejo Nacional de Planificación Económica.

Part II of this book, the Bibliographical Guide, is an attempt to bring together reference material from many disciplines. This will enable the user of the Dictionary to go beyond the information given, since many of the items listed were resource items for the Dictionary. All the titles included in the guide were inspected by the compiler to ensure an accurate description and for assurance that the books selected were useful source books. There were many items that appeared to be excellent resource items that are not included because the compiler was unable to procure a copy to inspect.

The items included in the guide were evaluated on their relevance for Guatemalan studies, their reliability, quantity of material, and general ease of use.

Large general sources that do not devote a significant portion to Guatemala have not been included, unless it was felt that the source was too important to pass over, as example the Handbook of Latin American Studies or the Bancroft Library Catalogue. Brief annotations are included to give the general scope of the work, as well as some indication of the arrangement and usefulness. The items in the guide have been indexed by subject and author. This index does not include items from the first part making up the Dictionary.

Latin America has too often been handled as a single area and this has generated various guides of a general nature. Persons interested in one specific area, like Guatemala, have had to glean bits and pieces from numerous guides, many of which are less than useful. The serious researcher needs first to become a bibliographer, then a subject specialist. This Dictionary and guide addresses itself to supplying a basic amount of information on one geographical area; it then provides a guide to other information in the event the user wishes to go beyond basic information.

Part I

HISTORICAL DICTIONARY

A. A.   see   ASOCIACIÓN DE AZUCAREROS.

A. E. D.   see   ASOCIACIÓN DE ESTUDIANTES DE DERECHO.

A. F. G.   see   ALIANZA FEMENINA GUATEMALTECA.

A. G. A.   see   ASOCIACIÓN GENERAL DE AGRICULTORES.

A. G. S. A.   see   ALGODONERA GUATEMALTECA, S. A.

A. G. U. A. P. A.   see   ASOCIACIÓN GUATEMALTECA DE
PRODUCTORES DE ALGODÓN.

A. J. D. G.   see   ALIANZA DE LA JUVENTUD DEMOCRATI-
CA DE GUATEMALA.

A. N. A. C. A. F. E.   see   ASOCIACIÓN NACIONAL DE CAFÉ.

A. N. F. A. L.   see   ASOCIACIÓN NACIONAL DE FABRI-
CANTES DE ALCOHOL Y LIQUORES.

ABASCAL, VALENTÍN, 1908- .   An instructor in public
schools and an artist, he was born in Escuintla.   In
addition, he has written Tierra nuestra (1935) Kukulcan (1939), Estampas de la Antigua (1943), and Santiago de los Caballeros de Goathemala (1961).

ABATE CAUSERIE, EL [pseudonym]   see   RODRIGUEZ
CERNA, CARLOS

ABAUNZA, ALVARO GOMEZ DE.   Acting governor of Guatemala, 1596-1598.

ABBOTSVILLE.   A town located in the old department of
Verapaz on the Río Polochic.   It was founded in 1836
by the Eastern Coast of Central America Commercial
and Agricultural Company, a British firm.   The firm

9

obtained a grant to the entire province of Verapaz,
some 14 million acres, and settled there about three
hundred immigrants, primarily from the poorer classes of London. Although the area was then sparsely
settled, the Indians looked upon the settlers as heretics
and usurpers, and the settlers were unable to acclimate
to the country. The management of the company was
inefficient and dishonest, and expected support from
the British government was not forthcoming. As a result, the settlement disintegrated in two years and the
charter was forfeited. The episode proved costly for
the liberal regime of Governor Mariano Gálvez, as it
added to the bitterness the poorer classes held toward
his reform government.

ABULARACH, RODOLFO, 1933- . Born in Guatemala City,
he is an artist who studied under González Goyri and
in California and Mexico. He began as an architectural student and now has art displayed in New York,
São Paulo, Guatemala, La Paz and the Pan American
Union in Washington, D. C. In 1967 he had six one-
man shows and was involved in several group shows.

ACADEMIA GUATEMALTECA. Founded in 1888 with the
purpose of furthering Guatemalan letters. Membership
is by election and is reserved for leading men of letters. Their tradition has been the encouragement of
Guatemalan studies, both historical and literary.

ACASAGUASTLÁN see SAN AGUSTÍN ACASAGUASTLÁN;
SAN CRISTOBAL ACASAGUASTLÁN.

ACATENANGO. Municipio in the department of Chimaltenango in south central Guatemala. The cabecera is
located at the northwestern foot of the volcano,
Acatenango, ten miles southwest of Chimaltenango.
Fuego Volcano can be reached from here. Population:
9254. Altitude: 5499 ft. Crops: coffee, grain,
sugar cane, henequen; livestock.

ACATENANGO VOLCANO. Altitude: 12, 992 ft. Located in
south central Guatemala on the Sacatapéquez-Chimal-
tenango border. It is north of Fuego Volcano and ten
miles west-southwest of Antigua. It has three craters,
one of which emits gasses. Last eruption was in 1925.

ACCIÓN CATÓLICA RURAL. Began as an agency of Acción
Católica to train and coordinate rural leaders for work

in the church. By using local leaders, the church can
communicate doctrine to a larger number of persons
than the priests are able to reach.

ACEÑA DURÁN, RAMÓN, 1898-1945. A newspaperman,
pharmacist and author, he was editor-in-chief of Ex-
celsior from 1921-24 and Diario de Guatemala, in
1930. He was later editor of Revista Universitaria and
Boletín Oficial de Ciencias Naturales y Farmacia. His
writings are primarily satirical and humoristic and fol-
low the modernistic school. They include El ensueño
del surtidor and Tierras floridas (1921), Estampas
desvaidas, Noderias (1925), Parque galante (1927), and
Tiruliro (1926). Pseudonyms: Cándido, El Principe
Féliz, Jacinto Galeón.

ACHIGUATE RIVER see GUACALATE RIVER.

ACHIOTE. A red dye used as food coloring. In colonial
days and earlier, it was a favorite paint for body decor
in celebrations.

ACINTAL see ASINTAL, EL.

ACTA CONSTITUTIVA DE 1851. Guatemala's fundamental
law for 20 years. Under it, the President was to
serve four years, elected by the Chamber of Deputies,
the Council of State, the justices of the Supreme Court
and the Archbishop. Suffrage was extended to male
citizens who were 25 years of age, or 21 and married,
who could read and write. The author of the Acta was
Luis Batres. The Acta was amended in 1854 to allow
Carrera to serve for life and to name his own success-
or. In 1855, it was broadened to permit the president
to initiate legislation and appoint council members without restriction.

ACTA DE PATZICIA. Proclamation of 3 June 1871 by
Justo Rufino Barrios and Miguel García Granados, de-
posing Vicente Cerna from power, appointing Granados
as provisional president, and calling for a constitutional assembly.

ACUÑA, DIEGO DE. Governor of Guatemala from 1626 to
1633.

ADELANTADO. The most important official in newly acquired territory, who usually held the title of governor

until the arrival of the viceroy. There were several
levels of power, as follows: adelantado mayor, governor with judicial, administrative and military power;
adelantado menor or fronterizo, often appointed by a
governor to act as military head at outposts in distant
regions; adelantado de la corte or del rey, official representative of the king; adelantado del mar, entrusted
to those in command of an expedition, granting them
the title of governor of the territories discovered or
conquered by them.

ADELANTO, EL. Municipio located in the department of
Jutiapa in highland southeast Guatemala. The cabecera
is south-southeast of Jutiapa. Population: 3325.
Altitude: 3300 ft. Crops: corn, beans; livestock.

AGRARIAN REFORM see LEY DE REFORMA AGRARIA.

AGUA BLANCA. Municipio located in the department of
Jutiapa in the southeast highlands of Guatemala. The
cabecera is 22 miles northeast of Jutiapa. Population:
10, 973. Crops: corn, beans; livestock.

AGUA VOLCANO. Altitude: 12, 310 ft. Located in south
central Guatemala, eight miles south of Antigua.
Guided tours to the top leave from Santa María on its
northeast base. Thought to have been active in 1541
and to have contributed to the destruction of the capital,
Almolonga, now called Ciudad Vieja.

AGUACATÁN. Municipio located in the department of Hue-
huetenángo in western Guatemala. The cabecera is in
the Cuchumatanes Mountains, 11 miles east of Huehuetenango. Local market center; textile milling. Population: 14, 691. Altitude: 5128 ft. Crops: rice,
avocados.

AGUACATEC. A linguistic group of the Mamean, located in
Huehuetenango.

AGUARDIENTE. A strong rum made from brown cane sugar.

AGUAS AMARGAS. Hot springs resort located in the depart-
ment of Quezaltenango, between San Felipe and Zunil.
Its natural hot springs flow from the inactive volcano,
Santo Tomás.

AGUECHE, Francisco.   An influential priest under Carrera.
    After Carrera's initial successful revolt, Agueche per-
    suaded him to continue his revolutionary activity.   Af-
    ter Carrera became president, he became a chief ad-
    visor.

AGUILAR, OCTAVIO, 1894-1962.   A jurist and mystery
    writer.   Works: Código de procedimientos civiles
    (1930), El juez Olaverri (novel, 1944), and Juan Ca-
    nastuj (novel, 1944).

AGUILAR, SINFOROSO, 1891-1949.   A journalist and poet,
    he founded the daily El Demócrata and weekly La Na-
    ción, 1920; was a member of the Boundary Commis-
    sion with Honduras, 1931-33; chief of the International
    Press Office from 1933 to 1945.   Author of El parque
    ensoñador (1921), Esfumes de opalo (1921), and Tem-
    plos abandonados y otros poemas (1923).   Pseudonyms:
    Ixto Xipate, Xavier de Ximenez.

AGUILAR GIRON, JOSÉ IGNACIO, 1920-1961.   A Guatemal-
    an agronomist and veterinarian, his works include
    Pinos de Guatemala (1953), Estudio de plantas forra-
    jesas en Guatemala (1944), La fiebre aftosa (1947), and
    Forrajes y plantas forrajeras (1946).

AGUIRRE, JUAN DE.   A 16th-century Franciscan monk
    noted for his carved wooden statues.   Best examples
    of his work are found in Quezaltenango in the churches,
    Jesús de la Candelaria and Justo Juez, as well as in
    several churches in Guatemala City and Antigua.

AGUIRRE VELÁSQUEZ, EDUARDO, 1881-1941.   A medical
    doctor, he wrote Contribución al estudio de la lepre,
    Discurso pronunciado en representación de la prensa
    (1909), and Refutación Febrero de 1922.

AGURTO Y ALVA, JUAN MIGUEL DE.   Governor of Guate-
    mala, 1682-1684; he led an unsuccessful power struggle
    against the Cabildo over appointments of office holders.

AHIJADO.   Child for whom an adult is a padrino or god-
    parent.   A padrino may have several children or ahija-
    dos in different families.   See also PADRINO.

AIRE (Evil Wind).   An Indian belief that an evil wind can in-
    vade the body of a weakened person and bring about an

illness.   The evil wind may emanate accidentally from
an unclean or sick person or it may be induced through
black magic by an enemy.

AJIT.   A young shaman who is not allowed to fully participate in the more elaborate rituals until he has more
fully proved his powers.   See also SHAMAN.

ALCABALA.   A colonial sales and turnover tax collected at
the custom houses whether or not the goods were actually sold.   Next to tobacco, this was the most fruit-
ful source of revenue for the crown.   It was first introduced in 1574 at 2 per cent, then doubled in 1632
to help pay for forces needed to protect America.
In 1635, another 2 per cent was added to the tax.   Between 1644 and 1754 and between 1780 and 1790, the
rate was 8 per cent.   The tax remains a major source
of revenue, although since then it has tended to be a
slightly lower rate.

ALCALDE.   During the colonial period, the mayor and
judge.   Alcaldes mayores were royal appointees chosen
at the recommendation of the viceroy for a period of
three years.   Alcaldes ordinarios were elected officials in each town, to handle routine duties.   The
Alcalde de la hermandad was a police magistrate for
rural areas.   Alcalde de barrio was the ward or parish supervisor in larger towns.   During the national
period, the alcalde was the municipio political leader
appointed by the national government through the departmental governors.   Since 1944 the position has been
elective.

ALCÁNTARA, GERMÁN, 1863-1910.   Guatemalan musician,
director of the National Conservatory of Music.   Best
known for his composition La flor de café.

ALDEA.   A small settlement of lesser importance than a
pueblo.   It usually contains a church, a school and a
cemetery, although not necessarily all three.   It is
governed by the alcalde of the municipio in which the
aldea is located.

ALEAS, FERMÍN.   A Dominican who, in 1780, charged the
Universidad de San Carlos with irregular teaching
methods and corrupt ethics.   The charges were brought
before the king; the university proved the charges to be

false.   The king expressed his confidence in the university and reprimanded Aleas for making such serious charges without first investigating.

ALFARO, ALFONSO [pseudonym]   see BRAÑAS, CÉSAR.

ALGODONERA GUATEMALTECA, S. A.   (A. G. S. A.).
Founded in 1953 to promote the development of cotton
milling, it is now involved in all aspects of cotton production and serves as a political influence organization.

ALGUACIL.   A municipal servant who performs menial duties; often assists in local law enforcement on special
occasions.

ALGUACIL MAYOR.   The local constable in colonial Spanish America, a lucrative post often obtained by pur-
chase.

ALIANZA DE LA JUVENTUD DEMOCRÁTICA DE GUATE-
MALA   (A. J. D. G.).   Founded in 1947 as a non-politi-
cal youth group to appeal to rural and urban youth.   It
became politically active in the early 1950's, and was
disbanded in 1955.

ALIANZA FEMENINA GUATEMALTECA (A. F. G.).   An organization to promote political action, founded in 1947
by Señoras Arbenz and Fortuny.   They published a
monthly newsletter "Mujeras."   Inactive since 1954.

ALMIRANTE DE LA MAR DEL SUR.   Honorary title given
to Pedro de Alvarado by Emperor Carlos V in 1538.

ALMOLONGA.   1) Municipio in the department of Quezaltenango in southwestern Guatemala.   The cabecera is
located two miles southeast of Quezaltenango in the
Cerro Quemado Mountains.   Population: 5551.   Altitude: 6808 ft.   Crops: truck produce, grain.
2) The second capital of Guatemala, founded November 25, 1527, on the site now known as Ciudad Vieja,
at the foot of Agua Volcano.   The city was destroyed
on September 8, 1541.   There were several hundred
Spaniards killed and an indeterminable number of Indians, possibly in the thousands.   The Spanish casualties
included Doña Beatriz de la Cueva, acting governor who
had taken control of the government at the death of her

husband, Pedro de Alvarado. Accounts of the destruction vary as to the cause. One version accepted by
many authorities is that hard, driving rains caused
streams to swell to the point of flooding, and this,
plus an earthquake, did the damage. At any rate,
there was no attempt to rebuild the town. The seat of
government was moved to a nearby valley and located
at the present city of Antigua.

ALMUD. An instrument for volume measurement which
holds about 12 and 1/2 pounds of goods; it is primarily
used in measuring grain.

ALOTENANGO see SAN JUAN ALOTENANGO.

ALTA VERAPAZ. Department located in central Guatemala.
The capital, Cobán, is in the northern highlands of the
Sierra de Chama Mountains, which slope north into the
Petén lowlands. It is bounded on the West by the
Chixoy River and the South and East by the Sierra de
las Minas Mountains. The area is drained by the Polochic and Cahabón Rivers. Most income comes from
agriculture: coffee, corn, beans, sugar cane, cacao,
vanilla, tropical fruit, livestock, lumbering and chicle.
Coffee processing, matting, weaving, and pottery making are the local industries. The main trade route is
the Verapaz railroad between Pancajche and Panzos,
continued by the Polochic River. Chief urban centers
are Cobán, San Cristóbal, and Carcha. There are
fourteen municipios in this department: Chahal, Chisec,
Cobán, Lanquín, Panzos, San Cristóbal Verapaz, San
Juan Chamelco, San Miguel Tucuru, San Pedro Carcha,
Santa Cruz Verapaz, Santa María Cahabón, Senahu,
Tactic, Tamahu. Population in 1950 was 189,812; in
1964 it was 260,572. Projected to 1980 as 388,800.
Area: 3353 square miles.

ALTAGUMEA, HILARIO DE [pseudonym] see IRISARRI,
ANTONIO JOSÉ DE.

ALTAMIRANO Y VELASCO, FERNANDO DE, d. 1657. Governor from 1654 to 1657.

ALTOS, LOS. The departments of Sololá, Totonicapán, and
Quezaltenango declared themselves detached from Guatemala on January 31, 1838, and a sixth state of the federation was formed. The state was recognized by the

federation.   Marcelo Molina was elected president;
a constitution was drawn up, and an assembly was established.   The state was forcibly reincorporated into
Guatemala on January 29, 1840, by an army led by
Rafael Carrera.

ALTOS RAILWAY, LOS.   An electric railroad running from
   Quezaltenango to San Felipe in the Pacific lowlands.
   An electric dam was built at Santa María to supply
   power, and in 1912, work began on the railroad.   In
   order to build the route to the highlands, many bridges
   and tunnels were built and the line was not completed
   until 1930, at the cost of $8,478,379.   The railroad
   lasted four years, before floods and earthquakes dam-
   aged part of the line and caused the whole line to be
   closed.   Even at the peak of its performance, the revenue of the railroad did not match the expense of day-
   to-day operation.

ALVARADO, ALONSO DE, d. 1556.   Cousin of Pedro de
   Alvarado, he took part in the conquest of Mexico and
   Guatemala and went to Peru in 1534, where he served
   under Pizarro.

ALVARADO, DIEGO DE.   Cousin of Pedro de Alvarado, he
   was on the conquest of Mexico and Guatemala.   He was
   in charge of the garrison at Sacatepequez when the rebellion of 1526 broke out.   In 1534 he went to Peru
   and served under Pizarro.

ALVARADO, FRANCISCO DE.   A cousin of Pedro de Alvarado, he took part in the conquest of Mexico and Guatemala.

ALVARADO, GÓMEZ DE, d. 1542.   Brother of Pedro de
   Alvarado, he took part in the conquest.   He later went
   on to Peru with Pedro and joined the ranks of Almagro
   in 1534.   He was made a prisoner at Salinas, then re-
   leased by Pizarro.   He participated in the battle of
   Chupas under the standard of Vaca de Castro.   He died
   of an illness contracted at Chupas.

ALVARADO, GONZALO DE.   Brother of the conquistador,
   Pedro, and one of his captains.   Founder of the town
   of Gracias a Dios, he became mayor of Guatemala and
   later, in 1535, a regidor.   He settled near Gracias a
   Dios on land granted to him.   He was acting governor

of Guatemala when the rebellion of 1526 broke out, a
result of his order to force Indian children to dig for
gold.

ALVARADO, HERCULANO, 1873-1921. A Guatemalan musician and composer, he studied in Italy and in 1910
became director of the National Conservatory of Music. His best remembered compositions are Electra,
Nocturno, and Las tardes de Abril.

ALVARADO, HERNANDO, d. 1526. A cousin of Pedro de
Alvarado, who accompanied him on the conquest. He
was killed during the Indian rebellion of 1526 while
making an assault on the fortress at Jalpatagua.

ALVARADO, JORGE DE. Brother of Pedro de Alvarado, he
joined Pedro in Guatemala in 1527. He was often left
in command as governor of Guatemala while Pedro was
absent. In 1528 when Pedro was in Spain, Jorge supervised a more just redistribution of land among the
conquerors.

ALVARADO, JUAN DE. Illegitimate brother of Pedro de
Alvarado, he accompanied him on the conquest and was
later named second adelantado of Guatemala. He received an encomienda at Chiribito in New Spain.

ALVARADO, DOÑA LEONOR DE. Daughter of Pedro de
Alvarado and the Indian Princess, Doña Luisa Xicotenga Tecubalsi, she married one of Alvarado's chief
lieutenants, Pedro de Portocarrero. After he died in
1547, Doña Leonór married Francisco de la Cueva,
brother of Doña Beatriz de la Cueva de Alvarado.

ALVARADO, PEDRO DE, 1485?-1541. Born in Badajoz,
Spain, Alvarado went to the new world in 1510, where
he accompanied the Grijalva expedition to Yucatan, and
the Cortés expedition to Mexico in 1519. Alvarado
was in charge at Mexico City when the revolt broke
out that led to noche triste. In December, 1523, he
left to conquer Guatemala for Cortés. Although the
initial conquest was handled rather quickly, his continued cruelty kept him occupied with rebellions. The
two reports which Pedro de Alvarado sent back to
Cortés are the only eye-witness accounts of the Guatemalan conquest. After he organized the Spanish government of Guatemala, and made a trip to Spain, Al-

varado led an expedition to Peru in 1533-1534. Almagro met him and Alvarado sold his equipment and fleet
to Almagro for 100,000 castellanos. In 1540, he
started to lead an expedition of discovery in the South
Seas, but instead, agreed to help quell an Indian rebellion in Mexico. During an assault he was crushed
by a falling horse and died a few days later. Alvarado had married twice. His first wife was a niece
of the Duke of Albuquerque, Doña Francisca de la Cueva. She died in 1528, shortly after their marriage.
He married Doña Beatriz, his first wife's sister, while
in Spain in 1538.

ALVARADO CONTRERAS, PEDRO see ALVARADO, PED-
RO DE.

ALVARADO MONZÓN, BERNARDO, d. 1966. The labor union representative on the I.G.S.S. Board of Directors
under Arbenz and secretary of the Partido Guatemalteco de Trabajadores. Prior to his death, he was a
political advisor for guerilla leader, Luis Turcios.

ALVAREZ, JOSÉ MARÍA, 1777-1820. An authority on the Just-
inian Code, he was held in high respect by his con-
temporaries. He wrote the first Guatemalan text on
jurisprudence, Instituciones de derecho real de Castilla
y de Indias (1818), in addition to several other essays
on law.

ALVAREZ, OSCAR MIRÓN see MIRÓN ALVAREZ, OSCAR.

ALVAREZ ALFONSO ROSICA DE CALDAS, SEBASTIÁN, d.
1672. Governor from 1668 to 1670. He was arrested
in 1670 for presenting fraudulent evidence to support
the arrest of cabildo members charged with selling offices. Alvarez was investigated by a residencia but
died in 1672 before any formal conclusions were made.

ALVAREZ DE TOLEDO, JUAN BAUTISTA, 1655-1725.
Fourteenth Bishop of Guatemala and first creole bishop
of the country. Born in Antigua, he was an orphan
when he entered the Franciscan monastery. He later
earned a doctorate from the University of San Carlos
and established a nunnery for the Capuchin Order in
Antigua, but died before the first of the sisters arrived. His published works include El prelado Quer-
ubin, modelo de un perfecto provincial.

ALVAREZ OVALLE, RAFAEL, 1858-1946.   A Guatemalan
musician, he wrote the music for the national hymn
in 1897.

ALZATATE VOLCANO.   Altitude: 9020 ft.   Located in east
central Guatemala, 13 miles south-southwest of Jalapa.
San Carlos Alzatate is located at its southeastern base.

AMATES, LOS.   Municipio located in the department of
Izabal in eastern Guatemala.   The cabecera is on a
railroad and on the Motagua River, 45 miles southwest of Puerto Barrios.   Population: 30,601.   Crops:
bananas, grain; livestock, lumber.

AMATIQUE, BAY OF.   An inlet of the Caribbean Sea on the
Guatemala-British Honduras border.   Ten miles wide
and 25 miles long, it is bounded on the east by Cabo
de Tres Puntes.   Puerto Barrios is on the south shore,
Livingston, on the southwest shore at the mouth of
Río Dulce.   The Sarstoon and Moho Rivers empty into
the bay.   British Honduran ports on the northwest
shore are Baranco and Punta Gorda.

AMATITLÁN.   Municipio located in the department of Guatemala in south central Guatemala.   The cabecera is in
the central highlands at the west end of Lake Amatitlán, 14 miles southwest of Guatemala City.   A major
year-around resort, it was the capital of the department of Amatitlán until new districts were set up in
1934.   It was formerly a cochineal producing center;
wool milling is now found there.   Population: 19,729.
Altitude: 3871 ft.   Crops: sugar cane, coffee, grain,
fruit.

AMATITLÁN LAKE.   Volcanic lake in south central Guatemala, located 11 miles south-southwest of Guatemala
City.   It is seven miles long, three miles wide, and
about 130 feet deep.   Its inlet is the Villalobos River
on the northeast and its outlet, the Michatoya River,
where the town of Amatitlán is located.   A popular
summer and weekend resort for Guatemala City, hot
springs are on its southern shore.   Altitude: 4085 ft.

AMAYO VOLCANO.   Extinct volcano near Jutiapa.   Altitude: 3444 ft.

AMIGO DE LA PATRIA, EL.   vol. 1, no. 1 to vol. 2, no.

24 (6 October 1820 to 15 April 1822). Weekly published in Guatemala City by Manuel Arévalo.

AMOLÍN, PEDRO. A lieutenant of Pedro de Alvarado on
the conquest of Guatemala, second in command under
Pedro Portocarrero on the conquest of Chimaltenango
in 1526.

ANDA. A wooden frame with shafts, used for carrying images in processions. Usually borne on the shoulders
of men.

ANDRINO, JOSÉ ESCOLÁSTICO, 1837-1862. A Guatemalan
organist and composer. His works include Misa del
pilar, Sagrada escritura, Lejos de la patria, Brisas
guatemaltecas, and an opera, La mora generosa.

ANDRINO, MÁXIMO, 1805-1873. Considered the best violinist from Guatemala. He opened a school of music
in 1825. José Andrino was his son.

ANDUJAR, MARTÍN DE. A Spanish architect, he planned
the Cathedral in Antigua in 1669 and was involved in
several other buildings in Antigua.

ANGULO, PEDRO. A Dominican priest who accompanied
Bartolomé de Las Casas on his missions to Chiapas
and the Lacondón area.

ANNALS OF THE CAKCHIQUELES (Memorial of Tecpán-
Atitlán). Pre-colonial legends and history first put into writing in the late 16th century by Francisco Hernández Arana Xajila and Francisco Díaz Gebuta Quej,
descendants of the ruling Indian families. The Annals
trace the chronology of the ruling houses for the Cakchiquel nation.

ANTIGUA. The full name given this third capital city of
Guatemala by Charles V, on March 10, 1566, was "Muy
Noble y Muy Leal Ciudad de Santiago de los Caballeros
de Goathemala." The city was established in 1541 and
came to be a religious center of the first order, with
a population of 80,000. The Audiencia was moved to
Antigua in 1549 from Gracias a Dios, Honduras. Antigua was destroyed by an earthquake in 1773 and the
decision was made to move the capital to the plains
at the present location. The clergy never regained the

strength it held prior to the destruction of the monas-
teries and the religious colony at Antigua.   Today
many of the old ruins still stand; some have been destroyed, others restored.   An attempt is being made
by the government to retain the 18th-century atmos-
phere, with the ruins intact.

ANTIGUA GUATEMALA.   Municipio located in the department of Sacatepequez in south central Guatemala.   The
cabecera is in the central highlands and rests on the
Pensativo River, 15 miles west-southwest of Guatemala City.   Sulphur springs are nearby, as are also
the volcanoes, Agua, Fuego, and Acatenango.   Pottery
and metal making are its primary industries.   Population: 22,317.   Altitude: 5029 ft.   Crops: coffee,
sugar cane, grain, fodder grasses, fruit, vegetables.

ANTONELLI, JUAN BAUTISTA.   Spanish architect, he arrived in Guatemala in 1541, after the destruction of
Ciudad Vieja, to inspect and decide upon a new site
for the capital.   The sites considered were: Jalapa,
Las Vacas (the present site), Tianguecillo and Panchoy
(Antigua).   Antonelli was the city planner for Antigua.
His work there is considered to be the best conceived
plans in Spanish America.   He returned to Spain in
the late 16th century.

APOSTLE DE LOS INDIAS   see   LAS CASAS, BARTOLOMÉ
DE.

ARANA, FRANCISCO JAVIER, d. 1949.   A military leader
of the 1944 revolutionary triumvirate and later, chief
of the army.   He was assassinated in July, 1949, near
Lake Amatitlán, shortly after he had declared his in-
tention to run for president in 1950.

ARANA, TOMÁS IGNACIO DE, d. 1744.   A judge on the
Audiencia, he published a good description of the destructive earthquake of 1717.

ARANA OSORIO, CARLOS, 1918- .   Born in Barbarena,
Santa Rosa, he was elected President and took office
on 1 July, 1970.   Prior to becoming President, he
was military governor of Zacapa.   Relieved of his duties by the then President Méndez in 1968, he was appointed ambassador to Nicaragua.   He was nominated
by the M. L. N. , the political party of Castillo Armas.

ARANA XAJILA, FRANCISCO HERNÁNDEZ, d. 1582. see ANNALS OF THE CAKCHIQUELES.

ARAUJO Y RÍO, JUAN DE. Governor from 1748 to 1751.

ARBENZ GUZMÁN, JACOBO, 1913-1970. Member of the revolutionary triumvirate, 1944-45, he served as Minister of Defense under President Arévalo. He was elected President in 1951 and deposed in 1954 by the U.S. backed forces of Castillo Armas. His strong stand against foreign economic interests led to an agrarian reform program that caused him to clash with U.S. -based companies, and brought about his fall.

ARCE, MANUEL JOSÉ, 1786-1846. Elected provisional president of Central America by the national constituent assembly in July, 1823. He was installed as president by an election of the representative congress in April, 1825. In 1828, he resigned after civil war broke out between the federal troops and El Salvador. The struggle was over federal versus state powers.

ARCE Y VALLADARES, MANUEL JOSÉ, 1907- . Poet and newspaperman, born in Guatemala. He has been editor of Diario de Hoy in San Salvador since 1929. His poetry has been published in El dolor supremo (1926), Romances de la barriada (1938), and Canto a la ciudad Antigua Guatemala (1943).

ARCOS Y MORENO, ALONSO DE. Governor from 1754 until 1760. In 1756, troops were required to quell a riot over prohibition of liquor. His published decree, "Relación individual de las fiestas" (1759), discusses the resulting regulations.

ARENALES, EMILIO, 1923-1969. Lawyer and diplomat, he served as Foreign Minister under Méndez Montenegro and President of the United Nations General Assembly in 1968-69.

ARÉVALO, JUAN JOSÉ, 1904- . He received a doctorate in education from the Universidad de La Plata in 1934. After working in Guatemala he returned to Argentina. During the revolution of 1944, he was elected President with 85 per cent of the votes. His six years as President (1945-51) were full of controversy. After his term in office he left the country, to return in

1963, causing the fall of the Ydígoras government.
He was appointed Ambassador to France in 1970, only
to be relieved in 1972.   He has written several books
on his political philosophy, two translated to English:
The Shark and the Sardines (1961) and Anti-Kommu-
nism in Latin America (1963).

ARÉVALO, SEBASTIÁN DE, d. 1772.   A Franciscan printer
in Guatemala from 1727 to 1772.

ARÉVALO MARTÍNEZ, RAFAEL, 1884- .   The leading contemporary Guatemalan poet and novelist whose poetry
carries a religious flavor, mixed with sentiment and
irony.   He is noted for psycho-zoological novelettes,
particularly, El hombre que parecía un caballo (1915).
Influenced by Rubén Darío, he is considered one of the
outstanding authors of Latin America.   He is a past
director of the Biblioteca Nacional.   His works include
El mundo de los maharachias (1938), Hondura (1946),
La oficina de paz de Orolandia (1925), Manuel Aldano
(1922), Viaje a Ipanda (1939), and many others.

ARGÜELLO, SANTIAGO, 1872-1940.   A leading educator and
director of the Escuela Normal Central Para Varones,
among his works is La juventud que yo busco.   He was
Minister of Public Instruction in Nicaragua at the time
of his death.

ARIAS, GASPAR.   On the conquest with Pedro de Alvarado,
he was sent in 1529 to Honduras to meet the expedition
sent by Pedrarias Dávila from Panama, and was successful in getting the expedition to return without making any permanent settlements.

ARIAS, LUÍS FELIPE, 1876-1908.   A Guatemalan musician
and composer, he is best remembered for his compositions, Moresque and Himno de Minerva.

ARIAS MALDONADO, RODRIGO DE   see   LA CRUZ, ROD-
RIGO DE.

ARIEL [pseudonym]   see   VALLE, RAFAEL.

ARISTONDO, JUAN DE DIOS.   Eighteenth-century builder
and architect, he was named master architect of Antigua in 1741.

ARRIOLA, MANUEL YSMAEL, 1873-1927. A Guatemalan
historian, he wrote Etimologias nacionales (1925).

ARRIOLA, OSMUNDO, 1881-1939. A poet from Quezaltenango,
best known for the poems, La fuente del bosque and
El poema de las rosas. His poetry was simple and
dealt with Indian life. He was the leading poet of the
Mondonovist movement.

ARROBA. A unit of measurement equal to 25 libra (pounds)
or 11.5 kilograms.

ARROYO, JOSÉ. Architect and director of the construction
of the Cathedral in Guatemala City, partially responsible for the plans.

ARZU HERRARTE, JOSÉ, 1888-1944. Newspaperman; Chief
of Consular Business for Guatemala and second secretary to the Guatemalan Legation, Paris, 1922-31. His
writings include Pepe Batres íntimo (1940) and El
diálogo de los bostezos (1945). Pseudonym: O.S.
Juárez.

ASINTAL, EL. Municipio located in the department of
Retalhuleu in southwestern Guatemala. The cabecera
is in the Pacific piedmont area, four miles northwest
of Retalhuleu. Population: 9749. Crops: sugar cane,
cotton, corn, rice. Sometimes spelled Acintal.

ASOCIACIÓN COORDINADORA DE ASOCIACIONES REGION-
ALES DE CAFECULTORES DEL OCCIDENTE (C.A.
R.C.O.R.). A regional coffee growers association
formed in 1964 to represent San Marcos, Quezaltenango
and Suchitepéquez in A.N.A.C.A.F.E. to ensure a
larger export quota for members.

ASOCIACIÓN DE AZUCAREROS (A.A.). From 1931 to 1948
known as Consorcio Azucarero. Reformed in 1957 to
protect the interests of sugar refineries. It is a sub-
group of the Cámara de Industrias (C.I.).

ASOCIACIÓN DE ESTUDIANTES DE DERECHO (A.E.D.).
The association of law students having considerable national influence through its public debates, free legal
service to the poor, and its tradition of political leadership. It is a sub-group of the A.E.U.

ASOCIACIÓN DE MAESTROS DE ENSEÑANZA SECONDARIA. A non-affiliated union formed in Guatemala City in 1958. Led by Rodolfo Ortiz, the organization claimed 50 members in 1962.

ASOCIACIÓN DE MAESTROS DE ESCUELAS NOCTURNOS. Formed in 1961, with a membership of 150 in 1962, this non-affiliated teacher's union of Guatemala City was led by Guillermo Giorgis Tobas.

ASOCIACIÓN DE TELEGRAFISTAS Y RADIOTELEGRAFIS-TAS DE GUATEMALA (A. T. R. G.). A non-affiliated radio operator's union in Guatemala City, led by Ricardo A. Guerra. Membership in 1962 was six hundred.

ASOCIACIÓN GENERAL DE AGRICULTORES (A. G. A.). An association of finca owners which acts as a political pressure group at the capital. Founded in 1920, it was dissolved by Ubico, but was re-established in 1944. The A. G. A. fought the labor act of 1948 and the agrarian law in 1952. Although unsuccessful then, it has proven to be an effective voice in the economic policy of the government.

ASOCIACIÓN GUATEMALTECA DE PRODUCTORES DE ALGODÓN (A. G. U. A. P. A.). Formed in 1955 as a protective organization of cotton growers, it has no regulatory powers and tends to be ineffectual except in immediate crisis periods.

ASOCIACIÓN MUSICAL JUVENIL DE GUATEMALA. Formed in 1944 to procure improved music education in Guatemala through better facilities, more concerts and conferences, and the publication of the review Música, January, 1945+.

ASOCIACIÓN NACIONAL DE CAFÉ (A. N. A. C. A. F. E.). Originally part of the A. G. A. , it became a separate unit in 1960. It has achieved control over coffee exportation and receives a per-bag export fee to regulate export licenses, to represent Guatemala at international meetings, and to keep statistics on national coffee production.

ASOCIACIÓN NACIONAL DE FABRICANTES DE ALCOHOL Y LIQUORES (A. N. F. A. L.). Formed in 1950 to draw

up liquor laws and production control, it is now the
political spokesman for the liquor companies.

ASTURIAS, MIGUEL ÁNGEL, 1899- . A leading Guatemalan author and poet, he was for ten years a corre-
spondent in Europe for El Imparcial. He has since
written numerous novels which have been translated into German, French, English and several other languages. His best known works are: Leyendas de
Guatemala (1930), El papa verde (1954), El señor
presidente (1946), Hombres de maiz (1949), Viento
fuerte (1950), and Weekend en Guatemala (1956).
He won the Lenin Peace Prize in 1966, the Nobel
Prize for Literature in 1967 and has been an ambassador to several countries, including France, up until
1970. He now lives in Paris and continues to write.

ASUNCIÓN MITA. Municipio located in the department of
Jutiapa in southeastern Guatemala. In the highlands,
the cabecera is 13 miles east-northeast of Jutiapa, on
the Inter-American Highway. Indian burial mounds can
be found here. Population: 23,833. Crops: beans,
corn, cotton; livestock.

ATABAL. Indian musical drum, consisting of several small
drums of various sizes and played with flexible sticks.
The Atabal is often used to accompany Indian poetry or
stories.

ATESCATEMPA. Municipio located in the department of
Jutiapa in the southeastern highlands of Guatemala.
The cabecera is 12 miles southeast of Jutiapa, near
the El Salvador frontier. Population: 8289. Crops:
corn, beans, rice; livestock.

ATESCATEMPA LAKE. Located in southeastern Guatemala
near the Salvadoran border, four miles northeast of
the municipio of Atescatempa. The Atescatempa River
flows into the lake; there is no draining river. The
lake dried up in 1893 but filled again a few years
later. Depth: 25 feet.

ATITLÁN see SANTIAGO ATITLÁN.

ATITLÁN LAKE. Located in the southwest central highlands
of Guatemala, it is one of the most picturesque lakes
in Latin America. On its shores are the volcanoes

Atitlán and Toliman on the south and San Pedro and
Santa Clara on the southwest.   There are nine villages
on the lake shore, several accessible only by boat.
The lake is 16 miles long and 11 miles wide.   Depth:
1050 feet.   Altitude: 4500 feet.

ATITLÁN VOLCANO.   Altitude: 11,565 ft.   An inactive volcano located in the department of Solola in southwest
central Guatemala, near Lake Atitlán.   The volcano
was active in 1469 (according to Indian tradition), 1717-
21, 1826-28, 1833, 1843, 1852 and 1856.

ATOLE.   A thin corn gruel flavored with spices or cocoa,
often used for special occasions.   It is also a common
breakfast drink of the Indians.   Atole elote is a drink
made from ground sweet corn in water.

ATZIQUINAHAY   see   TZUTUHIL.

AUDIENCIA.   The highest royal court of appeal within a
given district of colonial Spanish America, which also
served as a consultative council for the viceroy, or
captain-general; it had some legislative powers as well.
It could hear the complaints of individuals against vice-
roys and captains-general and often took measures to
restrain these officials.   The lesser audiencia had, by
law, three to five judges (oidores).   As a court of
justice, it tried civil and criminal cases.   Unusually
important cases could be appealed from the audiencia
to the Council of the Indies.   An important function of
the audiencia was to protect the interests of the Indians, and usually two days a week were set aside for
suits among Indians or between Indians and Spaniards.
The viceroy, or captain-general, was president of this
tribunal, but had no voice or vote in judicial decisions
unless he was a lawyer.   Next to the viceroy, the
audiencia was the most important institution in the government of the Spanish Indies.   It served as the principal curb upon the colonial governors.   The Audiencia
de Los Confines was moved from Panama to Gracias
a Dios, Honduras, then to Guatemala City in 1549.
It was again moved to Panama between 1564 and 1566.
It had jurisdiction over Chiapas, Yucatan (from 1549
to 1560) and colonial Guatemala, extending to the northern boundary of Panama.

AUGURTO Y ALAVA, JUAN MIGUEL DE.   Governor from

1682 to 1684.

AUXILIAR.   A public servant who assists the regidores in
   carrying out public works projects.

AVALOS Y PORRAS, MANUEL.   Medical doctor of the early
   18th century who was born in Antigua and who was
   called the "Harvey" of America.   He led one of the
   most important scientific periods in Guatemala.

AVENDAÑO, DIEGO DE, d. 1649.   Governor from 1642 to
   1649.

AVERÍA.   A colonial tax or duty required from the merchants to finance convoys.   At the time of the establishment of the Consulado de Comercio in 1793, 1 and
   1/2 per cent of the import-export profits was given to
   the Consulado for use on internal improvements.   The
   Avería tax was increased to 2 and 1/2 per cent by the
   end of the colonial period.

AVIATECA.   Compañia Guatemalteca de Aviación, the national airline with scheduled flights from Aurora air-
   field in Guatemala City to 14 cities in Central America
   and the U.S.

AVILA AYALA, MANUEL MARÍA, 1908-1960.   Guatemalan
   literary critic.

AXICUAT   see   AXOPIL.

AXOPIL.   Warrior leader of the Nahua immigrants driven
   from central Mexico, he conquered the Quiché, Cakchiquel and Tzutuhil nations of highland Guatemala.   He
   divided the conquered area into three parts, ruled by
   himself and his two sons, Jiutemal and Axicuat.   At
   Axopil's death, Jiutemal, who had been given the
   Quiché nation, proclaimed himself monarch of both the
   Quiché and Cakchiquel nations, the latter of which had
   been his father's domain.   Jiutemal then set about con-
   quering the Tzutuhil, who were led by Axicuat.   The
   action set the whole area into a state of civil war,
   which never ceased until after the arrival of the Spanish.

AYARZA LAKE.   Located in the department of Santa Rosa
   in southern Guatemala, 13 miles east-northeast of

Cuilapa. It is three miles long, two miles wide and
has no surface inlet or outlet. Depth: 1150 ft. Altitude: 6500 ft.

AYCINENA, JUAN FERMÍN, 1838-1898. A poet, born in
Guatemala City, he had a legal career, was a finquero
and a deputy in the Council of State. He was one of
the founders of the Academia Guatemalteca in 1888.
He published most of his poetry under pseudonyms:
Delius, L.D., Saulo, Talmiro, Tamiro, Vêritas. His
best known poems are Al pensativo, A mi amada, and
Al café. His best play is El hombre de bien (1887).

AYCINENA, JUAN FERMÍN DE, 1729-1796. Born in Sija,
Spain, he became the leading merchant of Central America, Alcalde de Ayuntamiento in 1759 and 1784, and
was given the title "Marques de Aycinena" in 1783.
He was patron of the poet García Goyena.

AYCINENA, JUAN JOSÉ DE, 1792-1865. Guatemalan composer of religious music, he studied music in New
York but did most of his work in Guatemala.

AYCINENA, MARIANO, 1789-1855. Governor of Guatemala
from 1827-1829, while it was a member of the Federation of Central America. He later became an advisor
to Rafael Carrera. He was on the Consejo Consultativo from its foundation in 1848 until his death in 1855.

AYCINENA, PEDRO DE, 1802-1898. Acting president from
the time of Carrera's death on April 14, 1865, until
the new president was selected and installed on May
24, 1865.

AYUNTAMIENTO. The council at the local level, made up
of property owners and heads of important families,
who elected officials to the Cabildo. After the conquest had ended, the local officials were appointed by
the central government as a means to undermine the
powers of the Ayuntamiento.

AYUTLA. Municipio located in the department of San Marcos in southwestern Guatemala. The cabecera is on
the Suchiate River opposite Suchiate, Mexico, and 18
miles west of Coatepeque. Rail terminus, customs
station. Population: 9939. Crops: sugar cane, rice,
grain, beans.

AZACUALPA   see   SAN JOSÉ ACATEMPA.

AZUL RIVER   see   HONDO RIVER.

-B-

B. N. A.   see   BANCO NACIONAL AGRARIO.

BACK-STRAP LOOM   see   STICK LOOM.

BACOS   see   GAZISTAS.

BAJA VERAPAZ.   A department located in central Guatemala. The capital, Salama, is in the northern highlands. It is bounded by the upper Motagua River on
   the south, the Chixoy River on the northwest. It is
   crossed east to west by the Sierra de Chuacus Mountains. Crops: corn, beans, coffee, sugar cane, fruit,
   vineyards. Some livestock is raised. Gold and mica
   are mined near the Motagua River. The main cities
   are Salama and Rabinal. There are eight municipios
   in this department: El Chol, Cubulco, Granados,
   Purulha, Rabinal, Salama, San Jerónimo, San Miguel
   Chicaj. Population in 1950 was 66,313; in 1964 was
   96,259. The projection for 1980 is 156,000. Area:
   1206 square miles.

BAJAREQUE.   A house wall of woven cane poles or wooden
   poles, smeared over with adobe.

BALANYA   see   SANTA CRUZ BALANYA.

BALSELLS RIVERA, ALFREDO, 1904-1940.   A Guatemalan
   novelist and poet, his works include El Venadeado,
   La sonrisa provisional, and Baraja (1938), all in free
   verse. Pseudonyms: Caracolillo, Paca Espinal.

BANCO DE GUATEMALA.   Founded during Arévalo's regime,
   the bank has become a powerful and liberalizing economic force even after the revolutionary period ended.
   It presently serves as the bank for the government and
   as the central bank for other banks in Guatemala. It
   is not opened to business for private firms, but serves
   as the banker's bank.

BANCO NACIONAL AGRARIO (B. N. A.).   Established in 1953

to provide credit, at low interest rates, to farm
workers receiving land under the agrarian reform program. While represented in most municipios, the
B.N.A. services are in competition in many areas with
S.C.I.C.A.S.

BARAHONA, SANCHO DE. A captain under Alvarado on the
conquest, he became an encomendero in the village of
Santa Catarina Barahona and served in the city government in Antigua on several occasions.

BARBERENA. Municipio in the department of Santa Rosa in
southern Guatemala. Its cabecera is located on the
Inter-American highway, northwest of Cuilapa. Population: 20,149. Crops: beans, corn.

BARCENA. A small experimental farm in the department
of Guatemala under the Ministry of Agriculture. Its
purpose is crop experimentation, especially in corn
and beans.

BARILLAS see SANTA CRUZ BARILLAS.

BARILLAS, MANUEL LISANDRO, 1844-1907. Appointed Provisional President after Sinibaldi resigned and was
later elected President (1885-1892). He was assassinated in Mexico.

BARNOYA GÁLVEZ, FRANCISCO, 1906- . Journalist,
diplomat and writer, he was born in Guatemala City.
He studied law at the universities of Guatemala and
Chile. He was a representative to Chile and Mexico
and later was Secretaria de Relaciones Exteriores under Ubico. He wrote Nabey Tokik (1937), Leyenda
del Ñandutí (1939), and Zipacna (1939).

BARREDA, HÉCTOR DE LA. On the conquest with Alvarado, he settled in the Valle de las Vacas. The valley
takes its name from a cattle herd that he built up
there in the 1530's.

BARRI, DAVID [pseudonym] see IRISARRI, ANTONIO
JOSÉ DE.

BARRIOS, JUSTO RUFINO, 1835-1885. Born in San Lorenzo, he received a notary public license in 1860 and
set up business in San Marcos. He fell out of favor

with the government and his ranch was burned by federal troops after he led revolutionaries against President Cerna. In 1869 he joined Serapio Cruz in Mexico
and they "invaded," with a few men. Gaining some
support, they made it as far as Palencia before being
routed. Barrios returned to Mexico where he later
met Miguel García Granados. With García Granados'
support, a "liberation army" was equipped, and Guatemala was invaded on March 28, 1871. After the Cerna
government fell, Barrios was made military commander
of Quezaltenango, where he began to carry out reform
measures. He won the election in 1873 and then began
to push through reform measures for the whole country.
All church holdings were confiscated; education reforms
were carried out; communications were improved; constitutional and agricultural reforms were begun. He
called a constituent assembly in 1878 and a reform
constitution was enacted in 1879. A railroad was completed from San José to Guatemala City in 1880. In
1882, Barrios toured the United States and Europe;
while in Washington, he signed a treaty with Mexico
settling their boundary line dispute. On his return to
Guatemala, he began to work for the unification of Central America. When the other countries did not re-
spond favorably, he called out the army and attacked
El Salvador. His death during the first battle ended
the movement. His wife, Doña Francisca, went to the
United States, then to Spain, where she remarried.
See also CARTA DEL GENERAL J. RUFINO BARRIOS.

BARRIOS PENA, ROBERTO, 1909-   . A military tactician,
    he wrote Principios de combate de la sección de fusi-
    leros (1939), Exploración y patrulla para infanteria
    (1937), and Nociones de táctica y logística (1945).

BARRIOS Y LEAL, JACINTO DE. Governor from 1688 to
    1695. He organized an unsuccessful expedition against
    the Lacandón Indians.

BARRUNDIA, JOSÉ FRANCISCO, 1784-1854. A member of
    the Belén Conspiracy, he later was senior senator of
    the National Assembly. In 1829, Morazán appointed
    him President to finish out the term of ousted Presi-
    dent Arce until 1830. Later elected governor of Guate-
    mala, he refused the office, preferring to remain a
    senator. In 1839 he traveled to Los Altos to protest
    the invasion of Carrera. When Guatemala formally re-

nounced the confederacion in 1848, he left Guatemala.
In 1852, he was appointed Minister Plenipotentiary to
New York to represent Honduras, where he remained
until his death.

BARRUNDIA, JUAN. Governor of Guatemala from 1824-
1826 and in 1829. He was forced to resign by President of Central America, Manuel Arce, only to be reinstated by Francisco Morazán when he gained power.
He was defeated in his bid for reelection in 1830 by
Mariano Gálvez.

BARRUTIA, SALVADOR, 1842-1889. Born in Antigua, he
was a military man, who became a brigadier general
in 1885. He is best remembered for poetry which
tended toward a free style, less restricted by tradition.

BATRES, LUIS, d. 1862. Author of the first constitution
of the Republic of Guatemala (1851). Between 1855
and 1862 he was a leading figure in policy formation
in the Carrera government.

BATRES, PEPE see BATRES Y MONTÚFAR, JOSÉ.

BATRES Y JÁUREGUI, ANTONIO, 1847-1929. Guatemalan
historian, best known for his three-volume work, La
America Central ante la historia (1916-49), and for
Cristóbal Colón y el nuevo mundo (1893).

BATRES Y MONTÚFAR, JOSÉ, 1809-1844. Born in San
Salvador, he is considered a leading poet of Guatemala. His writings reflect much local color, mixed
with skepticism. Often referred to as "Pepe" Batres,
his best known poems are El relox and Yo pienso en
ti. He also wrote Tradiciones de Guatemala.

BAUER PÁIZ, ALFONSO, 1917- . A labor lawyer, Minister of Economy, and representative to the U.N. in
1952. Active in politics during the revolutionary period. In 1970 an assassination attempt was made on
him because of his attacks on the Arana government.

BAUL, EL. Town in the department of Escuintla in southern Guatemala, three miles north of Santa Lucía.
Sugar mills are located here. Population: 1595.

BAUTISTA, EL [pseudonym] see HERNÁNDEZ DE LEÓN, FEDERICO.

BEATRIZ, DOÑA see CUEVA DE ALVARADO, DOÑA BEATRIZ DE LA.

BECERRA, BARTOLOMAÉ. A captain under Alvarado, he led several Spanish companies against the rebelling Indian chief, Sinacam, in 1526. He later was Alcalde of Guatemala City in 1534 and 1544. He led in the unsuccessful attempt to keep Bartolomé de Las Casas from settling in Guatemala. His only daughter, Teresa Becerra, married Bernal Díaz del Castillo.

BEDEL. A policeman, doorkeeper or proctor at the University.

BEDOYA DE MOLINA, MARÍA DOLORES, 1783-1861. Guatemalan "Mother of her country."

BELÉN CONSPIRACY (1813). A plan to seize Captain-General Bustamente, Archbishop Casaus and the principal military officers; to liberate the captured soldiers of the patriot army of Granada (Nicaragua); and to declare independence. The leaders met in the cells of the Convent de Belén, but were discovered and arrested by local soldiers and sentenced to death by garrote. Those captured were: Joaquín Yudice, Tomás Ruiz and Fray Victor Castrillo. A royal order of May 2, 1818 granted amnesty to these men. José Francisco Barrundia, who was never captured but was sentenced in absentia, spent six years in hiding in Guatemala. Ten of the lesser leaders were sentenced to hang, but were later pardoned, and the other participants were sent to Africa for ten years of hard labor.

BELICE. An independent member of the British Commonwealth since 1963, it is bounded by the Caribbean, Guatemala and Mexico and has an area of 8867 square miles and a population of 119,645. Exports are: mahogany logs, lumber, chicle. The British began cutting wood in the area as early as the mid-17th century and continually expanded their work area against the wishes of the Spanish. After the revolution, the wood-cutters refused to leave. Guatemala and Great Britain signed a treaty of limitations in 1859, placing

the boundary at the Sarstun River. In exchange, the
British were to build a road connecting Guatemala
City with Belice. This road was never built and,
since the 1930's, Guatemala has claimed Belice by de-
fault of the British. The situation was further com-
plicated when Belice was granted home rule, which
resulted in Guatemala breaking diplomatic relations
with Great Britain. Efforts to resolve the dispute have
been futile. Under arbitration Guatemala has offered
to recognize Belice if the foreign policy and national
defense would be managed by Guatemala, or if, as a
member of the Central American community, all six
nations would have a collective approach to foreign
policy for Belice. Britain has suggested complete independence within the commonwealth for Belice, which
is not acceptable to the people in Belice because of
the Guatemalan threat.

BELICE RIVER. Arises as the Mopán River near Dolores
in El Petén. Flows 180 miles northeast past Benque
Viejo and into the Caribbean at Belice. Navigable for
small craft which carry lumber and chicle. Called
"Old River" in British Honduras.

BELIZE see BELICE.

BELTRANENA, MARIANO, 1782?-1860. Appointed Vice-
President under Arce, he was made President when
Arce resigned in 1828. He remained in command un-
til April, 1829, when Guatemala City was captured by
General Francisco Morazán. He went into exile to
Cuba and remained there until his death.

BERGAÑO Y VILLEGAS, SIMÓN, 1781-1828. Probably a
Spaniard, he arrived in Guatemala under the name of
Simón Carreño. He was editor of the Gazeta de Guatemala from 1803 to 1808. His liberal attitude angered
many of the higher government officials and in 1808 he
was arrested and returned to Spain for creating dis-
sention among the creoles and the peninsulares. He
often argued with himself in the Gazeta under the
names, Engañado and Bañoger de Sagellíu y Gielblas.
He wrote Cuatro piezas poéticas (1803) and La vacuna
(1808).

BERROSPE, GABRIEL SÁNCHEZ DE. Governor from 1696
to 1700. The factional dispute which arose under Gov-

ernor Escals continued during his term, and in 1699,
a visitador was assigned to investigate. Berrospe was
replaced by the senior judge on the Audiencia. He refused to step down, however, and ordered the arrest
of the visitador. The two factions met in open fighting, which resulted in Berrospe's being relieved as
governor. The dispute was not completely settled until the visitador was replaced in 1702.

BETANCOURT, HERMANO PEDRO DE, 1626-1667. Born
in the Canary Islands, he went to Guatemala in 1650
and began study for the priesthood. He failed but was
later admitted to the order of the Franciscans. He
founded a hospital for the poor called Belen, which is
now operated by a congregation of Bethlehemites. For
his work, he was beatified by Pope Clement XIV in
1735. See also LA CRUZ, RODRIGO DE.

BETETA, IGNACIO, 1757-1827. Newspaperman, he founded
the progressive journal, Gazeta de Guatemala in 1797.
Pseudonym: I.B. His works include Kalendario y guia
de forasteros de Guatemala, published every two years
between 1792 and 1805.

BETETA, JOSÉ ANTONIO, 1861-1930. A Guatemalan novelist, best known for his romantic novel, Edmundo
(1896).

BIJAO see HOJA MAXÁN.

BLACK CHRIST OF ESQUIPULAS see CALVARIO, EL.

BLACK LEGEND. An exaggerated legend of the inhumane
treatment of the natives of America at the hands of
the Spanish, first publicly expounded by Bartolomé de
Las Casas. His purpose was to shock the king into
passing protective laws, which was done in 1542.
However, the Anglo-Saxon countries of Europe were
ready to believe the worst of Spain because of the
Spanish support of the Church after the Reformation,
and they accepted Las Casas' account at face value.
Contributing also toward this acceptance was the fact
that the Spanish government required detailed reports
from their colonies, and these records were later
used to document Spanish treatment of the Indians.
Other colonial powers kept few or no records, and
thereby were spared much embarrassment when their

files were opened.

BONDESIR [pseudonym] see CÓRDOBA, MATÍAS DE.

BONILLA RUANO, JOSÉ MARÍA, 1889-1958. Guatemalan
educator and writer, his works include Curso didáctico
y razonado de gramática castellana and Mosaico de
voces y locuciones viciosas.

BORLA. A doctor's bonnet or cap with a tassel. In the
vernacular, it refers to a doctorate degree.

BOUNDARY DISPUTES see BELICE; HONDURAN BOUND-
ARY DISPUTE; MEXICAN BOUNDARY DISPUTE.

BRAÑAS, CÉSAR, 1900- . A Guatemalan author who has
written many books, most of which are concerned with
decadence in contemporary Guatemala. He sometimes
uses the pseudonym Alfonso Alfaro. His works include Alba emerita (1920), La divina patoja (1926),
Paulita (1939), Sor Candelaria (1924), Tu no sirves
(1926), and Viento negro (1935).

BRAZA. A measurement of land equivalent to 36 square
feet.

BRICEÑO, FRANCISCO. Governor from 1564 to 1569.

BRITISH HONDURAS see BELICE.

BRUJO. A diviner commissioned to cast spells, usually of
the nature to cause misfortune to an opponent or enemy.

BURGOS, LAWS OF (1512). The first Spanish code of laws
concerned with the governing and instruction of native
Americans. King Ferdinand V promulgated the body
of 32 laws at Burgos, Spain, after a controversy had
arisen. The controversy was precipitated by the denunciation of the enslavement of the Indians. Under
the laws, the native working hours were limited, ade-
quate food and shelter were assured, and royal officials were appointed to ensure good treatment of the
Indians. The laws limited the working force in the
mines to a maximum of one-third the total work force
of an encomienda. The laws stipulated that the natives
were to work no more than nine months of the year for

the Spaniards. Although the laws were intended to
eliminate many abuses, they were never properly enforced, and the Indians continued to be exploited and
mistreated.

BUSTAMENTE Y GUERRA, JOSÉ. Governor from 1811 to
    1818. Before going to Guatemala, he was a naval of-
    ficer and governor of Montevideo. During his rule
    there were several revolts against the crown which
    were quickly put down. Bustamente kept a very close
    watch on all those suspected of having sympathy with
    the revolutionary cause. He granted reform measures
    from Spain only after delaying as long as possible.
    He quickly eliminated any threats of rebellion and left
    Guatemala one of the crown's most peaceful colonies.

                              -C-

C.A.C.F. see COMITÉ COORDINADOR DE ASOCIACIONES
    AGRÍCOLAS, COMERCIALES, INDUSTRIALES Y FIN-
    ANCIERAS.

C.A.N. see CONSEJO AGRARIO NACIONAL.

C.A.R.C.O.R. see ASOCIACIÓN COORDINADORA DE
    ASOCIACIONES REGIONALES DE CAFECULTORES
    DEL OCCIDENTE.

C.C.N. see COMITÉ CÍVICO NACIONAL.

C.E.U.A. see COMITÉ DE ESTUDIANTES UNIVERSI-
    TARIOS ANTICOMUNISTAS.

C.G.T.G. see CONFEDERACIÓN GENERAL DE TRABA-
    JADORES DE GUATEMALA.

C.N.C.G. see CONFEDERACIÓN NACIONAL DE CAMPE-
    SINO DE GUATEMALA.

C.N.D.C.C. see COMITÉ NACIONAL DE DEFENSE
    CONTRA EL COMUNISMO.

C.N.P. see COMITÉ NACIONAL DE LA PAZ.

C.N.U.S. see COMITÉ NACIONAL DE UNIDAD SINDICAL.

C. O. N. S. I. G. U. A.   see   CONFEDERACIÓN SINDICAL DE
GUATEMALA.

C. O. P. A.   see   CONFEDERACIÓN OBRERO DE PAN
AMERICA.

C. P. N. T.   see   COMITÉ POLÍTICO NACIONAL DE LOS
TRABAJADORES.

C. R A. G.   A conservative group of university students who
specialize in bombings.   The full name of the organization is not known.

C. S. G.   see   CONSEJO SINDICAL DE GUATEMALA.

C. S. L. A.   see   CONFEDERACIÓN SINDICATO DE LATINA
AMERICANA.

C. T. A. L.   see   CONFEDERACIÓN DE TRABAJADORES DE
AMÉRICA LATINA.

C. T. G.   see   CONFEDERACIÓN DE TRABAJADORES DE
GUATEMALA.

CABALLERÍA.   A land grant awarded by the Spanish crown
to mounted conquistadores (Caballeros) during the conquest.   Since 1732, it has referred to a unit of land
measurement equal to 64.75 manzanas or 111.07 acres.

CABAÑAS.   Municipio located in the department of Zacapa
in eastern Guatemala.   The cabecera is near the Motagua River, 17 miles west-southwest of Zacapa.   Railroad.   Population: 5352.   Crops: corn, sugar cane,
beans.

CABECERA.   The governmental capital of a municipio or
department.   Often it carries the department name and,
if the cabecera of a municipio, it almost always carries the name of the municipio.

CABILDO.   The town government of Spanish America.   The
term has been expanded to include the municipal building.   The cabildo supervised public works, sanitation
and health, enforcement of police regulations, administration of property, regulation of prices and wages,
and collected taxes.   Early in the colonial period, the
members were elected annually by the Ayuntamiento.

Later in the colonial period, the positions were sold.
The cabildo consisted of four to 12 regidores, two
alcaldes ordinarios (judges), an alferez (ensign), and
an alquacil (constable). The cabildo lost much of its
power in the late colonial period. The "cabildo abierto" was an extension of the cabildo, held when matters of grave importance were to be discussed. The
governor, at his own initiative or at the request of the
cabildo, called an open (abierto) meeting, usually with
members of the ayuntamiento and the cabildo present.
The cabildo abierto functioned more as an advisory
body for the governor.

CABRAL, MANUEL, 1847-1914. A Guatemalan author, his
best known novel is María, historia de una martir.
Pseudonym: Felipe de Jesús.

CABRAL DE LA CERDA, MANUEL, 1886-1933. A poet, he
translated into Spanish the poems of Tennyson, A.
Lavergne and others. His original works include:
Mi album, Retazos campesinos, En el sendero, and
El toque del angelus. Pseudonym: Miguel Trocoso.

CABRERA, FRANCISCO, 1781-1845. An artist of the late
colonial and early national period, noted for his miniature portraits. He served as "Maestro corrector" at
the Real Escuela de Dibuxo.

CABRERA, MANUEL ESTRADA   see   ESTRADA CABRERA,
MANUEL.

CABRICÁN. Municipio located in the department of Quezaltenango in southwestern Guatemala. The cabecera is
about 20 miles north-northwest of Quezaltenango.
Population: 5285. Altitude: 8241 ft. Crops: corn,
wheat, fodder grasses; livestock.

CABRILLO, JUAN RODRÍGUES, 149?-1543. A Portuguese
who took part in the conquest, he supervised the construction of Cortés's ships on the lakes at Mexico
City. He later had constructed for Alvarado 13 ships,
and was appointed commanding admiral on Alvarado's
exploration to the north. When Alvarado was killed,
the ships went to Antonio de Mendoza, Viceroy of
Mexico. The expedition was delayed until 1542 and
then left for present-day California, where Cabrillo
was killed by Indians. At Alvarado's death, Francisco

de la Cueva claimed the encomiendas given to Cabrillo. Cabrillo's son fought this in court for several years before finally receiving an encomienda as compensation.

CACAO. In the pre-colonial and colonial periods, the cacao bean was universally used as money by the Indians. It had no set exchange rate with silver. In the 16th century the beans could be exchanged at 80 to 100 cacaos per real.

CACASTE. A wooden carrying frame used by Indian men and boys for transporting goods on their backs. It usually has four legs to allow the user to easily set it down while resting. The rack is held on the back with the tumpline, which fits across the forehead of the bearer.

CACHURECO. Literally, "false coin," the term was applied by political enemies to Rafael Carrera and to those who followed him, between 1837 and 1839.

CACIQUE. A word of Indian origin referring to the local leader or chief. The Indian ruling class structure was quickly adopted by the Spanish, who retained Indian personnel to act as petty magistrates. Throughout the Spanish-speaking countries the word has been extended to apply to those individuals who exert too great an influence on local politics. Caciquismo, the system, has become a distinctive trait in many Latin American countries.

CACOS see GAZISTAS.

CAHABÓN see SANTA MARÍA CAHABÓN.

CAHABÓN RIVER. Left affluent of the Polochic River, about 60 miles in length. It flows through Cobán.

CAITES. Sandals worn by Indians.

CAJOLA. Municipio located in the department of Quezaltenango in southwestern Guatemala. The cabecera is eight miles northwest of Quezaltenango. Population: 4577. Altitude: 8500 ft. Crops: corn, wheat, fodder grasses; livestock.

CAKCHIQUEL. Second largest language group of the Quichean linguistic stock. The nation is now centered near
present-day Tecpán, and includes the departments of
Chimaltenango, Quiché, Guatemala, Solola, Escuintla
and Sacatepequez. Until the conquest, the capital was
at Iximche. The Cakchiqueles were continually fighting the Quiché and the Tzutuhiles. After the Spanish
defeat of the Quichés, the Cakchiqueles allied themselves with the Spanish to defeat the Tzutuhiles. The
Cakchiqueles soon grew to dislike Spanish rule and revolted. After a long fight, the Cakchiqueles were defeated but avoided surrender by taking to the mountains.
In 1526, under Chief Sinacam, the Cakchiqueles again
revolted and were again defeated. Those not killed
were scattered in the mountains. See also ANNALS
OF THE CAKCHIQUELES.

CALDERÓN AVILA, FÉLIX, 1891-1924. A modernist poet,
his works include Lire altiva and Cantos de América.

CALDERÓN PARDO, RODOLFO, 1885-1944. A poet, he
became one of the leading journalists of the 1920's.
His works include Alma bohemia and Sonfonia en blanco
menor.

CALVARIO, EL. When the Spanish conquistadors entered
the valley of Esquipulas, the Indian leaders promised
no resistance. As a reward, the Spanish made their
village a trading center and established a large religious center there. Quirio Cataño, a colonial sculptor, made a figure of the Saviour from balsam so that
the complexion would be dark like that of the Indians.
It was installed in 1595 and since then, the burning
candles and incense have turned it shiny black. In
1737, Pardo de Figueroa, Bishop of Guatemala, was
cured there of a severe chronic ailment, and the
shrine's reputation for curing ailments was established
among the Indians. The Bishop ordered a large edifice to be constructed around the figure; it was completed in 1758. Now, each January, thousands of pil-
grims visit the Black Christ to pray and to have their
ills cured. It is legendary that a stone idol is hidden
at Esquipulas and that it, not necessarily the Black
Christ, is the real reason for the Indians' pilgrimage.

CÁMARA DE COMERCIO. Founded in 1894 by decree of
José María Reyna Barrios, it did not become active

until 1921. It was disbanded by Ubico. Reorganized in 1944, it was made up of commercial leaders. In 1947, the name was changed to Cámara de Comercio e Industria in recognition of the growing influence of the industrial leaders. In 1950, the industrial group broke away to form the Cámara de Industria. The C.C. has operated as a political influence group for the commercial interests in matters of governmental policy.

CÁMARA DE INDUSTRIAS. Formed in 1950 as a separate group of the C.C. First called the Asociación General de Industriales, but was reorganized in 1959 as the C.I. when other members of the C.C. elected to join. The C.I. represents local industrialists and was particularly interested in the development of the Central American common market.

CAMEY HERRERA, JULIO, d. 1970. Assassinated in Guatemala City for his opposition to the Arana government. A professor of law at the Universidad de San Carlos, many believed him to be head of the clandestine communist party.

CAMOTÁN. Municipio in the department of Chiquimula in eastern Guatemala. Its cabecera is located near the Honduran border. Population: 16,223. Crops: corn, beans, rice, sugar cane.

CANCUEN RIVER see CONCUEN RIVER.

CÁNDIDO [pseudonym] see ACEÑA DURÁN, RAMÓN.

CANÍCULA. A relatively short dry period, usually in late July or early August, which falls in the period of heavy rainfall (from June through September) in the Guatemalan highlands.

CANILLA. Municipio located in the department of El Quiché in west central Guatemala. Its cabecera is in the south central part of the department, near the Baja Verapaz border and is not accessible by road. Population: 4093. Crops: corn, beans, coffee, sugar cane, tomatoes, chile, potatoes.

CANOA, LA. Town in the department of Baja Verapaz in central Guatemala. Located on the Motagua River, it

is 18 miles south-southwest of Salama.   Gold placers
are nearby.   Population: 1206.   Crops: coffee, sugar
cane, grain.

CANTEL.   Municipio in the department of Quezaltenango in
southwestern Guatemala.   On the Samala River, the
cabecera is five miles southeast of Quezaltenango.
Cotton milling center, flour milling.   Population:
10,989.   Altitude: 7890 ft.

CANTÓN.   A section or district in the municipio.   The term
is applied interchangeably with aldea or caserio.

CAPITULACIÓN.   A royal license contracted between the
Spanish crown and a conquistador.   In return for the
expense of the conquest, financed privately, the conquistador could take profits from the conquered land,
extract labor, appoint municipal officers for the first
year, and recruit soldiers and settlers.   The crown
received a fifth of the treasures taken or profits made.

CAPIXAI.   A long, dark, woolen robe similar to a poncho,
worn by the Indian men of several of the tribes.   It is
fastened at the waist with a sash.

CAPORAL.   Group or section leader on a large finca.   A
caporal is responsible to the manager or administrator of the finca.

CAPTAIN GENERAL.   The office was more that of a provincial viceroy, with as much autonomy as a viceroy
and with direct responsibility to the Council of the Indies, except in cases requiring important policy decisions, when the viceroy would be consulted.   The cap-
taincy-general of colonial Guatemala included Chiapas,
Belice, and the other states of Central America, ex-
cluding Panama.   In 1543 the New Laws designated the
captain-general of Guatemala as governor, with semi-
independent status from the viceroyalty of New Spain
and with closer ties to the Council of the Indies and
the King.

CARACAS CONFERENCE.   The tenth Inter-American conference, which met at Caracas, Venezuela in March,
1954 and which was attended by all American republics
except Costa Rica.   Among the 97 resolutions voted on
by the delegates, the most noteworthy was the anti-

Communist declaration which was approved by a 17 to
one vote, with Mexico and Argentina abstaining and
Guatemala dissenting. The resolution was brought before the conference by the United States because of
Communist influence in the Arbenz government of Guatemala and was officially called the "Declaration of
solidarity for the preservation of the political integrity
of the American states against international Communist
intervention." Although the United States won the vote,
Guatemalan Foreign Minister Guillermo Toriello received much unofficial support in his denunciation of
U.S. policy.

CARACOL. A large shell, blown into and used as a horn.
An instrument of pre-Columbian times that was used
to summon warriors to battle.

CARACOLILLO [pseudonym] see BALSELLS RIVERA,
ALFREDO.

CARCHA see SAN PEDRO CARCHA.

CARDOZA Y ARAGÓN, LUIS, 1902- . A critic and poet,
born in Guatemala, his many years in France and Mexico have given his poetry a surrealistic flavor. His
best poetry is: Luna Park (1923), Maelstrom (1926),
El sonambulo (1937) and his critical works are:
Pintara mexicana contemporana (1953), Guatemala, las
lineas de su mano (1955) and La revolucion guatemalteca (1955).

CARGA. A load or burden carried by porters on journeys.
In the colonial period, it referred to a unit of measurement used by the Aztecs and adopted by the Spanish.
A Carga de Cacao consisted of three xiquipiles of cacao
beans, making up about 24,000 beans weighing two
arrobas (50 pounds), and was worth 30 to 38 pesos
when used as a unit of money.

CARIBS see MORENOS.

CARRANZA, JESÚS ENRÍQUEZ, 1863-1902. A Guatemalan
historian, he wrote El General Justo Rufino Barrios.

CARRANZA DE CÓRDOBA, DIEGO FÉLIX. Public attorney
of Jutiapa who, in 1681, wrote several excellent descriptions of the churches of Guatemala.

CARREÑO, SIMÓN see BERGAÑO Y VILLEGAS, SIMÓN.

CARRERA, JOSÉ RAFAEL, 1814?-1865. Little is known of
    Carrera's early life beyond that he came from a fam-
    ily of the lower social level; he was not a full-blooded
    Indian; and he received no schooling. In the civil war
    of the 1820's, he was a drummer in the conservative
    army. His first "revolutionary" activity was in Santa
    Rosa in 1837, where his group was routed by the fed-
    eral troops. He joined with conservatives at Antigua
    and captured Guatemala City in 1838. He took control
    of the capital three times before he retained power,
    but he did not become President until 1844. Except
    for the period between 1848 and 1851, when he was
    the power behind the Presidency, he remained Presi-
    dent until his death in 1865. His power rested in the
    army, the Church, and the aristocracy. As a gener-
    al, his best action was against Salvador and Honduras
    in 1851 when he turned back their invasion. As a
    diplomat, his most controversial act was to sign a
    treaty with Great Britain in 1858, outlining the bounda-
    ries of Belice. See also PRONUNCIAMIENTO DE
    CARRERA.

CARRERA, RAFAEL see CARRERA, JOSÉ RAFAEL.

CARILLO DE MENDOZA, JERÓNIMO GARCES. Acting gov-
    ernor from 1657 to 1659.

CARRILLO RAMÍREZ, SALOMÓN, 1897-1939. A Guatemal-
    an author, he wrote El poeta Villegas (1937), Tierras
    de oriente (1927), and De mi sierra (1922).

CARTA DEL GENERAL J. RUFINO BARRIOS (February 24,
    1883). This statement marked the turning point at
    which President Barrios began to actively work for the
    Central American Union. In the statement, he calls
    for the formation of a liberal union and for a congress
    to discuss union. Costa Rica and Nicaragua refused,
    and Barrios' persuasive efforts were unsuccessful.
    This prompted him to attempt a union by force of arms
    which ended with his death on the second day of battle,
    at Chalchuapa.

CARVAJAL, DIEGO DE, d. 1596. Arch-deacon of the Ca-
    thedral, he was appointed to the inquisition for Guate-
    mala in 1571.

CASA DE CONTRATACIÓN. Often referred to as the Casa
de las Indias, it was set up by the crown in 1503 to
supervise commerce, navigation and emigration. It
was subordinated to the Consejo de las Indias. In the
18th century, the policy of the Casa de Contratación
was liberalized by the opening of new ports and the
formation of more trading companies to stimulate trade.
In Central America, all the legal traffic had to enter
through Panama and Veracruz, with some limited west
coast trade from Lima, Peru. The Casa was abolished in 1790.

CASA DE LAS INDIAS see CASA DE CONTRATACIÓN.

CASA DE MONEDA. The royal mint of Guatemala was
founded in 1733. The mint produced more than four
million silver doubloons, worth eight reales (about 12
and 1/2 cents a real). The doubloons were called
macacos (pieces of eight) because of their value and
because of their irregular shape. The monetary system, based on the real, was as follows: Ocha escu-
dos (16 reales), Doubloon (eight reales), Peso (eight
reales), Tostón (four reales), Peseta (two reales),
Medio real (one-half real), and Cuartillo (one-fourth
real or eight and one-half maravedí). These coins
were used until the reform era of 1873 when they were
outlawed. A system based on the peso was then used
until 1924, when a monetary study carried out under
President Estrada Cabrera was acted on and the present system based on the Quetzal was instituted. A
few of the Spanish coins could be found in use as recently as the late 1930's in the mountainous regions.

CASA ROJA [pseudonym] see RODRÍGUEZ CERNA, JOSÉ.

CASANOVA Y ESTRADA, RICARDO, 1844-1913. A poet, he
began study as a lawyer but changed to become a
priest. He was named Archbishop of the Metropolitan
Archdiocese. His poetry reflects his thoughts on death
and was written under the pseudonym Andrés Vigil.

CASAS, BARTOLOMÉ DE LAS see LAS CASAS, BARTOL-
OMÉ DE.

CASAUS Y TORRES, RAMÓN. Archbishop of Guatemala
when Morazán ousted the archbishop and most of the
monastic orders. He went to Cuba, where he remained.

CASERIO. A small rural community, usually of lesser importance and smaller than the aldea. Often made up
of only scattered dwellings.

CASILLAS. Municipio in the department of Santa Rosa in
southern Guatemala. The cabecera is in the Pacific
piedmont, ten miles north-northeast of Cuilapa and on
the Esclavos River. Population: 9402. Crops: sugar
cane, grain; livestock.

CASTAÑEDA, FRANCISCO, 1858- . Guatemalan historian,
he wrote Emilio Zola (1906), Una ciudad historica
(1907), Guia del viajero en la republica (1909), Nuevos
estudios, 2 vols. (1919), and many others.

CASTAÑEDA, RICARDO C., 1879-1932. Judge and member
of the national assembly. He wrote Análisis de Don
Mariano Salas (1905) and La política en Guatemala
(1931).

CASTAÑEDA PAGANINI, RICARDO, 1908- . A historian,
Minister of Public Education, delegate to the U.N. in
1950, he has written several books: Las ruinas de
Palenque (1946), Historia de la...Universidad de San
Carlos (1947), and Tikal (1962).

CASTELLANOS ROMERO, CARLOS, 1889- . Judge and
professor at the Universidad de San Carlos, editor of
El Derecho and author of a four volume work, Derecho
procesal guatemalteco (1936-1941).

CASTELLÓN, FRANCISCO DE. On the conquest as Royal
Treasurer, he was an outspoken opponent of Alvarado.
He attempted to take control of the government at Al-
varado's death but was thwarted by Doña Beatriz.

CASTILLO, JESÚS, 1877-1946. A Guatemalan composer and
teacher, he was an impressionist who used native
themes in a classical tradition. He was recognized as
the leading authority on Indian music and instruments.
His writings include La musica Maya-Quiché (1941)
and Legado folklórico a la juventud guatemalteca (1944).

CASTILLO, RICARDO, 1894- . A musician born in Quezaltenango who has worked many years at the Conservatorio Nacional. He has written several compositions
for the piano: Barcarola, Nocturno, and a ballet, La

doncella ixquic (1942).

CASTILLO ARMAS, CARLOS, 1914-1957. President of
    Guatemala from 1954-1957. At the death of Francisco
    Arana in 1949, he participated in an unsuccessful re-
    volt. After being imprisoned, he escaped to Honduras,
    where he gained the support of Guatemalan conserva-
    tives and the U.S. State Department. In 1954 he led
    his "army of liberation" to oust President Arbenz
    from power. Many reforms were then halted or
    slowed. His regime ended in July, 1957, when one of
    the palace guards assassinated him.

CASTRILLO, VICTOR see BELÉN CONSPIRACY.

CATAÑO, QUIRIO, d. 1595. Late 16th-century sculptor in
    Guatemala. He created the famous Black Christ of
    Esquipulas and the figure of Cristo Crucificado, lo-
    cated in Escuela de Cristo in Antigua. See also CAL-
    VARIO, EL.

CATARINA. Municipio in the department of San Marcos in
    southwestern Guatemala. The cabecera is 17 miles
    west-northwest of Coatepeque. Population: 12,264.
    Crops: coffee, sugar cane, tropical fruit; livestock.

CAUDILLO. "Leader." The term first referred to the
    leaders at the provincial level who led the movement
    for freedom. Because of social and political instabil-
    ity, it now refers to the concentration of political au-
    thority in the hands of one person. Caudillismo is the
    term applied to movements of this nature.

CAYAMUSIO [pseudonym] see VELA, DAVID.

CAYUCO. A dugout canoe or boat, usually 12 to 20 feet in
    length, carved from a single log. Gunwales made of
    heavy planks 12 to 15 inches in height are added for
    protection against the waves. These boats are found
    almost exclusively on Lake Atitlán.

CEBALLOS Y VILLAGUTIERRE, ALONSO. Governor from
    1702 to late 1703.

CENSUS OF GUATEMALA. The first census was taken in
    1778 under a Spanish order of 1776 requesting the
    church officials to count all inhabitants, especially the

Indians needing indoctrination. While not an accurate
count, the total was placed at 396,149 inhabitants for
that portion that is today Guatemala. The second census and the first republican census was made in 1880
under the order of President Barrios. The three departments of Totonicapán, Quezaltenango and Huehuetenango had a high percentage of Indians and were least
effectively surveyed. There were six categories:
race, sex, age, state of residence, whether illiterate
or not, and profession (art or industry). With an estimated 3 per cent error, the population was placed at
1,224,602 persons. The third census was conducted
in 1893 using the same categories as the previous census. There were 1,364,678 persons counted; however,
the total given was 1,501,145 because of an estimated
error of omission of 10 per cent. The fourth census,
conducted in 1921, was made upon a sampling of 15
per cent of the total of 2,004,900 persons established
as the official number.
    The fifth census in 1940 was the most comprehen-
sive to that point and would have been a good tabulation except that on the orders of President Ubico, the
official records were inflated by an estimated 900,000.
The published result in 1940 was 3,283,209 but currently it is given to be 2,221,923. Again, this census
can be no more than an estimate. The sixth census in
1950 was the most comprehensive and accurate. It
contained categories for race, age, sex, income,
municipio of residence, profession by department, religion, language spoken (at home), literacy, etc. The
total population was established to be 2,790,868. The
first agricultural census was conducted to establish a
statistical base for production, growth, etc. The
seventh census in 1964 was based upon a 5 per cent
sampling by department and covered race, age, sex,
education and profession. A population of 4,210,000
persons was established. The second agricultural census was conducted at the same time to further expand
the statistical base for economic growth. The Consejo
Nacional de Planificación Económica has projected the
population growth through 1980 to be 7,107,800 persons. The statistics used are on a departmental basis
and can be found with the description of each department.

CENTRAL AMERICAN FEDERATION see PROVINCIAS
    UNIDAS DEL CENTRO DE AMÉRICA.

CENTRAL AMERICAN NATIONAL WAR.   In 1854 William
Walker, a U.S. citizen, went to Nicaragua with 300
men to help liberal leaders gain control of the government.   Walker soon gained control of the government
for himself.   By mid-1856 a mixed group, with troops
from all five of the Central American republics, was
fighting against Walker.   The greatest burden fell on
Costa Rica, with Guatemala supplying 500 troops.
With his army defeated and supplies cut off in May,
1857, Walker escaped to surrender to a U.S. war vessel.   He returned to Nicaragua in late 1857 but was
arrested by the U.S. navy as soon as he landed.   He
again returned in 1858 and was arrested by a British
war vessel.   He was then turned over to Honduran authorities, who executed him.   This was the only genu-
ine unified action made in Central America and has
thus become known as the national war.

CERDA, VICENTE LAPARRO DE LA, 1831-1905.   A poet,
born in Guatemala City, he is considered to be the
founder of the national theater.   He wrote most of his
poetry as a young man but did not publish until his
later life.

CERNA, ISMAEL, 1856-1901.   A Guatemalan author and con-
stant critic of the liberal government.   His works include Lucila (lyric poem), La penitenciaria de Guatemala, and Poesias.

CERNA, VICENTE.   President of Guatemala from 1865 to
1871.   A general under Rafael Carrera, he was picked
to become president by Carrera.   Although Cerna attempted to continue the policies of Carrera, he did not
command the same power; an increasing number of revolts kept the country in turmoil until Cerna was
forced from power by García Granados and Barrios.

CERRATO, ALONSO LÓPEZ.   Governor from 1548 to 1555.
Although relieved of his duties in 1553, the new governor did not actually arrive to take up his post until
1555.   In 1549 the Audiencia was moved from Gracias
a Dios to Guatemala.   Cerrato stepped up the policy
of forcing the scattered Indians to live in municipios
so that better control of the countryside could be main-
tained.

CERRO QUEMADO VOLCANO.   Altitude: 10,430 feet.   In-

active volcano in southwestern Guatemala, three miles
south of Quezaltenango. It was active between 1785
and 1818.

CHACHACLÚN   see   SAN FRANCISCO.

CHACÓN, LÁZARO, 1873-1931.   President from 1926-30.
He took office as first designate and was later elected
President. He resigned because of illness and died in
New Orleans.

CHACÓN GONZÁLEZ, LÁZARO see CHACÓN, LÁZARO.

CHAFANDÓN. A not too affectionate nickname given to Miguel García Granados by the soldiers of the liberation
army. Probably a variation of the colonial term
"chapetones," which was a slang expression that referred to people in the colonies actually born in Spain,
as was García Granados.

CHAHAL. Municipio in the department of Alta Verapaz in
central Guatemala. The cabecera is located in the
easternmost part of the department. Population: 3961.
Crops: corn, beans, chile, rice, sugar cane.

CHAJUL. Municipio in the department of El Quiché in west
central Guatemala. The cabecera is located at the
east end of the Cuchumatanes Mountains, 11 miles
north-northeast of Sacapulas. Population: 13,497.
Crops: corn, beans; livestock.

CHALCHUAPA, BATTLE OF. A battle fought in 1885 at
Chalchuapa, El Salvador, between the Guatemalan army
under President Justo Rufino Barrios and the forces of
El Salvador. The engagement resulted in the death of
Barrios, thus ending his efforts to unite Central Amer-
ica by force under his leadership.

CHALCHUAPA, TREATY OF (May 8, 1876). A treaty of
friendship between El Salvador and Guatemala conclud-
ing a series of minor battles between the two countries.
No reparations were paid. The only stipulation required Justo Rufino Barrios' approval of the Salvadoran
president.

CHAMELCO see SAN JUAN CHAMELCO.

CHAMPERICO. Municipio located in the department of Retalhuleu in southwestern Guatemala. The cabecera is
23 miles southwest of Retalhuleu. Pacific port, rail
terminus, beach. Population: 11,459. Crops: grain;
livestock, fisheries, game hunting. Exports: cotton,
coffee, lumber, sugar.

CHAPARRÓN see SAN MANUEL CHAPARRÓN.

CHAPETONA, LA. The shortened name of the figure of the
Virgen de la Concepción at the Cathedral of Ciudad
Vieja.

CHAPETONE. A colonial term referring to peninsulars or
Spanish-born inhabitants.

CHAPÍN. A person born in Guatemala City.

CHAS-CARRILLO [pseudonym] see VALLADARES Y
RUBIO, ANTONIO.

CHÁVEZ, JUAN DE. A captain under Pedro de Alvarado
during the conquest, he lived near the capital and was
elected regidor in 1531 and Alcalde in 1546. In 1544
he was appointed royal attorney to enforce the new
laws but refused the commission.

CHÉVEZ, AMALIA, 1896- . An author, born in Coban,
she married Carlos Wyld Ospina. Best known for her
novel Mah-rap (1946) written under the pseudonym,
Malín de Echevers.

CHÉVEZ, J. ADELAIDA, 1846- . He wrote for many of
the literary journals of the period. Best known for
his work on a monograph dealing with domestic economics entitled Llave de oro, compendio de economia
doméstica (1887).

CHIANTLA. Municipio located in the department of Huehuetenango in western Guatemala. The cabecera is in the
Cuchumatanes Mountains, two miles north-northeast of
Huehuetenango. Lead mining nearby, market center,
tanning, wool processing. Population: 21,489. Altitude: 6250 ft. Crops: corn, beans; livestock.

CHIAPAS. Territory, including Soconusco, that is now a
part of Mexico, but in colonial times was a part of

Guatemala. When the Central American Federation
seceded from Mexico at the fall of Emperor Iturbide,
both of these provinces were retained by Mexico. In
1825, both parties (Mexico and Guatemala) agreed that
the southernmost province, Soconusco, should govern
itself until an election could be held and a boundary
established. In 1842 General Santa Anna of Mexico
sent troops to occupy the disputed land and decreed
its annexation to Mexico. Guatemala entered into negotiations over the territory, and through the years
Mexico continually pressed its claims and occupation
deeper into Guatemalan territory. Under Justo Rufino
Barrios, the United States agreed to arbitrate and a
settlement was negotiated giving much of the territory
to Mexico. The treaty was very unpopular in Guatemala, but Barrios pushed it through the Assembly,
partially because he wanted to get on with the unification (by force if necessary) of Central America, and
did not wish any threat from Mexico.

CHICABAL VOLCANO. In the municipio of San Martín
    Sacatepéquez, Quezaltenango. It has a crater partial-
    ly filled with water forming Lake Chicabal. Altitude:
    9572 ft.

CHICACAO. Municipio in the department of Suchitepéquez
    in southwestern Guatemala. The cabecera is on the
    left branch of the Nahualate River, 12 miles east of
    Mazatenango. Population: 20,804. Crops: cotton,
    coffee, sugar cane, grain; livestock.

CHICHA. A fermented drink made from maize, with fruits
    added.

CHICHE. Municipio in the department of El Quiché in west
    central Guatemala. Located in the western highlands,
    the cabecera is on the upper Motagua River, four
    miles east of Quiché. Population: 8218. Altitude:
    6610 ft. Crops: corn, beans; livestock.

CHICHI. A shortened, commonly used form of Chichicaste-
    nango.

CHICHICASTENANGO see SANTO TOMÁS CHICHICASTE-
    NANGO.

CHICLE. The main ingredient of chewing gum, chicle is

extracted from the Sapote tree (Achras Sapote), which
is found in forested regions of Mexico, British Honduras and Guatemala (Petén). The plantations are at
a great distance from the coast and the gum has to be
carried on muleback or by airplane to ports for shipment. The United States is the biggest customer in
the world market, but the high cost of the raw material, the fact that the trees have been successfully
grown in Florida, and the possibility that a substitute
product may be used in the making of chewing gum,
all combine to threaten the future of the chicle industry.

CHILAM-BALAM. Native books from the Yucatan area,
tracing the Mayan history for about 1400 years.

CHIM see MATATE.

CHIMALTENANGO. A department located in south central
Guatemala. Its capital is Chimaltenango. In the central highlands, sloping southward to about one thousand
feet elevation, it is bounded on the north by the Motagua River and on the west by the Madre Vieja River.
Acatenango Volcano is the outstanding peak in the area.
In the higher areas, crops are: corn, wheat, black
beans. Sugar cane and coffee grow on the southern
slope. Also: cattle, hog, sheep raising. Industries
are coffee processing, flour milling, and saw milling
around Tecpán and Patzicia. Chief urban centers are
Chimaltenango, Comalapa and Patzún. There are 16
municipios in the department: Acatenango, Chimaltenango, Comalapa, Parramos, Patzicia, Patzún, Pochuta, San Andrés, Itzapa, San José Poaquil, San Martín
Jilotepeque, San Pedro Yepocapa, Santa Apolonia,
Santa Cruz Balanya, Tecpán Guatemala, El Tejar,
Zaragoza. Population in 1950 was 121,480; in 1964
was 163,484, and projected to 1980 is 227,300. Area:
764 square miles.

CHIMALTENANGO. Municipio located in the department of
Chimaltenango in south central Guatemala. The cabecera is on the Inter-American highway, 20 miles west
of Guatemala City. Market center; brick making, tanning; agricultural school in the outskirts. Founded in
1526 just south of an old Indian fortress. Population:
15,673. Altitude: 5860 ft. Crops: grain, sugar
cane.

CHIMÁN   see   SHAMAN.

CHINABUJUL   see   MAM.

CHINAMIT   see   TINAMIT.

CHINANDEGA   see   PACT OF CHINANDEGA.

CHINAUTLA.   Municipio in the department of Guatemala in
    south central Guatemala.   The cabecera is four miles
    north of Guatemala City.   Pottery making, charcoal
    production.   Population: 20,663.   Altitude: 3800 ft.
    Crops: corn, black beans; livestock.

CHINCHILLA AGUILAR, ERNESTO, 1926- .   A Guatemalan
    historian, graduate of the Universidad de Mexico.   His
    leading works are Sor Juana de Maldonado y Paz
    (1949), La inquisición en Guatemala (1953), El ayunta-
    miento colonial de la ciudad de Guatemala (1961), His-
    toria y tradiciones de la ciudad de Amatitlán (1961),
    and Historia del arte en Guatemala, 1524-1962 (1963).

CHINGO VOLCANO.   Altitude: 5840 ft.   An extinct volcano
    on the Guatemala-Salvador border, 16 miles southeast
    of Jutiapa.

CHINIMTAL.   Quiché for marriage spokesman; see also
    KALPÚL.

CHINIQUE.   Municipio in the department of El Quiché in
    west central Guatemala.   Located in the Sierra de
    Chuacus Mountains, the cabecera is five miles north-
    east of Quiché.   Population: 3957.   Altitude: 6200 ft.
    Crops: corn, beans; livestock.

CHIQUIMULA.   1) A department located in eastern Guate-
    mala on the Honduran border.   It is bounded on the
    south by El Salvador and on the east by the highlands.
    Its capital is Chiquimula.   Drained by the Chiquimula
    River, it has two notable volcanoes, Ipala and Quezal-
    tepeque.   Crops are: corn, beans, fodder grasses,
    wheat; some livestock.   In the warmer valleys coffee,
    sugar cane, bananas, tobacco and rice are grown.
    Main urban centers are: Chiquimula, Esquipulas,
    Quezaltepeque.   There are 11 municipios in this de-
    partment: Camotán, Chiquimula, Concepción las Minas,
    Esquipulas, Ipala, Jocotán, Olopa, Quezaltepeque, San

Jacinto, San José la Arada, San Juan Ermita. Population in 1950 was 112,841; in 1964 was 149,910; and
projection to 1980 is 204,600. Area: 917 square
miles.
   2) Municipio located in the department of Chiquimula in eastern Guatemala. The cabecera is on the
Chiquimula River, 65 miles east-northeast of Guatemala City. Railroad; agricultural center in fruit and
cattle-raising region. Ruins of colonial church destroyed in the 1765 earthquake; city also suffered in
the 1773 earthquake. Population: 36,167. Altitude:
1378 ft. Crops: tobacco, sugar cane, corn, wheat,
cotton.

CHIQUIMULA RIVER. In eastern Guatemala, it is formed
   at Chiquimula by the confluence of two branches.
   Flows about 45 miles north to the Motagua River, five
   miles north of Zacapa. Often called "Río Grande de
   Zacapa."

CHIQUIMULILLA. Municipio in the department of Santa
   Rosa in southern Guatemala. Located on the coastal
   plain, the cabecera is near the Esclavos River, 14
   miles south-southwest of Cuilapa. Population: 24,280.
   Crops: coffee, cotton, grain; livestock.

CHIQUIMULILLA CANAL. In the department of Santa Rosa,
   it is part of the coastal lagoon of southern Guatemala,
   separated by low, sandy islands from the Pacific
   Ocean. Serves coastal fish and salt trades. Length:
   about 70 miles between San José and the Salvadoran
   border.

CHIRIMIA [pseudonym] see IRISARRI, JUAN BAUTISTA
   DE.

CHIRIMÍA. A reed instrument similar to the oboe, it often
   accompanies a drum at fiestas. Not an indigenous instrument.

CHIRUCHIPEC RIVER. Begins near Chahal, forming the
   boundary between Alta Verapaz and Izabal. It joins
   with the Seninlatíu River to form the Sarstún.

CHISEC. Municipio in the department of Alta Verapaz in
   central Guatemala. The cabecera is located in the
   northern part of the department. Population: 2925.

Crops: corn, beans, chili, rice, platanos, yuccas, pumpkins.

CHIXOY RIVER. Begins in southwestern Huehuetenango as the Río Negro and becomes the Chixoy when it forms the border between Quiché and Baja Verapaz and between Quiché and Alta Verapaz. The Chixoy becomes the Río Salinas and defines the boundary between Petén and Mexico for a short distance before joining the Río de la Pasión to form the Usumacinta River.

CHOCOLA. An experimental farm near Suchitepequez, sponsored by the Ministry of Agriculture to improve coffee production in addition to working with fruits and vegetables.

CHOL, EL. Municipio in the department of Baja Verapaz in central Guatemala. The cabecera is located in the southern part of the department. Population: 5226. Crops: corn, beans, rice, coffee, sugar cane.

CHORTI. A language group making up part of the Cholán linguistic stock of the Proto-Chiapas-Tabasco family of the Mayan language area. The Chorti are located in Chiquimula and Copán, Honduras, the only group of this linguistic stock south of the Quiché-Mam language area.

CHUARRANCHO. Municipio in the department of Guatemala in south central Guatemala. The cabecera is 13 miles north of Guatemala City. Market center. Population: 6027. Crops: corn, black beans, sugar cane, fruit.

CHUJ. A linguistic group of the Proto-Chiapas-Tabasco family of the Mayan language area. The Chuj, or Chuh, are located in Huehuetenango. The Chuj dialect is a transitional language and is sometimes classed with the Mamean linguistic group.

CHUJ, MIGUEL. A wood carver noted for his artistic ability in making the wooden masks used in the various celebration dances. His shop was in Totonicapán; his best work was produced in the 1930's and 1940's.

CINTAS see TOYACALES.

CIUDAD. A settlement often made up only of small stores

and artisan shops. Often the only distinction between
a ciudad, villa or pueblo is that a ciudad is the department capital where the government offices for the department and the local municipio are located.

CIUDAD VIEJA. Municipio located in the department of
Sacatepequez in south central Guatemala. The cabecera
is found at the northern foot of Agua Volcano, on the
Guacalate River, three miles south-southwest of Antigua. Hydroelectric station, road center; has the oldest
cathedral of Guatemala, built in 1534. Founded in
1527 on the Indian site of Almolonga. Population:
7233. Altitude: 4974 ft. Crops: coffee, grain, fodder grasses; livestock.

CLARO [pseudonym] see LAINFIESTA, FRANCISCO.

COATEPEQUE. Municipio located in the department of
Quezaltenango in southwestern Guatemala. The cabecera is found on the coastal plain, on the Naranjo
River and 25 miles west-southwest of Quezaltenango.
Railway and road center in the agricultural area. Population: 41,857. Crops: coffee, sugar cane, pineapples, plantains.

COBÁN. Municipio located in the department of Alta Verapaz in central Guatemala. The cabecera, the capital
of the department, is found in the northern highlands,
60 miles north of Guatemala City. Founded in 1538
and named after an early Indian chieftain, Cabaón,
there are Mayan ruins nearby and a 17th century
church. It developed into the chief urban center of
northern Guatemala, exporting its products via the Polochic River valley. Textiles, net and rope making,
tanning, coffee processing. Population: 38,461. Altitude: 4330 ft. Crops: coffee, vanilla, tea, cacao,
spices, grain; livestock.

COBOS, EUFORIO [pseudonym] see HERNÁNDEZ COBOS,
JOSÉ HUMBERTO.

COCHINEAL. Often referred to as grana, it is dyestuff
made from dried bodies of female scale insects that
live on nopal, a species of cactus. Used in the colonial period by the Indians as tribute payment, it probably predates the conquest. It makes a bright red dye.

COCOA   see   CACAO.

CODICES.   Ancient Mayan books of pre-conquest culture having hieroglyphs painted on skins and folded, accordian-
like.   Three Mayan codices survived the destructive
zeal of the priests, the conquest, and time: the Codex
Dresdensis at Dresden, Germany; the Codex Peresianus
in Paris; and the Codex Tro-Cortesianus in Madrid.

CODO.   A unit of measurement approximately two-thirds a
vara, or about 22.11 inches; sometimes called Cubit.

COFFEE.   First introduced to the Caribbean in the late
18th century in Haiti.   In Central America, it was first
planted in Costa Rica during the late colonial period.
In 1845, the semi-official Consulado de Comercio began to encourage the development of coffee plantations.
In 1853, Carrera subsidized the crop.   By 1860, the
exportation of coffee had begun and increased rapidly
to replace indigo as the chief export crop.   Coffee now
makes up 80 per cent of Guatemala's export.   The
first crops were raised in Guatemala near Antigua and
Amatitlán.   It now takes up most of the cultivated highland area.   Brazil is the leading world coffee producer
and has attempted to set a world price for coffee.
This has led to some stability in prices as most Latin
American countries cooperate; however, the Africa
producers are a threat.   Since the end of World War
II, coffee production has doubled, much of it coming
from Africa to the United States.   Under U.N. aus-
pices, an International Coffee Agreement was signed
in 1959 which set up export quotas for coffee producing nations.   Guatemala signed and ratified this agreement.

COFRADIA.   A religious brotherhood organized about a particular saint.   The job of the cofrades, or members,
is the care of their saint.   They carry out proper de-
votions such as Mass, and procure stocks of candles,
incense, and clothing for the saint.   The celebration
of the saint's day and the display of the saint's image
in processions are also arranged by the cofrades.

COHETERO.   One who fires rockets and sets off fireworks
in processions.

COJULÚM, LUCAS TIBURCIO, 1863-1914.   A Guatemalan

teacher and mathematician. Works: Aritmetica elemental (1885) and Algebra elemental (1890).

COLEGIO DE ABOGADOS DE GUATEMALA. Established in
    1810, reorganized in 1945, it is a professional union
    for lawyers, who must belong to practice. It concerns
    itself with protection of members and issues statements
    commenting generally on laws as they are enacted or
    questioned. In 1968 there were over 900 members
    with about 85 per cent of the membership living in
    Guatemala City.

COLOMBA. Municipio located in the department of Quezalte-
    nango in southwestern Guatemala. The cabecera, in
    the Pacific piedmont, is 17 miles southwest of Quezalte-
    nango. Population: 29,894. Crops: coffee, sugar
    cane; livestock.

COLONO. A worker hired by contract to live and work on
    a rural property. This is usually a four-year con-
    tract, and can be a permanent or lifetime position for
    the colono.

COLOTENANGO. Municipio located in the department of
    Huehuetenango in western Guatemala. The cabecera is
    west of Huehuetenango and just off the Inter-American
    Highway. Population: 7331. Crops: corn, beans,
    sugar cane.

COMA, PERSIXTO DE [pseudonym] see SAMAYOA AGUI-
    LAR, CARLOS.

COMAL. Used for baking tortillas, it is a saucer-shaped
    griddle of fired clay.

COMALAPA. Municipio in the department of Chimaltenango
    in south central Guatemala. The cabecera is nine
    miles north-northwest of Chimaltenango. Road and
    market center; brick-making, cotton weaving. Popula-
    tion: 14,845. Altitude: 6200 ft. Crops: corn,
    beans, wheat.

COMAPA. Municipio in the department of Jutiapa in south-
    eastern Guatemala. Its cabecera is located in the cen-
    tral part of the department, near the Salvadoran border.
    Population: 11,528. Crops: corn, beans, rice, chili,
    henequen.

COMITANCILLO. Municipio located in the department of
San Marcos in southwestern Guatemala. The cabecera
is in the northern part of the department, near the
border of Quezaltenango. Population: 14,490. Crops:
corn, wheat, potatoes, beans, green peas, apples,
peaches, quinces, figs.

COMITÉ CÍVICO NACIONAL (C.C.N.). An organization
formed in 1951 for the purpose of unifying opposition
against President Arbenz Guzmán.

COMITÉ COORDINADOR DE ASOCIACIONES AGRÍCOLAS,
COMERCIALES, INDUSTRIALES Y FINANCIERAS
(C.A.C.I.F.). Founded in 1957 by a broad group of
business and economic leaders. Members are representatives of various associations who use C.A.C.I.F.
as a forum to promote business and liberal economic
practices at the national level.

COMITÉ DE ESTUDIANTES UNIVERSITARIOS ANTICOMU-
NISTAS (C.E.U.A.). A political opposition group set
up in 1951.

COMITÉ NACIONAL DE DEFENSE CONTRA EL COMUNIS-
MO (C.N.D.C.C.). An agency set up by the Castillo
Armas government in 1954 to investigate and eliminate
communist sympathizers from government employment.

COMITÉ NACIONAL DE LA PAZ (C.N.P.). An organization to support political action, founded in 1949 by José
Fortuny Arana, their most significant activity was to
collect 175,974 signatures on a peace petition in 1954.

COMITÉ NACIONAL DE UNIDAD SINDICAL (C.N.U.S.). A
labor unity organization formed in 1946 for the purpose
of acting as spokesman for labor at the national level.

COMITÉ POLÍTICO NACIONAL DE LOS TRABAJADORES
(C.P.N.T.). Labor unity organization, the principal
task of which was to prevent workers from splitting
into small parties and voting for various candidates in
the election of 1950. They endorsed Arbenz in the
election.

COMPADRAZCO see PADRINO.

COMPADRE see PADRINO.

COMPAGNIE BELGE DE COLONISATION see SANTO TOMÁS.

COMPAÑIA AGRÍCOLA DE GUATEMALA. An incorporated (1928) Delaware subsidiary of the United Fruit Company, with its headquarters at Tiquisate. See UNITED FRUIT COMPANY.

CONCEPCIÓN. 1) Municipio located in the department of Huehuetenango in western Guatemala. The cabecera is in the Cuchumatanes Mountains, 25 miles north-northwest of Huehuetenango. Population: 6800. Altitude: 7871 ft. Crops: corn, wheat, beans; sheep raising.
2) Municipio, with a 17th-century church, located in the department of Sololá in southwest central Guatemala. The cabecera is four miles east of Sololá. Population: 1283. Altitude: 8199 ft. Crops: grain, beans, vegetables.

CONCEPCIÓN CHIQUIRICHAPA. Municipio in the department of Quezaltenango in southwestern Guatemala. The cabecera is one mile southwest of Ostuncalco. Population: 5031. Altitude: 8465 ft. Crops: corn, wheat, fodder grasses; livestock.

CONCEPCIÓN LAS MINAS. Municipio located in the department of Chiquimula in eastern Guatemala. The cabecera is in the highlands, 20 miles south-southeast of Chiquimula; road center. Population: 6964. Crops: corn, wheat, coffee; livestock.

CONCEPCIÓN TUTUAPA. Municipio located in the department of San Marcos in southwestern Guatemala. Its cabecera is in the north central part of the department, northwest of San Miguel Ixtahuacán. Population: 18,196. Crops: corn, wheat, beans, potatoes, peanuts, peaches, apples, avocados, limes.

CONCUÉN RIVER. Begins in Petén, flows south to form part of the boundary between Petén and Alta Verapaz before emptying into the Río de la Pasión.

CONFEDERACIÓN CENTROAMÉRICA see PACT OF CHINANDEGA.

CONFEDERACIÓN DE TRABAJADORES DE AMÉRICA

LATINA (C. T. A. L.).   Labor organization to encourage union development.   Founded in 1938 as a continu-
ation of C. S. L. A. , its headquarters are in Mexico
and its leading spokesman is Vicente Lombardo Tole-
dano.   During the union development in Guatemala between 1944 and 1954, the C. T. A. L. gave much aid and
assistance to Guatemalan unions.

CONFEDERACIÓN DE TRABAJADORES DE GUATEMALA
(C. T. G.).   Labor organization composed of several
unions which banded together in late 1944 under the
leadership of Víctor Manuel Gutiérrez.   The C. T. G.
moved steadily to the left politically, until it was disbanded in 1954.   At its peak, in 1949, it included 39
unions having a membership of over 10, 000.

CONFEDERACIÓN GENERAL DE TRABAJADORES DE
GUATEMALA (C. G. T. G.).   Labor organization founded
at a unity conference held by labor and agricultural
unions in October, 1951.   It strongly supported labor
reform legislation, along with the agrarian reform
measure of 1952.

CONFEDERACIÓN NACIONAL DE CAMPESINO DE GUATE-
MALA (C. N. C. G.).   Labor organization of rural
workers founded in 1950, it worked toward benefits to
the small rural worker who could not join unions designed for the large farm worker.   At its peak in
1954, it had 1785 small local campesino unions making
up its membership.

CONFEDERACIÓN OBRERO DE PAN AMÉRICA (C. O. P. A.).
An inter-American labor organization founded in La-
redo, Texas in 1918, through the encouragement of the
American Federation of Labor.   It ceased in the 30's
and accomplished little beyond meeting six times.
Guatemala was a member of this organization.

CONFEDERACIÓN SINDICAL DE GUATEMALA (C. O. N. S. I.
G. U. A.).   Formed in 1955 as the Consejo Sindical de
Guatemala (C. S. G.), promoted by O. R. I. T. , its primary purpose was to get out urban votes for candidates being endorsed.

CONFEDERACIÓN SINDICATO DE LATINA AMERICANA
(C. S. L. A.).   Labor organization founded in 1928 for
the improvement of labor conditions in Latin America.

It later changed its title to Confederación de Trabajadores de América Latina.

CONGREGA.   A forced Indian settlement common during the
colonial period.   To better control the Indians, the
Spanish, from the mid-16th century on, pursued a policy of concentrating the widely scattered Indians into
congregaciones or congregas.   The Indians frequently
reacted violently toward this system, but were unable
to prevent it.   See REDUCCION.

CONGUACO.   Municipio in the department of Jutiapa in
southeastern Guatemala.   The cabecera is located in
the southwestern part of the department, near the Salvadoran border.   Population: 7492.   Crops: corn,
beans, rice.

CONQUISTA, LA.   A dance, created in 1542 by a Spanish
priest, and first presented in Antigua.   Its theme is
the defeat of the Quiché by the Spanish and the death
of the last great Indian leader, Tecum Uman.

CONQUISTADOR.   Name given to the Spaniards who took
part in the expeditions of conquest in the New World.

CONSEJO AGRARIO NACIONAL (C. A. N.).   Established by
the Agrarian Reform Law in 1952, the consejo set the
policy and largely determined what land would be distributed to whom.   At the national level, a nine-mem-
ber consejo was appointed by the President to set policy.   There were committees in each department, except Petén, and local committees in each municipio.
One of the first acts of Castillo Armas was to disband
the whole structure in Decree no. 21 of July 16, 1954.

CONSEJO DE LAS INDIAS.   "El Real y Supremo Consejo de
las Indias" was set up in August, 1524, as the supreme
legislative and judicial control, responsible only to the
King.   Queen Isabella had, in 1493, appointed Juan
Rodríguez de Fonseca to head affairs relating to the
new territories.   He held the post until his death in
1524.   The Consejo then came into being and controlled
all functions of government for the New World.   It
handled important cases brought up through the audi-
encias and had jurisdiction over cases proceeding from
the Casa de Contratación.   The Consejo lacked unity of
action, however, since it was not responsible for the

enforcement of regulations. Decisions could be held
up by the Consejo for an unlimited amount of time. In
1714, a Ministry of Navy and Indies was created to
take over affairs pertaining to America, with the Consejo subordinate to it. In 1790, the power of the Consejo was restricted to that of advisory capacity. It
was abolished in 1812, re-established in 1814, and
permanently ended in 1834.

CONSEJO SINDICAL DE GUATEMALA (C.S.G.). A trade
union council formed in 1955 in affiliation with the International Confederation of Free Trade Unions. In 1964 it
claimed 25 per cent (4,000) of the total union members
in Guatemala. In 1965 the name was changed to C.O.
N.S.I.G.U.A. Since then it has received funds for
operation from O.R.I.T.

CONSORCIO AZUCARERO see ASOCIACIÓN DE AZUCARE-
ROS.

CONSULADO DE COMERCIO. A guild of merchants formed
for the purpose of encouraging trade and profitable
crops. It had its own law courts to handle matters of
contract, freights, bankruptcy, etc. It was established
in Guatemala in 1793, abolished in 1826, only to be
re-established in 1839 and to last then until 1871, when
the mercantile courts were established to handle commercial matters under the direction of the Ministerio
de Fomento. The consulado was influential in encouraging the development of coffee, when chemical dyes
threatened indigo profits.

CONTLE see ZONTLE.

CONTRERAS VÉLEZ, ALVARO, 1923- . Born in Costa
Rica, he studied in Guatemala and the United States.
Since 1951 he has worked on the newspaper Prensa
Libre. As a novelist, he has written Humour (1942),
El cooperativismo en la postguerra (1946), Suicido
barato se necesita (1949), Memorias de un amnesico
(1955), and El blanco que tenía el asma negra.

COPAL. A tree from which a resin is extracted and used
for incense.

CÓRDOBA, ALEJANDRO, 1888-1944. A novelist, born in
Huehuetenango, editor of the newspaper, El Imparcial

and member of the National Assembly from 1934 to
1944. His best effort was Espigas al viento (1926).
Pseudonym: Adan Vigil.

CÓRDOBA, MATÍAS DE, 1750-1828. A Dominican born in
Chiapas, he held the chair of rhetoric at the Univer-
sity of San Carlos. He was one of the founders of the
Sociedad Económica in 1795. He went to Spain in 1803
and witnessed the Spanish uprising against Bonaparte.
Upon his return to Guatemala, he edited the periodical
Para-rayos and assisted in another entitled El Expe-
ciero. His works include La tentative del León.
Pseudonym: Bondesir.

CÓRDOBA GONZÁLEZ, Jacinto, 1877-1950. An author
from Quezaltenango, he wrote Papeles íntimos (1907)
and Proemio al periodico "La propaganda" (1910).

CÓRDOVA, JOSÉ FRANCISCO, 1786-1856. A leader in the
independence movement, he presented the act of independence to the assembly in 1823. He later helped to
edit the conservative newspaper El Indicador.

CORREGIDOR. Local official with administrative and judicial powers. In Spanish America there were two types
of corregidores: the Corregidor de Españoles and the
Corregidor de Indios. The former was appointed by
the crown and lived in the Spanish settlements. The
latter was appointed by the viceroy and lived in Indian
villages. Each presided over his respective cabildo or
municipal council. The duties of the corregidor were
to foster economic development of his district, to make
at least one tour of his district during his term of office, and to resolve administrative and judicial problems. Special duties of the corregidor de indios were
the collection of tribute from the Indians, the supervi-
sion of forced labor which was demanded of the Indians, and the protection of the natives from the Spaniards. The system was set up in 1530 to replace the
encomienda, but due to the short-term appointments
of corregidores, they never developed a paternal attitude toward the welfare of the natives as did most of
the encomenderos. The tyranny and corruption of the
corregidores, especially in their relations with the Indians, was often extreme. Charles III, in his reform
measures, gradually replaced the corregidores with
intendentes, and by 1790, the new system was in opera-

tion throughout Spanish America.

CORTÉS, HERNANDO, 1485-1547.   Spanish conqueror of
    Mexico.   In 1523-24 he sent two expeditions into Cen-
    tral America, one of which, led by Pedro de Alvarado,
    overcame the Mayan civilization in Guatemala.   Cortés
    led the second expedition to Honduras in 1524-26, by
    way of the lowland jungle, passing through Yucatan and
    Petén.   He embarked by ship from the Honduran coast
    on his return trip to Mexico.

CORTEZ Y LARRAZ, PEDRO, 1712-1786.   Archbishop of
    Guatemala from 1767 to 1779, he left 50,000 pesos to
    found a college of surgery at the Universidad de San
    Carlos.   He wrote several religious tracts.

COSIO Y CAMPA, TORIBIO JOSÉ DE.   Governor from 1706
    to 1716.   He led an expedition against the Tzendal re-
    bellion in Chiapas and was successful in putting it
    down.

COSTA CUCA.   The northwestern Pacific coastal lowlands
    lying between the town of Retalhuleu, the Pacific coast,
    and the Mexican border.

COSTA DE GUAZACAPAN.   The coastal area in the south-
    eastern Pacific lowlands of Guatemala.   It extends
    from the widest part of the lowland piedmont area
    southward to the border.

COSTUMBRISMO.   A prose fiction movement beginning in
    Latin America in the 1840's, influenced by Spain: usu-
    ally, short essays in prose or verse, depicting man-
    ners, customs or characters of a social or provincial
    setting.   The movement gave rise to the later region-
    al novelistic trend.   An early leading Guatemalan cos-
    tumbrista writer was Antonio José de Irisarri (El Cris-
    tiano errante, 1847).

COTA, BLAS.   A lawyer and leading member of the Ayunta-
    miento of 1541, which elected Francisco de la Cueva
    and Bishop Marroquín joint governors of Guatemala af-
    ter the deaths of Pedro de Alvarado and his wife, Doña
    Beatriz.

COTON see HUIPIL.

COTZAL   see   SAN JUAN COTZAL.

CREOLES.   The Spanish-American non-Indians born in America.   Although there was no law barring them from public office, they were usually excluded from high administrative positions in both Church and State in the Spanish colonies; this fact contributed much toward the antagonism between creoles and the Spaniards.   Sometimes called Criollos.

CRESPO JUÁREZ, PEDRO, d. 1646.   Postmaster of Guatemala; he left 20,000 pesos to augment the university fund left by Bishop Marroquín.   The university was not founded until 1679.

CRIADO DE CASTILLA, ALONSO, d. 1611.   Governor from 1598 to 1611.   Although appointed in 1596, he did not assume his duties until 1598.   In 1605 the Caribbean port of Santo Tomás was built, but was later moved to Puerto Dulce where better health conditions existed.

CRIOLLISMO.   A literary movement beginning in Venezuela in the late nineteenth century.   It emphasized native (creole) characters and background and was most often realistic or naturalistic in style and was concerned with social reform.   Best representative of this movement in Guatemala is the work of Miguel Ángel Asturias.

CRIOLLOS   see   CREOLES.

CRISTO DEL GOLGOTA, EL.   A favorite shrine of the Quiché Indians in Chajul, in the department of Quiché. It is visited on the second Friday of Lent, mostly by Indians.

CRUZ, MARÍA, 1876-1915.   A Guatemalan poetess, her only volume of poetry is entitled Cartas de la india.

CRUZ, VICENTE, d. 1849.   One of Carrera's earliest followers, he was made Vice-President when Carrera took the office of President.   Cruz held the post until November 28, 1848, when he resigned because he was not appointed President after Carrera's resignation.   He was killed while fighting rebels led by Augustín Pérez.

CRUZ SAMAYOA, FERNANDO, 1845-1902.   A lawyer, he

held several high government posts. His writings include works on civil law, and poetry published under
the title A mi hijo.

CUADRILLERO. A migratory worker hired as day labor.
The term comes from the coffee finca area where day
labor is hired to clear new land for cultivation. In
one day, one man is expected to clear one cuadrillo,
an area of about 28 vara square. See also TEMPORA-
DISTA JORNALERO and TAREA.

CUAJATINTA see SACATINTA.

CUAJINIGUILAPA see CUILAPA.

CUARENTIÑO. A short, two-month growing season for
maize.

CUARTILLO. A unit of colonial money equal to about one-
fourth a real or a 32nd part of a silver peso. There
is no accurate way to calculate the value of the money
by present-day standards. One 16th century writer
considered one cuartillo an excessive day's wage for
weeding.

CUBIT see CODO.

CUBULCO. Municipio located in the department of Baja
Verapaz in central Guatemala. The cabecera is in the
northern highlands, 21 miles west of Salama. Population: 19,707. Crops: grain; livestock raising.

CUERDA. A measure of land, usually 32 vara square,
which is between one-fifth and one-sixth of an acre.
On coffee fincas, a cuerda of 28 varas square is often
used as the standard to determine a day's work for
the cuadrillero.

CUEVA, FRANCISCO DE LA, 1501?-1576. He went to
Guatemala with Alvarado in 1539 after Alvarado had
married his cousin, Doña Beatriz. He was made acting governor when Alvarado went to Mexico, and lieutenant governor after Alvarado died. When Doña Beatriz died, he was made co-governor with Bishop Francisco Marroquín until the arrival, in May, 1542, of
the new governor, Alonso de Maldonado. He later
married Doña Leonor, illegitimate daughter of Pedro

de Alvarado, and widow of Pedro Portocarrero.

CUEVA DE ALVARADO, DOÑA BEATRIZ DE LA, d. 1541.
Wife of Pedro de Alvarado, she had herself appointed
governor at his death and was the only woman governor in the history of the Spanish colonial period. She
signed her name, "La sin ventura." Two weeks after
taking office, she was killed in the destruction of Almolonga. She was buried in Antigua along with the remains of her husband.

CUILAPA. Municipio in the department of Santa Rosa in
southern Guatemala. The cabecera is on the Inter-
American highway, 27 miles southeast of Guatemala
City, in a bend formed by the Esclavos River. The
department capital was moved here in 1871 from Santa
Rosa. Following destruction (1913) of Cuilapa by
earthquake, Barbarena was temporary capital until
1920. Two miles southeast of the cabecera, on the
Esclavos River, is a massive 16th-century stone bridge.
Commercial and agricultural center in coffee and sugar
cane. Population: 13,314. Sometimes called Cuajiniguilapa.

CUILCO. Municipio located in the department of Huehuetenango in western Guatemala. The cabecera is on the
Cuilco River, 33 miles west of Huehuetenango. Population: 15,042. Altitude: 3445 ft. Sugar refining,
fishing, livestock raising.

CUILCO INCENSE. Incense from the area around Cuilco,
made from the best grade copal.

CUILCO RIVER. Headstream of the San Miguel River; it
flows into Mexico and eventually empties into the Gulf
of Mexico. Sometimes called the Grijalva River.

CULEBRA, LA. Snake dance. see LOS GRACEJOS.

CUNÉN. Municipio located in the department of El Quiché
in west central Guatemala. The cabecera is at the
eastern end of the Cuchumatanes Mountains, five miles
north-northeast of Sacapulas. Population: 8248. Altitude: 5600 ft. Crops: corn, beans; livestock.

CURANDERO. A native healer, herbalist, masseur or shaman whose treatments include the application of medi-

cines or herbs along with the performance of a religious ritual.

CUYOTENANGO. Municipio located in the department of Suchitepequez in southwestern Guatemala. The cabecera is on a railroad, four and a half miles west of Mazatenango. Population: 17,932. Crops: coffee, cotton, sugar cane, grain, fodder grasses; livestock raising, lumbering.

-D-

D. A. N.   see   DEPARTAMENTO AGRARIO NACIONAL.

D. A. R.   [pseudonym] see GARCÍA REDONDO, ANTONIO.

D. C. G.   see   DEMOCRACIA CRISTIANA GUATEMALTECA.

DANCE (ceremonial) see under CONQUISTA, LA; GRACE-JOS, LOS; MOROS, LOS; PALO VOLADOR; SON; VENADO, EL.

DÁVILA, FERNANDO ANTONIO, 1783-1851. A Guatemalan Franciscan who wrote several religious tracts. The best known, Bosquejo del curato de Quezaltenango (1846), deals with statistics of the area.

DE ECHEVERS, MALÍN [pseudonym] see CHÁVEZ, AMALIA.

DELGADO, JOSÉ MATÍAS, 1787-1832. A priest who became an early leader in the movement against Spain. He led an unsuccessful revolt in 1811. He later became provisional governor of San Salvador and was quite active in the politics of the federation as the first Bishop of Salvador.

DELIUS [pseudonym] see AYCINENA, JUAN FERMÍN.

DEMOCRACIA, LA. Municipio located in the department of Escuintla in southern Guatemala. The cabecera is 12 miles southwest of Escuintla, near the railroad. Population: 11,088. Crops: sugar cane, grain, cotton.

DEMOCRACIA, LA. Municipio located in the department of Huehuetenango in western Guatemala. Its cabecera is is in the western part of the department, between the Inter-American Highway and the Trapichillo River. Population: 8961. Crops: corn, beans, sugar cane, coffee, rice, peanuts.

DEMOCRACIA CRISTIANA GUATEMALTECA (D. C. G.). First appeared as the Movimiento de Afirmacia Nacional de Cristianidad (M. A. N. C.) during the administration of Arbenz as a political support party for the Church. In 1955 the name was changed and the organization received open support of Castillo Armas. The D. C. G. remains the church political party and has in recent years taken a liberal approach to social and economic affairs.

DEPARTAMENTO. The department is the largest political division within the republic, the equivalent of a state in other countries. Each departamento is broken up into municipios, which is the base for the local governmental unit. There are 22 departments in Guatemala (counting Belice, 23): Alta Verapaz, Baja Verapaz, Chimaltenango, Chiquimula, Escuintla, Guatemala, Huehuetenango, Izabal, Jalapa, Jutiapa, El Petén, El Progreso, Quezaltenango, El Quiché, Retalhuleu, Sacatepéquez, San Marcos, Santa Rosa, Sololá, Suchitepéquez, Totonicapán, Zacapa.

DEPARTAMENTO AGRARIO NACIONAL (D. A. N.). A government agency in the Ministry of Agriculture which was established between 1952 and 1962 to assist in overcoming agricultural problems. The D. A. N. , through a branch agency, the Consejo Agrario Nacional, controlled the agrarian land distribution program. The reorganization of 1962 replaced D. A. N. with I. N. T. A.

DÍAZ, VICTOR MIGUEL, 1865-1940. A Guatemalan journalist and author. He often wrote under the pseudonym El Viejo Reporter. His works include La romántica ciudad colonial (1927), Las belles artes en Guatemala (1934), Historia de la imprenta en Guatemala (1930), Barrios ante la posteridad (1935), and Conmociones terrestres en la América Central, 1469-1930 (1931).

DÍAZ DEL CASTILLO, BERNAL, 1496-1584. A Spanish soldier and Guatemalan historian. His eyewitness account of the conquest told of his participation in the 1517 Yucatan expedition of Francisco de Córdoba and in

the 1518 expedition under Juan de Grijalva. He also
took part in the conquest of Mexico under Hernán
Cortés, 1519-1521, and went on to Honduras with Cortés in 1524-1526. His account was entitled Historia
verdadera de la conquista de la Nueva España and
earned him the title of historian of the conquest. In
1541, Díaz settled at Antigua where he later married
Teresa Becerra, a daughter of a fellow conquistador.
In 1552, Díaz began to write the true history of the
conquest, after reading the official account written by
Francisco de Gómara. He believed that the common
soldier was not given enough recognition in Gómara's
work and set out to correct the errors. He finished
the first draft in 1575, but it remained unpublished
until 1632. The closest copy to an original known today is located at the Archivo Nacional in Guatemala.
This is the copy used by Genaro García in his edition
of 1904-05, from which the Hakluyt Society's translation was made. The "true history" is now considered
to be one of the major contributions to historical scholarship.

DÍAZ GEBUTA QUEJ, FRANCISCO, d. 1597. Thought to be
one of the authors of the Mayan epic Annals of the
Cakchiqueles (1554).

DÍAZ ROZZOTTO, JAIME, 1918- . Born in Quezaltenango,
he attended the Universidad de San Carlos. He was
general secretary to President Arbenz. He wrote El
carácter de la revolución guatemalteca (1958).

DÍAZ VASCONCELOS, LUIS ANTONIO, 1906- . A lawyer
and historian, born in El Salvador, he was educated
and lived in Guatemala. He wrote Apuntes para historia de la literatura guatemalteca (1942), De nuestro
antaño historico (1948), and Norma e institución jurí-
dicas Mayas (1953).

DIÉGUEZ, MANUEL, 1821-1861. A Guatemalan poet, he
translated the French novel Rico y pobre (1858) by
Emilio Souvestre.

DIÉGUEZ FLORES, MANUEL, 1856-1922. Guatemalan author and diplomat, he died in New York while serving
as consul general to the United States.

DIÉGUEZ OLAVERRI, JUAN, 1813-1866. A Guatemalan

poet, his selected works were published in A los
cuchumatanes (1893).   His leading poem is entitled Las
tardes de Abril, reprinted in his Poesias de ... (1893)
and the second edition of 1957.

DÍEZ DE NOVARRO, LUIS.   A Spanish architect and military
engineer, he arrived in Guatemala in 1741.   He conducted a geographical survey of Guatemala in 1756, and
built the Palace of the Captains General in Antigua in
1764.   After the destruction of Antigua in 1773, he
drew up the town plans for Guatemala City.

DIEZMO.   Church tithe, meaning "one-tenth."   This ecclesiastical tax was collected in the American colonies by
the Spanish government for the purpose of defraying the
cost of maintenance and construction of churches and
other religious buildings.

DOLORES.   Municipio in the department of El Petén in northern Guatemala.   The cabecera is located 40 miles
southeast of the city of Flores.   Population: 1180.
Crops: chicle, agricultural products; lumber.

DOMAS Y VALLE, JOSÉ, d. 1802.   Governor from 1794 to
1801.

DOMINICAN.   A Catholic Order which was very powerful in
colonial Guatemala.   The Dominicans were active edu-
cators and led in the protection of native races from
exploitation by the Spaniards.   Bartolomé de Las Casas
was their outstanding spokesman.   The Order believed
that conversion by force or en masse was not true conversion, that only through peaceful preaching of the
gospel would true conversion occur.   The Order had its
start in Guatemala in 1528 and led in the struggle to
found the Universidad de San Carlos.   The ruins of the
Dominican Church and Convent in Antigua are monumental.   The Dominicans were forced out of Guatemala
along with other religious orders during the liberal revolution of 1871.

DONADIU   see   TONIATIUH.

DOVALLE, GONZALO.   A captain in the Pánuco expedition
to Mexico led by Garay against Cortés.   He was on the
conquest of Guatemala under Alvarado and was appointed
alcalde (mayor) of Guatemala by Orduña in 1529 while

Alvarado was in Spain. He attempted to revoke some
land grants made by Alvarado but was unsuccessful due
to Alvarado's return. Dovalle was again Alcalde in
1539.

DRAGO-BRACO, ADOLFO, 1893- . Guatemalan dramatist,
he has written some 80 plays, farces and skits, mostly commercial productions. His more serious works
include Farandula sentimental (1915), San Luis Gonzaga
(1921), Colombina quiere flores (1928), and Se ban
deshojado en el jardín las rosas (1938).

DUEÑAS see SAN MIGUEL DUEÑAS.

DULCE RIVER. Located in the department of Izabal in
eastern Guatemala, the Dulce River leaves the northeastern end of Lake Izabal at San Felipe and flows 22
miles northeast to the gulf at Livingston. It widens
in the middle to form a small lake, ten miles long
and two to four miles wide.

-E-

E.A.H. [pseudonym] see HIDALGO, ENRIQUE AGUSTÍN.

EARTHQUAKES. Between 1541 and 1773, 14 prolonged, destructive quakes rocked Antigua before the capital was
moved to its present location. Besides the devastating quake of 1773, which leveled the city, one in 1717
leveled almost 3000 buildings and homes. In 1874,
Guatemala City was battered by a severe earthquake.
In 1902, an earthquake destroyed Quezaltenango, causing much of its leading industry to move to Guatemala
City. In 1913, a quake destroyed the capitol of Santa
Rosa, Cuilapa, causing the official offices to be moved
for several years. Between Christmas Eve, 1917, and
the end of January, 1918, Guatemala City was almost
leveled by earthquakes and, as a result, much of the
city is extremely modern in structure today. Earthquakes are frequent but normally only slight damage
results.

EASTERN COAST OF CENTRAL AMERICA COMMERCIAL
    AND AGRICULTURAL COMPANY see ABBOTSVILLE.

ECHEVERS, MALÍN DE [pseudonym] see CHÉVEZ, AM-
    ALIA.

ECHEVERS Y SUVISA, ANTONIO PEDRO DE, d. 1734.
Governor from 1724 to 1733.

ECONOMIC SOCIETY   see   SOCIEDAD ECONÓMICA DE
AMIGOS DE GUATEMALA.

EL.   Phrases and place names beginning with an article
are found under the word following the article.

EMPRESA ELÉCTRICA DE GUATEMALA.   On July 1, 1918,
the government of Guatemala took control of the German Compañía Eléctrico de Guatemala by decree number 737.   By decree number 742 of October 2, 1918,
it nationalized the property.   In May, 1919, the Electric Company was leased to Henry W. Catlin.   In
March, 1920, the government authorized the sale of
the company to the Electric Bond and Share Company
of New York for $495,000.   The Central American
Power Company, as it was known under Catlin, was
incorporated as Empresa Guatemalteca de Electricidad,
with a capital stock of $3,250,000, after the company
received a 50-year contract under which it could operate.   The company operated under three titles at
various times, the last being Empresa Electrica de
Guatemala.   It is a subsidiary of the American and
Foreign Power Company which operates in several
Latin American countries.   Most of the electricity
used in Guatemala goes for lights and cooking stoves,
making up three-fourths of all the electric power used
in Guatemala City.   The Empresa Eléctrica supplies
about four-fifths of the electricity in Guatemala from
its six hydroelectric, and one steam, plants (in 1950).
Under President Jacobo Arbenz, several labor strikes
were called, resulting in the company's labor being
among the highest paid in Guatemala.   Before Arbenz
was overthrown, Congress passed tax claims, chal-
lenged its 1923 contract, threatened expropriation and
enacted an "absentee tax" against foreign countries.
The company's monopolistic position in the capital city
and its high rates to electricity users gave rise to the
Arbenz action.   All such action was suspended with
the fall of Arbenz from power, and plans were made
to install additional hydro-electric and thermal gener-
ating facilities.

ENCOMIENDA.   A system of forced labor whereby the Spanish encomenderos were granted allotments of natives

to indoctrinate into the ways of the Church and to protect.   The grants were rewards for the conquistadors
and could be passed on to descendants.   The encomendero received the right to demand labor or payment in
kind.   No grant of land accompanied the encomienda,
but often the encomendero eventually appropriated the
Indian lands.   The New Laws of 1542 was an attempt
to correct the injustices of the system, but the encomenderos prevented its enforcement.   A royal order of
1720 set up a method to gradually eliminate the encomienda and by the end of the colonial period, this
was accomplished.

ENGANCHE.   From the word "enganchamiento" (enlisting in
the army), it refers to a system of labor contract
whereby a quantity of money is advanced to the worker
to ensure and obligate his appearance at the finca when
needed to work.   First used in Guatemala in official
legislation after the revolution of 1871.

ENGAÑADO [pseudonym]   see   BERGAÑO Y VILLEGAS,
SIMÓN.

ENRÍQUEZ DE GUZMÁN, ENRIQUE.   Governor from 1684
to 1688.   After an epidemic in Guatemala City, he ordered construction of hospitals.

ENRÍQUEZ DE RIBERA, PAYO, 1612-1685.   From Seville,
he was one of the outstanding bishops of Guatemala
(1657-1668).   He was responsible for having the press
of José de Pineda Ibarra taken to Guatemala.   Ribera's
Explicato (1663) was the first major item published on
the press.   He became Archbishop of Mexico after
leaving Guatemala.

ENTRADA.   Literal Spanish meaning: an entrance or arrival at a place.   Also: conversion of Indians to Christianity made by military coercion (also known as Con-
quistas de Almas).   Concerning property or money:
the placement in a treasury or under the control of another person.

ENVIDIA.   A state of being envied, believed by the Indians
to be caused by witchcraft.   The victim is secretly attacked by a person envious of the victim or of his position.   The threat of an envidia is one of the few anx-
ities of the Indians.

ESCALS, JOSÉ DE. Acting governor from 1695 to 1696.
He took office at the death of Governor Barrios. A
dispute arose over his right to the governorship and
continued into the next administration of Governor Berrospe.

ESCLAVOS RIVER (Río de los Esclavos). Begins in the
highlands of southern Guatemala, near Mataquescuintla;
flows about 75 miles south past Santa Rosa, then to
the Pacific, 37 miles east-southeast of San José. It
forms the border between the departments of Santa
Rosa and Jutiapa in its lower course. Near Cuilapa,
a large 16th-century stone bridge crosses the river.

ESCOBAR, JOSÉ BERNARDO. A noted orator, he held the
office of president during part of the time Carrera
was in voluntary exile. His term of office lasted from
November 28, 1848 to January 1, 1849. He wrote
Apelación al tribunal de la opinión pública.

ESCOBEDO, FERNANDO FRANCISCO DE. Governor from
1672 to 1682. He revised the constitution of the Audiencia, built up coastal fortifications, and upon his
return to Spain, used his influence to liberalize trade
regulations for Guatemala.

ESCOBILLA. A small lowland shrub, the fibrous bark of
which is used in making fish nets.

ESCUINTLA. 1) A department located in southern Guatemala,
on the Pacific coast. The capital is Escuintla. Located in the Pacific piedmont, it slopes southward into the coastal plain and is drained by the Nahualate,
Madre Vieja, Guacalate and Michatoya Rivers. The
volcano Pacaya is in the northeast. Crops include:
sugar cane, with mills at Pantaleón, El Baul, Concepción and Salto; bananas at Tiquisate; coffee, corn,
citronella and tropical fruit. Some cattle raising.
The area is served by the Guatemala to San José railway. Main centers are Escuintla, Santa Lucía, Palín,
and the port of San José. There are 12 municipios in
this department: La Democracia, Escuintla, La Gómera, Guanagazapa, Iztapa, Masagua, Palín, San José
(Puerto), San Vicente Pacaya, Santa Lucía Cotzumalguapa, Siquinala, Tiquisate. The population in 1950
was 123,759; in 1964, 270,059 and the projected population to 1980 is 588,400. Area: 1692 square miles.

2) Municipio located in the department of Escuintla, in southern Guatemala. The cabecera is near
the Guacalate River, 28 miles southwest of Guatemala
City, on the railroad. It is a commercial and agricultural center in a rich sugar cane, cotton and coffee
district. Also: citronella, lemongrass, tropical fruit
(coconuts, pineapples, mangos); cotton gin. Sugar
mills of Concepción and Salto are nearby. Winter resort (mineral baths). Flourished as a political and
indigo-trading center in the 17th and 18th centuries.
Population: 55,192. Altitude: 1109 ft.

ESPANTO. Fright. An Indian folk medicinal belief is that
a sudden fright or shock may cause a mental or
physical breakdown. Sleeplessness, apathy, loss of
appetite, partial paralysis or headaches may be caused
by a sudden clap of thunder, a sudden meeting with a
snake, a fall, or anything that produces a sudden fright
in a person. Sometimes besets a person who is out
of touch with others or one who is no longer integrated
in the social group. Often called Susto.

ESPARRAGOSA Y GALLARDO, NARCISO, 1759-1819. Born
in Venezuela, he went to Guatemala in 1785 to become
a leading medical scholar at the University of San
Carlos. He was a student of José Felipe Flores. Esparragosa developed an elastic forceps to be used in
breech births. He left his library, tools, and money
to the college of surgery. His works include Memoria
sobre una invención (1798) and Medicina operatoria
(1802).

ESPERANZA, LA. Municipio in the department of Quezaltenango, in southwestern Guatemala. The cabecera is
two miles northwest of Quezaltenango, and is the site
of the Quezaltenango airport. Population: 3232. Altitude: 7831 ft. Crops: corn, wheat, fodder grasses;
livestock raising.

ESPINAL, PACA [pseudonym] see BALSELLS RIVERA,
ALFREDO.

ESPINOSA DE LOS MONTEROS, JOSÉ OSORIO. Governor
from 1704 to 1706.

ESQUILACHES. A group of students formed in 1934 to protest the Ubico government. They later formed the

nucleus of the opposition, leading to the 1944 revolution.

ESQUIPULAS. Municipio located in the department of Chiquimula in eastern Guatemala. The cabecera is in the highlands, near the Honduras and Salvador borders, 20 miles southeast of Chiquimula. It is the mecca of greatest religious pilgrimages, Indian and Ladino, in Central America (see CALVARIO, EL). Church dates from 1737. Population: 17,130. Crops: corn, beans, rice, potatoes, sugar cane, coffee, tobacco, cotton.

ESQUIPULAS PALO GORDO. Municipio in the department of San Marcos in southwestern Guatemala. Its cabecera is located just southwest of San Marcos. Population: 2740. Crops: corn, wheat, potatoes, vegetables.

ESTACHERIA, JOSÉ DE. Governor from 1783 to 1789.

ESTADO. A measurement equal to slightly over five and one-half feet.

ESTADO DE SITIO see STATE OF SIEGE.

ESTANCIA. A large farm, generally a cattle ranch.

ESTANCO. A store where aguardiente is sold.

ESTANZUELA. Municipio in the department of Zacapa in eastern Guatemala. The cabecera is near the Motagua River, three miles northwest of Zacapa. Population: 3697. Crops: corn, beans, sugar cane; livestock.

ESTOR, EL. Municipio located in the department of Izabal in eastern Guatemala. The cabecera is on the northwestern shore of Lake Izabal, 50 miles west-southwest of Puerto Barrios. The municipio was transferred from the department of Alta Verapaz in 1945. Population: 5550. Crops: grain, bananas; fisheries, lumbering.

ESTRADA, DOMINGO, 1855-1901. Born in Amatitlán, he held several high governmental posts under President Reyna Barrios and President Barrillas. He spent much of his life in Europe in diplomatic posts. He was a close friend and follower of Fernando Cruz, and is known in the literary field for his poetry (best known

is his Las campañas) and his translations of poetry.
His writings were of the early modernistic school.
Pseudonym: Julius.

ESTRADA CABRERA, MANUEL, 1857-1924. Born in Retalhuleu, he became a lawyer in Quezaltenango. He was
named Minister of Gobernación in the cabinet of President Reyna Barrios and was first designate. When
Reyna Barrios died, Estrada Cabrera was in Costa
Rica; he returned and with the help of the army, was
constitutionally appointed President and was inaugurated on October 2, 1898. He was "re-elected" in
1904, 1910 and 1916. On April 8, 1920, the legislature found him unfit to carry on his duties because of
mental disturbances, and elected Carlos Herrera as
substitute president. Estrada Cabrera was relieved of
his office on April 15, 1920. During his stay in office, he continued to extend roads and railroads, improved educational facilities, increased crop yields and
instituted measures to support public health. The novel El señor presidente by M. A. Asturias portrays
Guatemala under Cabrera.

-F-

F. A. N.   see FRENTE ANTICOMMUNISTA NACIONAL.

F. A. R.   see FUERZAS ARMADAS REBELDES.

F. A. S.   see FEDERACIÓN AUTONOMÍA SINDICAL.

F. A. S. G. U. A.   see FEDERACIÓN AUTONOMÍA SINDICAL
DE GUATEMALA.

F. D. E.   see FRENTE DEMOCRÁTICO ELECTORAL.

F. D. N.   see FRENTE DEMOCRÁTICO NACIONAL.

F. E. C. E. T. R. A. G.   see FEDERACIÓN CENTRAL DE
TRABAJADORES DE GUATEMALA.

F. E. S. C.   see FEDERACIÓN ESTUDIANTIL SOCIAL CRIS-
TIANO.

F. F. D. E.   see FRENTE FERROVIARIO DEMOCRÁTICO
ELECTORAL.

F. L. A. see FRENTE LIBERACIÓN DE ANTICOMMU-
NISTS.

F. L. A. G. see FEDERACIÓN DE LABOR AUTÓNOMO
DE GUATEMALA.

F. O. G. see FEDERACIÓN OBRERA DE GUATEMALA
PARA LA PROTECCIÓN LEGAL DEL TRABAJO.

F. P. L. see FRENTE POPULAR LIBERATADOR.

F. R. T. see FEDERACIÓN REGIONAL DE TRABAJADORES.

F. S. G. see FEDERACIÓN SINDICAL DE GUATEMALA.

F. U. D. see FRENTE UNIVERSITARIO DEMOCRÁTICO.

F. U. P. A. see FRENTE UNIDAD DE PARTIDOS AREVA-
LISTAS.

FALLA, SALVADOR, 1845-1935. A Guatemalan author and
economist, he collected the poems of Juan Diéguez
Olaverri, but is best known for his Orientación económica (1899), and Conversión monetaria de Guatemala (1913).

FANEGA. A unit of measurement for grain, equal to about
one and one-half bushels.

FEDERACIÓN AUTONOMÍA SINDICAL (F. A. S.). Organized
in 1954 after the revolution, it was the leading trade
union federation under Castillo Armas. In 1957,
F. A. S. became F. A. S. G. U. A.

FEDERACIÓN AUTONOMÍA SINDICAL DE GUATEMALA
(F. A. S. G. U. A.). Formed in 1957, the only labor
federation to have recognition under President Peralta.
Led by Enrique Cruz Ramírez, the federation claimed
14 affiliated unions with 1500 union members. Leon-
ardo Castillo Flores was one of the more active leaders until his death in 1966.

FEDERACIÓN CENTRAL DE TRABAJADORES DE GUATE-
MALA (F. E. C. E. T. R. A. G.). Formed in 1962 with
12 affiliated unions claiming 500 members in 1964.
Led by Julio Celso de León Flores; formerly called
Frente Cristiano de Trabajadores de Guatemala.

FEDERACIÓN DE CENTROAMÉRICA (1921). An attempt to
reunite Central America, led by Guatemala, El Salvador and Honduras. The agreement was called the pact
of San José, although Costa Rica refused to join.
United States intervention in Nicaragua at that time
prevented Nicaragua from attending the conference.

FEDERACIÓN DE LABOR AUTÓNOMO DE GUATEMALA
(F. L. A. G.). A short-lived union federation formed
in 1952 as an opposition group to the C. G. T. G.   The
movement failed when its leaders were discredited.

FEDERACIÓN ESTUDIANTIL SOCIAL CRISTIANO (F. E. S. C.).
Formed as a student body political subgroup of Acción
Católica in 1944 under the name Congregación Mariana
Universitaria, then changed to Juventud Católica Centroamericana at the fall of Arbenz. As the F. E. S. C. in
1966, they elected the student body president and vice-
president of the Law School, marking the first defeat
of the A. E. D.

FEDERACIÓN NACIONAL DE OBREROS EN LA INDUSTRIA
TEXTIL DE VESTIDO Y SIMILARES. A federation of
seven textile unions in Guatemala City, led in 1962 by
Señora Leticia Najarro de Flores and claiming membership of 1, 024 persons.

FEDERACIÓN OBRERA DE GUATEMALA PARA LA PRO-
TECCIÓN LEGAL DEL TRABAJO (F. O. G.). Founded
in 1927, it was the only recognized labor union in
Guatemala in the 1930's but was little more than an
aid society for workers. Its headquarters building became the central union house in the late 1940's.

FEDERACIÓN REGIONAL DE TRABAJADORES (F. R. T.).
Founded in 1926 as an outgrowth of the S. G. P., it
joined the C. T. A. L. in 1929, only to be driven under-
ground in 1932.

FEDERACIÓN SINDICAL DE GUATEMALA (F. S. G.). Labor
organization founded in 1946 by 15 unions that had left
the C. T. G. It was made up of most of the urban
skilled workers. Its power and influence was broken
in 1950, when the railway union (S. A. M. F.) withdrew
its support. At the peak of its power, in 1949, it had
15, 000 members.

FEDERATION OF CENTRAL AMERICA   see   PROVINCAS UNIDAS DEL CENTRO DE AMÉRICA.

FELIPILLO [pseudonym] see HIDALGO, ENRIQUE AGUSTÍN.

FERIA. An annual fair or animal market. Usually considered the most important fiesta of the year in the smaller communities.

FERNÁNDEZ, JUAN DE JESÚS, d. 1846. A Guatemalan violinist and composer, he is best known for his religious music: Misa de Nuestra Señora de los Dolores.

FERNÁNDEZ DE CÓRDOBA, GÓMEZ. Bishop of Guatemala from 1574 to 1598.

FERROCARRILES INTERNACIONALES DE CENTRO AMÉRICA see INTERNATIONAL RAILWAY OF CENTRAL AMERICA.

FIESTA TITULAR. A festival held in celebration of a community's patron saint, scheduled on the saint's day.

FIGUEROA MARROQUÍN, HORACIO, 1904- . A medical historian, he wrote Enfermedades de los conquistadores (1957), Antología de la poesía médica (1962), Historia de la enfermedad de Robles (1963), and Viente sonetos (1967).

FILÍSOLA, VICENTE, 1779?-1850. An Italian commander of the Mexican troops in Central America from June 12, 1822 to June 24, 1823. He tried to get Central America to join the Mexican Empire, headed by General Iturbide. At the downfall of Iturbide, General Filísola called an assembly to set up a local government on June 24, 1823, and on the first of July, the fundamental act of emancipation of Central America was issued.

FINCA. Usually, a large plantation or coffee producing farm. The size may range from a single family farm to a plantation containing several hundred inhabitants.

FINCA HELVETIA. A finca located on the Pacific Piedmont owned by Roberto Alejos which was used for the train-

ing of Cubans for the Bay of Pigs invasion. The U.S.
military mission to Guatemala was especially active
in this operation.

FINQUERO. The owner of a finca.

FLAMENCO, JOSÉ, 1865-1918. A Guatemalan poet-politi-
cian best remembered for his volume of poetry entitled Intimas.

FLORES. Municipio in the department of El Petén in northern Guatemala. The cabecera is on an island in the
south part of Lake Petén, 160 miles north-northeast
of Guatemala City. It is a trading center for towns in
the lake area, the collection point for chicle, rubber,
sugar cane, cacao. Once the capital of the Itza Indians, it came under Spanish rule in the 17th century.
Population: 4100. Altitude: 449 ft.

FLORES, CIRILO, 1779-1826. Acting governor of Guatemala
when it was part of the Federation. Flores took office in 1826 when Governor Juan Barrundia was forced
from office by President Arce. Flores moved the capital to Quezaltenango in an effort to minimize federal influence. He was assassinated by a mob soon after reaching Quezaltenango.

FLORES, DOMINGO, 1825-1864. A poet from Antigua, he
held a medical degree but practiced infrequently. He
is best remembered for his poetry.

FLORES, JOSÉ FELIPE, 1751-1824. The leading medical
scholar at the University of San Carlos, he developed
a wax anatomical figure that could be disassembled by
its various organs. It is thought to be the first of its
kind. He went to Europe to study and died in Spain.

FLORES AVENDANO, GUILLERMO, 1898- . President of
Guatemala from 1957-1958.

FLORES COSTA CUCA. Municipio in the department of
Quezaltenango in southwestern Guatemala. Its cabecera
is located five miles south of Coatepeque. Population: 7992. Crops: corn, coffee, cotton, rice, beans,
chile, plantains, vegetables.

FLORES LAKE see PETÉN LAKE.

FLORES Y FLORES, JOSÉ, 1864-1908. A Guatemalan judge, he wrote Extracto de derecho internacional (1902).

FRAIJANES. Municipio located in the department of Guatemala in south central Guatemala. The cabecera is on the Inter-American Highway, 11 miles south-southeast of Guatemala City. Population: 5872. Altitude: 5670 ft. Crops: grain, cattle raising, beekeeping.

FRANCISCAN. An important Catholic order in colonial Guatemala, led by Fray Toribio de Motolinía, who founded the first Franciscan monastery in Guatemala in 1533. The Franciscans continually opposed the Dominicans concerning the best method of ecclesiastical policy. The Franciscans felt that a benevolent system of Christian servitude could best convert the natives and were not opposed to the use of armed forces and mass baptism to Christianize the population. The order continued to be a force in Guatemala until 1871, when most of the Catholic orders were expelled.

FRENTE ANTICOMMUNISTA NACIONAL (F.A.N.). Supporters of Castillo Armas, who attempted to coordinate efforts within Guatemala to oust President Arbenz in 1954.

FRENTE CRISTIANO DE TRABAJADORES DE GUATEMALA see FEDERACIÓN CENTRAL DE TRABAJADORES DE GUATEMALA.

FRENTE DEMOCRÁTICO ELECTORAL (F.D.E.). A coalition of several political parties for the congressional elections of 1952.

FRENTE DEMOCRÁTICO NACIONAL (F.D.N.). Political party founded in 1952 to unify leftwing splinter groups. It disbanded in 1954 after having been very influential with President Arbenz Guzmán.

FRENTE FERROVIARIO DEMOCRÁTICO ELECTORAL (F.F. D.E.). A group within S.A.M.F. which banded together to defeat Morales Cubas in 1953, when he attempted to be re-elected as secretary-general of the S.A.M.F.

FRENTE LIBERACIÓN DE ANTICOMMUNISTS (F.L.A.). An exile group working in Honduras in 1954 for the overthrow of the regime of President Arbenz.

FRENTE POPULAR LIBERTADOR (F. P. L.). A major political party of students formed in 1944 with the support of some middle-class workers. It merged with
the R. N. party in 1945 to form the P. A. R., but withdrew in 1947. It supported Victor Manuel Giorani for
President in the election of 1950. The F. P. L. became
part of the P. R. G. in 1952.

FRENTE UNIDAD DE PARTIDOS AREVALISTAS (F. U. P. A.).
A loose political organization having the purpose of
getting Arévalo elected in 1944.

FRENTE UNIVERSITARIO DEMOCRÁTICO (F. U. D.). An organization to support political action, formed in 1952
on the University campus. Published a monthly periodical entitled "Nuestra Lucha."

FRONTERIZO see ADELANTADO.

FUEGO VOLCANO. Altitude: 12,582 ft. (crater level at
11,854 ft.). Located in south central Guatemala on the
Sacatepequez-Chimaltenango border, 12 miles southwest
of Antigua. It was very active when the Spanish arrived in the 16th century and has erupted more than 20
times since then. The worst eruption was that of 1773
when an accompanying earthquake destroyed Antigua,
then the capital city of Guatemala. Last erupted in
1932.

FUENTES GEORGINAS. Natural hot spring resort five miles
southeast of Zunil, on the northern slope of Santo
Tomás Volcano.

FUENTES Y GUZMÁN, ANTONIO FRANCISCO DE, 1643-1700.
Guatemalan historian, great-great-grandson of Bernal
Díaz. Best known for his Recordación florida del
Reyno de Guatemala and Presceptos historiales.

FUEROS. A system in colonial America whereby the clergy,
military, and certain civil officials received the special privilege of maintaining their own civil and criminal courts. The conflict of overlapping jurisdictional
procedure often led to confusion and violent quarrels.
The special courts were not abolished until the late
18th century.

FUERZAS ARMADAS REBELDES (F.A.R.). Formed by Luis
Turcios in 1960 as part of MR-13 under the leadership of Yon Sosa. Turcios and Cézar Montes led the
F.A.R. away from MR-13 in an ideology fight. At
the death of Turcios in 1966, Montes continued as the
leader and began more urban terror activities under
the name of ojo por ojo. They took credit for the assassination of U.S. Ambassador John Mien in 1968.

-G-

GABÁN. A man's short jacket of natural black wool; the in-
side seams of the sleeves are split as are the sides,
for freedom of arm movement.

GAINZA, GABINO, 1760-1824. Acting governor in 1821-22.
He presided over the congress which adopted the declaration of independence and was elected the new civil
and military commander of Guatemala at a salary of
10,000 pesos per year. He held the position until
June, 1822, when he was relieved by General Filísola.
He went to Mexico to become an aide-de-camp to Mexican Emperor Iturbide.

GALEÓN, JACINTO [pseudonym] see ACEÑA DURÁN,
RAMÓN.

GALEOTTI TORRES, RODOLFO, 1912- . A sculptor born
in Quezaltenango, he studied in Italy. His work is in
the Palacio Maya and in the national palace. His stone
carvings have exaggerated limbs which give them an
air of vigor and activity. He helped to compile Indice
de pintura y escultura (1946) which contains illustrations and brief biographies.

GALICH, MANUEL, 1913- . Professor of literature at the
Universidad de San Carlos. He was one of the leaders
in the 1944 revolution, Minister of Foreign Relations
in 1951 and 1952. He has written several plays:
Papa natos, Gentes decentes, El canciller cadejo, and
others. His political writings include Del pánico al
ataque (1949) and Porque lucha guatemala (1952), two
of the more objective accounts of the revolutionary
periods.

GALINDO, JUAN. Born in England, he took up Guatemalan

citizenship in order to gain a tract of one million
acres in northern Petén and Belice in 1834. He became embroiled in a boundary controversy with Great
Britain and failed to colonize and develop the claim.

GÁLVEZ, MARIANO, 1794-1862. Elected governor under
the Federation of Central America in 1831 and re-
elected in 1835, he was forced to resign in 1838. Under Gálvez, the Church was restricted, the Livingston
Code adopted, and a settlement plan in Verapaz was
attempted.

GÁLVEZ, MATÍAS DE, 1717-1783. Governor from 1779 to
1783. When the war with England broke out in 1779,
Gálvez built up the militia to oppose any British land-
ings on the coast of Nicaragua and Honduras. He was
transferred to the Viceroyalty of New Spain before any
action took place.

GÁLVEZ SUÁREZ, ALFREDO, d. 1946. A Guatemalan artist and teacher, he painted some of the murals in the
National Palace. He held several personal exhibitions
in Guatemala City, Mexico, and the United States.
Much of his work appeared in 1942 in a collection entitled Indios de Guatemala, artistic album.

GANDARA DURÁN, CARLOS, 1899-1962. Co-founder of the
newspaper El Imparcial, in 1922. He wrote a biography of Pedro Molina, besides poems which appear under the title Etopeyas. Pseudonym: Razumikin.

GARAVITO, HUMBERTO, 1897- . Artist born in Quezaltenango, he studied in Mexico and Europe. He was Director of the Academia de Belles Artes, 1928-1935,
and wrote Francisco Cabrera, miniaturista guatemalteco, 1781-1845 (1945).

GARCI-AGUIRRE, PEDRO, d. 1809. A colonial sculptor
and architect of late 18th-century Guatemala, where he
directed the construction of the Cathedral in 1802.

GARCÍA GOYENA, RAFAEL, 1766-1823. A Guatemalan poet, he was born in Guayaquil, Ecuador, but went to
Guatemala to study and later became a citizen. He
wrote many short stories and satirical essays but is
best known for his poetry. Leading poem: El pavo
real, el guarda, y el loro.

GARCÍA GRANADOS, JORGE, 1900-1961. Author, journalist and diplomat, he was a grandson of Miguel García
Granados and became a deputy to the legislature under
President Chacón.   Under Ubico, he was imprisoned
for political reasons.   Upon his release from prison,
he went to Mexico in exile and remained there, except
for a brief period when he worked for Republican
Spain, until Ubico's fall from power.   He considered
himself a non-Marxist Socialist.   He was the presiding
officer of the Constituent Assembly of 1945.   In 1950
he ran a poor second as a socialist to Jacobo Arbenz
in the presidential race.   Editor of several newspapers, his works include El gobierno del Dr. Mariano
Gálvez, Evolución sociológica de Guatemala, and Los
veneros del diablo.   He died in Chile while attending
a conference.

GARCÍA GRANADOS, MARÍA JOSEFA, 1796-1848.   Guatemalan poet, born in Spain but moved to Guatemala before the revolution.   He wrote in all fields of literature, although he is best known for his poetry.

GARCÍA GRANADOS, MIGUEL, 1809-1878.   Born in Spain,
his parents went to Guatemala when he was young.
He aided in bringing Rafael Carrera to the Presidency
and for this received considerable freedom of political
activity.   Under President Cerna, he went into exile
and teamed up with Barrios to lead the movement
against Cerna.   He was President from 1871-1872 and
is one of the heros of Guatemalan history because of
his work with Barrios in setting up a revolutionary
government.

GARCÍA PELÁEZ, FRANCISCO DE PAULA, 1785-1867.
Archbishop of Guatemala between 1846 and 1867.   As
a historian, he wrote Memorias para la historia del
antiguo reyno de Guatemala (3 vols., 1852) and Vindi-
cación del sistema federal de Centro-América (1825).

GARCÍA REDONDO, ANTONIO.   Early 19th-century Guatemalan priest and author; born in Spain.   He advocated
the education of Indians; was professor of mathematics
at the University of San Carlos during the late colonial
period.   He wrote several treatises on economics, including Sobre el fomento de las conchas de caldo en
la provincia de Guatemala (1799) and Impugnación al
impreso ... (1831).   He often wrote under the pseu-

donym, D.A.R.

GARRIDO, FRANCISCO. A 19th-century Guatemalan musician, noted for his ability on the guitar.

GARRIDO, J. CESAR DE. A 19th-century Guatemalan novelist, best known for Recuerdos de una temporada.

GAZETA DE GUATEMALA, TOMO 1-14 (1797-1810). The founder and publisher of this progressive journal was Ignacio Beteta. It was dedicated to the dissemination of useful knowledge in the fields of philosophy, economics, medicine, literature and commercial affairs. Leading intellectuals of the period from all the colonies contributed to the journal, often under pseudonyms. The series began to appear weekly on February 13, 1797. Authorities suspended the Gazeta soon after it began publication, but renewed its license in February of 1798, at which time Alejandro Ramírez became editor until 1802. Simón Bergaño y Villegas was editor from 1803 until 1809, when he was arrested by the Inquisition. The journal was suspended soon after his arrest.

GAZISTAS. One of two leading political factions of the late colonial period, from which later developed the important political groups of the Federation period. The Gazistas were locally referred to as Bacos (drunks) while the opposition group was known as Cacos (thieves). The Cacos were in good standing with the last two Spanish governors (Urrutia and Gainza) and were led by Pedro Molina and the Aycinena family. Through the newspaper spokesman of the Cacos, El Editor Constitucional, the party led in the cry for independence. When this was achieved, they rallied against the union with Mexico and for a republican form of government. The Gazistas were led by José del Valle, who edited the newspaper El Amigo de la Patria. The Gazistas favored a "with Mexico" policy in the independence movement. After the split with Mexico, the Gazistas advocated a centralized government, less democratic in its make-up. They were largely unsuccessful in their efforts, due primarily to lack of aggressive leadership. After the Federation period, the political parties became less distinctive because of the crossing of issues and the charismatic qualities of the political leaders.

GENOVA. Municipio in the department of Quezaltenango in southwestern Guatemala. The cabecera is six miles south-southeast of Coatepeque, on a railroad. Population: 15,070. Crops: coffee, cotton, sugar cane, grain; livestock.

GOICOECHEA, JOSÉ ANTONIO, 1735-1814. A Franciscan, born in Costa Rica, he received his bachelor's degree in 1767 from the University of San Carlos. He taught for many years at San Carlos, traveled in Europe, and worked as a missionary among the Indians of Central America. He taught physics, geometry, optics, astronomy and geography. He proposed a course in 1782 which included study of the natural philosophers of 18th-century Europe. His writings include Acto público de teologia dogmática (1792), Memoria sobre los medios de destruir la mendicidad (1797), Relación sobre los indios gentiles de Pacura, and others. Pseudonyms: Licornes, El Viejo Licornes.

GOLFO DULCE see IZABAL LAKE.

GÓMERA, LA. Municipio located in the department of Escuintla in southern Guatemala. In the coastal plain, the cabecera is 23 miles southwest of Escuintla. Population: 28,870. Crops: cotton, corn; livestock.

GÓMERA, CONDE DE LA see PERAZA AYALA CASTILLA Y ROJAS, ANTONIO.

GÓMEZ, IGNACIO see GÓMEZ MENENDEZ, IGNACIO.

GÓMEZ CARRILLO, AGUSTÍN, 1838-1908. Guatemalan historian and father of Enrique Gómez Carrillo.

GÓMEZ CARRILLO, ENRIQUE, 1873-1927. A major Guatemalan writer of the modernistic school. Most of his works were short, for newspaper publishing, and dealt with sex and the Bohemian group in Paris. He represents a break away from the historical novel in Guatemala. His works include Tres novelas inmorales, Treinta años de mi vida, Flores de penitencia, El evangelio de amor, Bohemia sentimental, Del amor, del dolor y del vicio, and Maravillas.

GÓMEZ MENÉNDEZ, IGNACIO, 1813-1879. Guatemalan author and newspaperman, he edited La Revista de la Universidad.

GÓMEZ ROBLES, JULIO, 1896- . Jurist and diplomat,
    born in Guatemala City. He served as a judge, Min-
    ister to Costa Rica, 1931-32. He wrote Ensayo de
    sociología jurídica (1936), Concepciones y metodos de
    Bodín (1939), and El amparo en Materia Agraria
    (1953).

GONZÁLEZ, ANTONIO. Governor between 1570 and 1572.
    The audiencia was re-established in Guatemala in
    1570, largely due to the support of Bartolomé de Las
    Casas.

GONZÁLES BUSTILLO Y VILLASEÑOR, JUAN. Acting gov-
    ernor of Guatemala from 1771 to 1773. As senior
    judge on the audiencia, he took over the governorship
    at the death of the previous governor, Salazar, in
    1771. He wrote several reports on the destruction of
    Antigua in 1773 (published in 1774). He later became
    a member of the Audiencia of Mexico, then a member
    of the Council of the Indies.

GONZÁLEZ CAMPO, FRANCISCO, 1832-1904. Guatemalan
    author and politician, he wrote Corona funebre dedi-
    cado a la ... literato don José Milla (1885) and as-
    sisted with Galería poética Centroamericana (1880).
    His best known poem is A Centro-América.

GONZÁLEZ GOYRI, ROBERTO, 1924- . Guatemalan sculp-
    tor influenced by Yela Gunther, he has done much bas-
    relief on government buildings and erected a statue of
    Tecun Uman. His works are displayed in the New
    York Museum of Modern Art. He wrote biographies
    of R. Abularach and Carlos Mérida.

GONZÁLEZ JUÁREZ, HUMBERTO, 1913-1970. Union or-
    ganizer and diplomat, he was born in Jutiapa. He par-
    ticipated in the revolution of 1944 and helped to form
    several political parties. He held several diplomatic
    posts and went to Mexico at the fall of Arbenz. He
    and two associates broadcasted criticisms of the Arana
    government from his station TGJA and were assassi-
    nated by a conservative terrorist group, "Mano blanco."

GONZÁLEZ LÓPEZ, LUIS ARTURO, 1900-1965. President
    of Guatemala in 1957 (July to October). As Supreme

Court judge in 1952, he fought Arbenz and the agrarian reform and was dismissed for his efforts.

GONZÁLEZ MOLLINEDO Y SARAVIA, ANTONIO. Governor from 1801 to 1811. He went to Mexico to command the Spanish forces in 1811, and while there, was captured by the rebels and shot.

GONZÁLEZ SARAVIA, ANTONIO, 1852-1922. A Guatemalan judge, he wrote Derecho patrio (1914) and Lecciones de derecho administrativo (1882).

GORRIZ DE MORALES, NATALIA, 1868-1941. Guatemalan geographer. Writings: Vida y viajes de Colón (1895) and Compendio de geografía descriptiva (1904). Pseudonym: Noel.

GOUBAUD CARRERA, ANTONIO, 1902-1951. A Guatemalan anthropologist, his works include, Guajraquip bats (1935). He committed suicide while serving as ambassador.

GOVERNORS OF COLONIAL GUATEMALA (57). (Includes acting governors. Dates indicate terms of office.)
Alvarado Contreras, Pedro de, 1525-1541.
Cueva de Alvarado, Doña Beatriz de la, 1541.
Marroquín, Francisco, 1541-1542, jointly with
Cueva, Francisco de la, 1541-1542.
Maldonado, Alonso de, 1542-1548.
Cerrato, Alonso López, 1548-1555.
Quesada, Antonio Rodríguez de, 1555-1558.
Ramírez de Quiñones, Pedro, 1558-1559.
Landecho, Juan Nuñez de, 1559-1563.
Briceño, Francisco, 1564-1569.
González, Antonio, 1570-1572.
Villalobos, Pedro de, 1573-1578.
Valverde, García de, 1579-1589.
Rueda, Pedro Mallén de, 1589-1592.
Sande, Francisco de, 1593-1596.
Abaunza, Alvaro Gómez de, 1596-1598.
Criado de Castilla, Alonso, 1598-1611.
Peraza Ayala Castilla y Rojas, Antonio, 1611-1626.
Acuña, Diego de, 1626-1633.
Quiñones y Osorio, Alvaro de, 1634-1642.
Avendaño, Diego de, 1642-1649.
Lara y Mogrobejo, Antonio de, 1649-1654.
Altamirano y Velasco, Fernando de, 1654-1657.

Carrillo de Mendoza, Jerónimo Garces, 1657-1659.
Mencos, Martín Carlos de, 1659-1667.
Alvarez Alfonso Rosica de Caldas, Sebastián, 1668-1670.
Sáenz de Mañosca y Murillo, Juan de Santo Matía, 1670-1672.
Escobedo, Fernando Francisco de, 1672-1682.
Augurto y Alava, Juan Miguel de, 1682-1684.
Enríquez de Guzmán, Enrique, 1684-1688.
Barrios y Leal, Jacinto de, 1688-1695.
Escals, José de, 1695-1696.
Berrospe, Gabriel Sánchez de, 1696-1700.
Heduardo, Juan Jeronimo, 1701-1702.
Ceballos y Villagutierre, Alonso, 1702-1703.
Espinosa de los Monteros, José Osorio, 1704-1706.
Cosio y Campa, Toribio José de, 1706-1716.
Rivas, Francisco Rodríguez de, 1716-1724.
Echevers y Suvisa, Antonio Pedro de, 1724-1733.
Rivera y Villalón, Pedro de, 1733-1742.
Rivera y Santa Cruz, Tomás de, 1742-1748.
Araujo y Río, Juan de, 1748-1751.
Montaos y Sotomayor, José Vasquez Prego, 1752-1753.
Velarde y Cienfuegos, Juan, 1753-1754.
Arcos y Moreno, Alonso de, 1754-1760.
Heredia, José Fernández de, 1761-1765.
Salazar y Herrera Nájera y Mendoza, Pedro de, 1765-1771.
Gonzales Bustillo y Villaseñor, Juan, 1771-1773.
Mayorga, Martín de, 1773-1779.
Gálvez, Matías de, 1779-1783.
Estachería, José de, 1783-1789.
Troncoso Martínez del Rincón, Bernardo, 1789-1794.
Domas y Valle, José, 1794-1801.
González Mollinedo y Saravia, Antonio, 1801-1811.
Bustamente y Guerra, José, 1811-1818.
Urrutia, Carlos, 1818-1821.
Gainza, Gabino, 1821.

GOVERNORS OF FEDERATED GUATEMALA. (Dates indicate terms of office.)
Barrundia, Juan, 1824-1826, 1829.
Flores, Cirilo, 1826.
Aycinena, Mariano, 1827-1829.
Molina, Pedro, 1829-1830.
Rivera Cabezas, Antonio, 1830-1831.

Gálvez, Mariano, 1831-1838.
Velenzuela, Pedro J., 1838.
Rivera Paz, Mariano, 1838-1839; President, 1839-
    1844.

GOYENA PERALTA, RAFAEL, 1852-1883. Guatemalan poet
    and politician, he held several high government posts.
    He is best remembered for his part in writing Galeria
    poética Centroamericana (1880).

GOYOM. Indian name for the marimba.

GRACEJOS, LOS. Dance of the Jesters. Dating from be-
    fore the conquest, the dance is often called La Culebra
    (the Snake). The shamen go to the hills and while
    performing a ritual, capture snakes. The participants
    dress in old clothes and dance in the festival with
    much clowning. In the climax, the snakes are re-
    leased and permitted to twine themselves around the
    dancers' necks and arms. After the dance, the snakes
    are released in the hills. The snakes are symbolic of
    the plumed serpent, the rain god, and the dance is to
    ensure enough rain for good crops.

GRACIAS A DIOS, HONDURAS. The seat of the Audiencia
    de los Confines, which was later the Audiencia of
    Guatemala. It was founded by Gonzalo de Alvarado in
    1536. The ciudad is located in northwestern Honduras
    near the Guatemalan-Salvadoran border.

GRANA see COCHINEAL.

GRANADOS. Municipio in the department of Baja Verapaz
    in central Guatemala. The cabecera is located on the
    highway between Rabinal and Guatemala City. Popula-
    tion: 7251. Crops: corn, sugar cane.

GRAY, DORIAN [pseudonym] see VALLE, RAFAEL.

GRIJALVA RIVER see CUILCO RIVER.

GUACALATE RIVER. In southern Guatemala, it begins
    near Chimaltenango and flows about 50 miles south to
    the Pacific Ocean near San José. It flows between the
    volcanoes Fuego and Agua. A hydroelectric station is
    located on the river near Ciudad Vieja. Sometimes
    called Achiguate.

GUACALE.   A round gourd used for bowls or dippers by
the Indians and obtained from the Morro tree.

GUALÁN.   Municipio in the department of Zacapa in eastern
Guatemala.   The cabecera is on the railroad and near
the Motagua River, about 15 miles northeast of Zacapa.
Important port for small craft before the founding of
Puerto Barrios.   Population: 21,618.   Crops: corn,
wheat, cotton, coffee, sugar cane; livestock.

GUANAGAZAPA.   Municipio in the department of Escuintla
in southern Guatemala.   The cabecera is 11 miles
east-southeast of Escuintla.   Population: 6661.   Crops:
coffee, sugar cane, grain; livestock.

GUARO.   A sweet drink made of cane, widely used at religious ceremonies.

GUASTATOYA   see   PROGRESO, EL, def. 3.

GUATEMALA.   1)   The republic: made up of 23 departments, counting Belice, and further divided into 324
municipios.   Spanish is the predominant language although in many of the Indian municipios, one or another of the Mayan dialects is still used except in official business.   Catholicism is the most common religion, although many Protestant sects are represented.
The President is elected for a four-year term by direct vote and cannot be re-elected for two terms (i.e.,
eight years).   The legislature is made up of one chamber with representatives for four-year terms from
each department or for every 50,000 inhabitants there-
in.   The largest cities are: Guatemala City (the capital), Quezaltenango (highland Indian center), and Puerto
Barrios on the Caribbean coast.   The Motagua River
is the longest waterway, stretching 250 miles inland
from the Caribbean.   Coffee, cotton, bananas, sugar
cane and beans are the major agricultural crops in
that order of importance commercially.   From the
forest, chicle gum, cinchona bark, wood and some rubber are harvested.   Guatemala exports coffee and bananas mainly to the United States, and imports textiles,
petroleum, drugs, and automobiles, primarily from the
United States.   The census for 1950 placed the population at 1,950,000; the 1964 census, at 4,210,000 and
the projected population for 1980 is 7,107,800.
    2)   A departamento located in south central Guate-

mala, its capital is the capital of the Republic, Guatemala City. In the central highlands, it includes Lake Amatitlán in the south. Its crops are: corn, black beans, coffee, fodder grasses, and sugar cane. Some cattle and hogs are raised. Home industries produce pottery and textiles. The railroad crosses the department from northeast to southwest. Chief cities are Guatemala City, the center of manufacturing, and Amatitlán, a summer resort. There are 17 municipios in this department: Amatitlán, Chinautla, Chuarranco, Fraijanes, Guatemala, Mixco, Palencia, San José del Golfo, San José Pinula, San Juan Sacatepequez, San Miguel Petapa, San Pedro Ayampuc, San Pedro Sacatepequez, San Raymundo, Santa Catarina Pinula, Villa Canales, Villa Nueva. The population in 1950 was 438,913; in 1964 the population had grown to 810,186 and the projected population to 1980 is 1,555,300. Area: 830 square miles.

3) A municipio located in the department of Guatemala in the central highlands. The cabecera is the capital city for the Republic and is connected by road and by railway with Mexico and El Salvador, as well as both sea coasts. It is a major commercial center, with manufacturing of cement, furniture, leather goods, soap, textiles, cigars, beer and food products. The capital city was first located at Iximche in 1524 by Pedro de Alvarado, but was soon moved to Xepán. In November, 1527, acting governor Jorge de Alvarado moved the capital to Almolonga, now Ciudad Vieja. When the city was destroyed by floods in 1541, the capital was moved to present-day Antigua. Antigua was destroyed in 1773, and the site again moved, this time to its present location. The city is built on the classical Spanish gridiron pattern which centers about a park. Facing the central park is the National Palace (built in 1943), the Cathedral (built from 1782-1815), and the city hall. The central market place is located behind the Cathedral. In the southern part of the city are located the botanical gardens, archeological museum, museum of history and art, the observatory, and the airport. The city was severely battered by earthquakes in 1874 and 1917-18. As a result, few of the original buildings remain, giving the capital an air of modern sophistication. Population: 573,254. Altitude: 4872 ft.

GUATEMALTECO, EL, 1875-1931, 1950- . An official

bulletin of Guatemala for the publication of constitutional amendments and official acts. It published,
chronologically, the laws as they were enacted. Between 1931 and 1950, the Seccion Oficial of the Diario
de Centro América continued this function. In 1950
the title was changed to El Guatemalteco, and the volume numbering of the first series was resumed.

GUATEMALTECO, UN [pseudonym] see MONTÚFAR Y
CORONADO, MANUEL.

GUAZACAPÁN. Municipio located in the department of Santa
Rosa in southern Guatemala. In the coastal plain, the
cabecera is three miles west-southwest of Chiquimulilla. Population: 7663. Crops: coffee, cotton,
sugar cane, grain; livestock raising center.

GÜIJA LAKE. On the Salvador-Guatemala border, it is 20
miles long, six miles wide, and 150 feet deep. Twenty per cent of the lake is in Guatemala. A summer
resort area, it has ancient Indian ruins on its large
island. Altitude: 2000 ft.

GUILLÉN, FLAVIO, 1871-1933. A journalist and professor
of Economics at the Universidad de San Carlos.
Works: Gramática bisoya ... (1898), Un fraile procer
y una fábula poema (1932).

GUMARKAEJ. Early Indian name for the Quiché capital of
Utatlán.

GUNTHER, RAFAEL YELA see YELA GUNTHER, RAFA-
EL.

GUTIÉRREZ GARBÍN, VICTOR MANUEL, 1922-1966. Born
in Barbarena, he was a school teacher at the time of
the revolution. He became a labor organizer, a member of the Assembly from 1946 to 1954, Secretary General of the C.G.T.G. in 1954, Chairman of the Assembly Committee on Agrarian Reform, 1952-53. He
wrote numerous union articles. It was reported that
he was arrested and executed while returning from exile in 1966, shortly before Méndez Montenegro's taking
office.

-H-

HALL, EDUARDO, 1832-1885. A Guatemalan poet, he
translated into Spanish many works of the leading English poets.

HATUNNAH. The Mayan name for Lake Petén.

HEDUARDO, JUAN JERÓNIMO. Acting governor, 1701 to
1702.

HEREDIA, JOSÉ FERNANDEZ DE, d. 1782. Governor from
1761 to 1765.

HERMANI [pseudonym] see RODRÍGUEZ CERNA, JOSÉ.

HERMANO SERAPIO, EL [pseudonym] see SÁNCHEZ,
SERAPIO.

HERNÁNDEZ COBOS, JOSÉ HUMBERTO, 1905- . Writer,
poet and journalist, he was the interim director of
Diario de Centro América. He wrote Balandro en tierra
(verse), El resucitado (1962), Lores al hermano Pedro,
La crisis de la democracia, ensayo (1950), and Las Casas
sin parendes (1965). Pseudonym: Euforia Cobas.

HERNÁNDEZ DE LEÓN, FEDERICO, 1883-1959. Born in
Quezaltenango, he was an author and newspaperman.
He served in the legislative assembly. His works include Viajes presidenciales (2 vols., 1939; on the trips
of Jorge Ubico), Dos crepusculos (1919), El libro de las
entrevistas (1922), and El libro de los enfermerides
(3 vol., 1925-27). He had several pseudonyms or
sobriquets: El Ixcamparic, El Bautista, Juan de Mayor-
aga, Señor de Portales.

HERRERA, CARLOS, 1856-1930. President of Guatemala,
1920-1921. Elected by the national legislature after
Estrada Cabrera was declared unfit to govern, Herrera
resigned and was replaced by General José Orellana.

HERRERA, FEDERICO, 1874-1905. A Guatemalan artist
and poet, his poetry was published under the title,
Recuerdos del colegio (1901).

HERRERA, FLAVIO, 1895- . Author and lawyer, he wrote

La lente opaca (1921), El ala de las montanas (1921), Cenizas (1923), Trópico (1932), Bulbuxya (1934), El Tigre (1934), Poniente de sirenas (1937), La tempestad (1935), Caos (1949), Solera (1962), and Oros de otoño (1962).

HIDALGO, ENRIQUE AGUSTÍN, 1876-1915. Guatemalan newspaperman and poet, his writings were satirical. His poetry was published under the title, Latas y latonees. Pseudonyms: E. A. H. and Felipillo.

HINCAPIE MELÉNDEZ, CRISTÓBAL DE, 1689-1772. A Guatemalan printer from 1739 to 1748, a Franciscan, and creative writer and scientist, he wrote about the 1717 earthquake. He was a collector of botanical specimens for a natural history which he compiled.

HOJA MAXÁN. Often called Bijao, it is a leaf from a broad-leaved Marantaceous plant found in the Pacific lowlands; it is sold throughout Guatemala for food wrappings.

HOMICIDA (Society) see KOPESKWI PLOT.

HONDO RIVER. Arising as the Río Azul in El Petén, northeast of Uaxactún, the Hondo flows about 130 miles to the northeast into Mexico and empties into the Caribbean. It forms the Mexico-Belice border.

HONDURAN BOUNDARY DISPUTE. The only boundary established in the colonial period followed generally the Copán Mountain range between Honduras and Guatemala. In 1845, an agreement was reached, making the boundary the same as the diocese boundary of 1786; however, the exact line was left in question. When Honduran companies began to operate in the Motagua River valley in the early 20th century, both countries began to press their claims. The U. S. offered to mediate in 1923, but the offer was turned down. By 1928, armed warfare threatened. An arbitral tribunal met in Washington in 1931 and worked out the present boundary; a survey was conducted and the boundary marked by April, 1933.

HONDURAS, WAR OF 1850 see SALVADOR, WAR OF 1850.

HONDURAS, WAR OF 1853. Border skirmishes led to one
    battle at Atulapa in July of 1853. Salvador led as
    mediator between Guatemala and Honduras and a peace
    treaty was finally signed in February, 1856, after lit-
    tle fighting and much political maneuvering in each of
    the capitals.

HONDURAS, WAR OF 1872. Salvador and Guatemala formed
    an alliance against Honduras because the Honduran gov-
    ernment was giving active support to the conservative
    exiles from both countries. When Honduras broke re-
    lations with Salvador, the allied forces invaded Hon-
    duras and captured Comayagua. Later defeats were
    suffered by Honduras at Potrerillos and Santa Bárbara,
    ending the campaign in late July, about two months af-
    ter actual hostilities began. The peace treaty, besides
    ending the conflict, contained clauses of little impor-
    tance.

HUASTATOYA see EL PROGRESO.   (Municipio in the de-
    partment of El Progreso).

HUEHUETENANGO. 1) A department located in western Guate-
    mala on the Mexican border. Its capital is Huehuete-
    nango. It is drained by the headstreams of the Cuilco
    system in the west and the Lacantún River in the north
    and east. The highest part of the Cuchumatanes
    Mountains is in the western part. Wheat, corn, beans
    and sheep are raised on the slopes; coffee, sugar cane
    and tropical fruit, on the lower plains. Textile weav-
    ing and pottery-making comprise the local industry,
    along with some lead mining near Chiantla and San
    Miguel Acatán. The department is made up of 31
    municipios: Aguacatán, Chiantla, Colotenango, Con-
    cepción, Cuilco, La Democrácia, Huehuetenango, Jac-
    altenango, La Libertad, Malacatancito, Nentón, San
    Antonio Huista, San Gaspar Ixchil, San Ildefonso Ixta-
    huacán, San Juan Atitán, San Juan Ixcoy, San Mateo
    Ixtatán, San Miguel Acatán, San Pedro Necta, San Ped-
    ro Soloma, San Rafael la Independencia, San Rafael
    Petzal, San Sebastián Coatan, San Sebastián Huehuete-
    nango, Santa Ana Huista, Santa Bárbara, Santa Cruz
    Barillas, Santa Eulalia, Santiago Chimaltenango, Tec-
    titán, Todos Santos Cuchumatan. Population in 1950
    was 200,101; in 1964, 288,104; and the projected pop-
    ulation for 1980 is 445,700. Area: 2857 square miles.

2) Municipio located in the department of Huehuetenango in western Guatemala. Near the headstreams of the Chiapas River, its cabecera is 80 miles
northwest of Guatemala City. It is the commercial
center of the northwestern highlands and Cuchumatanes
Mountain area. Flour milling, tanning, wool processing and wool milling are leading industries, as are
trades in pottery, leather and textiles. The cabecera
was founded in the 17th century, after the downfall of
the old Indian capital of Zaculeu, one mile west.
Population: 24,989. Altitude: 6200 ft.

HUIPIL. Sleeveless tunic or blouse-like upper garment worn
by Indian women. It is of varying length, reaching to
just above the waist or as low as the knee. Sometimes
called Coton.

HUITÁN. Municipio in the department of Quezaltenango in
southwestern Guatemala. Its cabecera is located in
northern Quezaltenango near the border of San Marcos.
Population: 2754. Crops: apples, corn, wheat,
beans, potatoes.

HUITÉ. Municipio in the department of Zacapa, established
in 1958 in the western part of the department. The
main industry is agriculture, with corn, beans and
fruit raised. Population: 3988. Altitude: 984 ft.

HURAKÁN. Literally, the heart of the heaven, in the rituals and concept of present-day Mayans. One of the
deities pre-dating the conquest, Hurakan is closely akin
to the Christian concept of God. In some areas, Hurakan is worshipped as god of earthquakes.

-I-

I. A. N. (Instituto Agropecuario Nacional) see SERVICIO
COOPERATIVO INTERAMERICANO DE AGRICULTURA.

I. B. [pseudonym] see BETETA, IGNACIO.

I. G. S. S. see INSTITUTO GUATEMALTECO DE SEGURI-
DAD SOCIAL.

I. N. F. O. P. see INSTITUTO DE FOMENTO DE LA PRO-
DUCCIÓN.

I. N. T. A.   see   INSTITUTO DE TRANSFORMACIÓN AG-
RARIA.

I. P.   [pseudonym]   see   LAINFIESTA, FRANCISCO.

I. R. C. A.   see   INTERNATIONAL RAILWAY OF CENTRAL
AMERICA.

INANA I TORRE, JOSÉ ISIDRO   [pseudonym]   see   IRIS-
ARRI, ANTONIO JOSÉ DE.

INDEPENDENCE.   The first movement occurred in 1811 in
San Salvador, where several men, led by Fray Matías
Delgado, captured the Royal Treasury and some arms.
The expected support was not forthcoming, however,
and the movement died.   The next attempt broke out
in Nicaragua and was led by León and Granada.   At
the first show of force, León surrendered.   Granada
held out for one day, then surrendered in April, 1812.
Next was the Belén conspiracy of 1813 in Guatemala
City.   All except one of the leaders were captured and
exiled before the conspiracy got well under way.   In
1814, Manuel José Arce was arrested for raising a
revolt in San Salvador.   Further movement was suppressed until Urrutia became governor and more freedom of expression was permitted.   It was not until
Mexico had succeeded in freeing herself and Gainza became governor that the movement became a positive
force.   When the Mexican Plan de Iguala was proclaimed, a similar measure was adopted in Guatemala.
Independence was declared on September 15, 1821, and
Guatemala elected to join with Mexico in the hope that
being part of a larger empire would bring her more
stability and prosperity.   This did not prove to be the
case and when Iturbide fell from power, Central America elected to go its own way on July 1, 1823.

INDEPENDENCIA, LA.   The name given the port of Iztapa
after independence was declared.   The name did not
last.

INDIAN.   The Mayan Indian civilization makes up the back-
bone of the numerous groups of Indians in Guatemala.
The word "Indian" came from Columbus, and the most
widely accepted theory concerning the origin of the American Indian is that he is of Asiatic origin.   At one
time the Indians crossed over the Bering Strait and,

over a period of several thousand years, spread throughout the Western Hemisphere before the natural bridge
was broken. At the time of the Spanish conquest, the
Mayan civilization had broken and declined, leaving only ruins hidden in the jungles. The Indian of today
largely remains outside the influence of western culture,
although enough assimilation has occurred to cause the
anthropologist frustrations. With improved internal
communications, the influence of western culture is becoming more pronounced, making the isolated Indian
community a rare exception.

INDIGO. A crop from which dark blue dyestuff was made.
Referred to as Jiquilite in many areas, the crop was
grown in the hot, lowland areas, processed, and
shipped to Europe, where it was used as a textile dye.
Chemical dyes replaced it in the early nineteenth century. Next to cacao, Indigo was the most important
commercial crop in colonial Guatemala. It was cultivated for local use before the conquest and was first
grown on plantations for export in the 16th century.

INQUISITION. The inquisitorial tribunals were set up to
combat heresies against the faith, but became a royal
defensive instrument, both religiously and politically,
because tribunal powers were never clearly defined.
The Spanish Inquisition played a relatively inconspicu-
ous role in Guatemala. Most of the population was Indian and fell outside the sphere of interest of the tribunal. Guatemala was not on main trade routes nor
was it populous enough to warrant a regular full-time
tribunal. The first inquisitor arrived in 1572 and the
last representative was requested to leave in 1813.

INSTITUTO AGROPECUARIO NACIONAL (I. A. N.). see
SERVICIO COOPERATIVO INTERAMERICANO DE AG-
RICULTURA.

INSTITUTO DE FOMENTO DE LA PRODUCCIÓN (I. N. F.
O. P.). A government agency founded in late 1948 to
encourage production of manufactured goods and crop
diversification. Through the efforts of the I. N. F. O. P.
cotton has become a major export crop. The I. N. F.
O. P. price program ended in 1954 when it began only
to back loans and act as a branch of the Banco de
Guatemala, which established easy loans for crop development.

INSTITUTO GUATEMALTECO DE SEGURIDAD SOCIAL
(I. G. S. S.). A government agency founded in late 1946
to handle medical and retirement insurance. It is an
autonomous agency which covers on and off the job ac-
cidents, retrains disabled through workshops, and provides benefits for females. In most cases, benefits
are available only to workers in or around the capital
city.

INSTITUTO NACIONAL DE TRANSFORMACIÓN AGRARIA
(I. N. T. A.). Broadly responsible for development of
agricultural programs from extension training to road
and school building. Set up in 1962 to replace the de-
funct Consejo Agrario Nacional, I. N. T. A. has taken
over land resettlement, primarily in El Petén and Alta
Verapaz.

INTENDENCIA. An administrative division at the provincial
level, set up in the late 18th century to replace the
decadent positions of corregidores, governadores, and
alcaldes mayores. The intendente was named by the
central government and had the power over military,
political and judicial questions in his respective area.
His primary duty was to collect taxes and he was more
successful than his predecessor, largely because better salaries helped to alleviate economic temptation.

INTENDENTE see INTENDENCIA.

INTENDENTE MUNICIPAL. A political chief of a municipio.
Between the years of 1935 and 1944, this system replaced the elected alcalde with an appointee of the departmental governor. In the Ladino municipios, the
intendente was always a Ladino. In the municipalidades
Indigene, the position was filled by Indians. In municipios with a small percentage of Ladinos, the intendente was usually an Indian.

INTERNATIONAL RAILWAY OF CENTRAL AMERICA (I. R.
C. A.). (Also, Ferrocarriles Internacionales de Centro
América). Through the impetus given by President
J. R. Barrios, the construction of the first Guatemalan
railroad began in 1880 at San José and pushed through
to Guatemala City by 1884. The Occidental Railroad
was begun in 1882, completed in 1884; it connected
Champerico and San Felipe. A railroad was begun at
Puerto Barrios in 1883 but only about 20 miles was

completed by 1885, when President Barrios died.
Nothing more was done until 1894 when President José
María Reyna Barrios had the line extended to El Rancho,
136 miles inland from the Caribbean.   Minor C. Keith,
of United Fruit Company fame, contracted to finish the
railroad over the 61-mile stretch of mountains to
Guatemala City.   This was completed by 1908 and a
transcontinental railroad was in operation.   In 1898 the
Ocos Railroad was completed between Ocos on the Pacific coast, and Ayutla on the Mexican border.   In
1900, the Guatemalan Central extended its lines to
Retalhuleu and connected with the Occidental Line.   In
1912, all four lines were connected and a merger contracted.   In 1929, the opening of a line from Zacapa
to El Salvador connected the two countries and in 1942,
the I. R. C. A. was connected with the Mexican system
when a bridge over the Suchiate River at Ayutla was
completed.   Presently the I. R. C. A. owns about 908
miles of railroad in Guatemala and El Salvador.   In
1936, the United Fruit Company (UFCo) acquired 42.68
per cent of I. R. C. A. 's stock.   The agreement was
that UFCo would not build a Pacific port, as it was
given permission to do by the Ubico government, but
would instead use the I. R. C. A. to haul its bananas
from Tiquisate to Puerto Barrios.   UFCo purchased
for I. R. C. A. 41 steam locomotives and much costly
equipment.   In return, the I. R. C. A. gave UFCo special preferential rates amounting to less than half that
of other I. R. C. A. customers.   This agreement stood
until 1955, when the United States Supreme Court ordered the UFCo to divest itself of all I. R. C. A. stocks
and properties.

INVIERNO.   The winter season, although it falls between
the months of May and October, which is actually summer.   It is so named because the rains, which come
during this season, keep the temperature at a lower
level than during the months from November through
April.

IPALA.   Municipio located in the department of Chiquimula
in eastern Guatemala.   Its cabecera rests at the foot
of the volcano Ipala, 14 miles south-southwest of Chiquimula.   Road center.   Population: 12,598.   Crops:
corn, wheat; livestock raising.

IPALA VOLCANO.   Altitude: 5480 feet.   An extinct volcano, located in the department of Chiquimula in eastern Guatemala.

IRISARRI, ANTONIO JOSÉ DE, 1786-1868. Born in Guatemala, he left in 1805 and began to travel over much of Latin America, spending considerable time in Chile where he was active politically. He was a journalist, a philologist, a diplomat, and an author. In 1827 he returned to found the periodical, El Guatemalteco, to defend the cause of the Federation, and was appointed Minister of War by President Arce. In 1846, his autobiographical novel, El cristiano errante, was the first literary work of the Latin American romantic movement. His major literary works include also Historia del perinclito epaminondes del Cauca (1864) and Poesías satiricas y burlescas (1867). He used the pseudonyms: Romualdo Villapedrosa, Fray Adrián de San José, José Isidro Inana i Torre, Dionisio Terrasa y Rejón, Dionisio Isrraeta Rejón, Hilario de Altagumea, and David Barri.

IRISARRI, JUAN BAUTISTA DE, d. 1805. A liberal merchant and founder of a rich, colonial commercial house, he contributed many articles on political economy to the Gazeta, using the pseudonym, Chirimia.

ISRRAETA REJÓN, DIONISIO [pseudonym] see IRISARRI, ANTONIO JOSÉ DE.

ITZA see TAYASAL.

ITZAPA see SAN ANDRÉS ITZAPA.

IXCAMPARIC, EL [pseudonym] see HERNÁNDEZ DE LEÓN, FEDERICO.

IXCHIGUÁN. Municipio in the department of San Marcos in southwestern Guatemala. The cabecera, in the Sierra Madre Mountains, is 16 miles north-northwest of San Marcos. Population: 6127. Altitude: 10,325 ft. Crops: corn, wheat, fodder grasses; livestock.

IXHUATÁN see SANTA MARÍA IXHUATÁN.

IXIL. A linguistic group of the Mamean, located in Huehuetenango and Quiché.

IXIM.   The Mayan word for maize in almost all of the 22
dialects in Guatemala.

IXIMCHE.   Stronghold capital of the Cakchiquel Indians,
captured and destroyed by Pedro de Alvarado.   Near
here, at Tecpán, Alvarado built the first Spanish capital called Santiago.   See also SANTIAGO and TEC-
PÁN GUATEMALA.

IXTAHUACÁN   see   SAN ILDEFONSO IXTAHUACÁN.

IXTAMÁL.   Quiché word for the colander used to strain
boiled corn.

IZABAL.   Department in eastern Guatemala.   Located on
the Caribbean gulf coast, the department includes
Lake Izabal and its outlet, Río Dulce.   It is separated
from the lower Motagua River valley by the Sierro del
Mico.   Its capital since 1920 has been Puerto Barrios.
It has a hot, humid climate.   Crops are bananas,
abaca, corn, beans and coconuts; some lumbering.
Puerto Barrios is the chief port and rail terminus,
and Livingstón is a developing port near Puerto Barrios.   There are five municipios within the department:
Los Amates, El Estor, Livingstón, Morales, Puerto
Barrios.   Population in 1950 was 55,032; in 1964,
116,649; and projected to 1980:   226,500.   Area:
3489 square miles.

IZABAL LAKE.   Largest lake in Guatemala, it is located
20 miles southwest of the Bay of Amatique, into which
it drains via the Río Dulce.   It is 30 miles long, 15
miles wide and 69 feet deep.   It receives the Polochic
River on the west.   Earlier it was called Golfo Dulce,
and in colonial times, it carried much trade between
the highlands and the sea.   Altitude: 26 ft.

IZTAPA.   Municipio in the department of Escuintla, in
southern Guatemala.   The cabecera is located on the
Pacific Ocean at the mouth of the Michatoya River,
seven miles east of San José.   Sometimes called
Puerto de Iztapa.   Renamed La Independencia after
the revolution but the name did not last.   Altitude is
sea level.   Population: 3808.

-J-

J. N. E.   see   JUNTA NACIONAL DE ELECTORAL.

JACALTEC.   A linguistic group of the Mamean, located in
Huehuetenango.

JACALTENANGO.   Municipio located in the department of
Huehuetenango in western Guatemala.   The cabecera,
on the western slope of the Cuchumatanes Mountains,
is 30 miles northwest of Huehuetenango.   Some manufacturing: palm-leaf hats, textiles; crude sugar production; livestock raising.   Population: 12,357.   Altitude: 5700 ft.

JALAPA.   1) Department in east central Guatemala.   Its capi-
tal is Jalapa.   Located in the eastern highlands, on
the Continental Divide, it is drained by affluents of the
Motagua River in the north and in the south, the Ostua
River, which makes up a part of the Lake Güija inlet.
It has two volcanoes, Alzatate and Jumay.   A live-
stock raising region, the crops are: corn, wheat,
beans, tobacco, rice, dairying and chees production.
Some lumbering.   Chromite is mined north of Jalapa.
The main urban centers are Jalapa and Jilotepeque.
The department consists of seven municipios: Jalapa,
Mataquescuintla, Monjas, San Carlos Alzatate, San
Luis Jilotepeque, San Manuel Chaparrón, San Pedro
Pinula.   Population in 1950 was 75,190; in 1964, was
99,242, and projected to 1980:   148,200.   Area: 796
square miles.
    2) Municipio in the department of Jalapa in the high-
lands of east central Guatemala.   The cabecera is 36
miles east of Guatemala City.   Commercial and road
center in an agricultural and livestock area.   Population: 36,637.   Altitude: 4530 ft.   Crops: corn, cotton, beans, wheat; cattle, hogs; dairying.

JALPATAGUA.   Municipio located in the department of
Jutiapa in southeastern Guatemala.   In the highlands,
the cabecera is 13 miles southwest of Jutiapa.   Population: 11,416.   Crops: corn, beans; livestock.

JASPE.   A method of dyeing thread.   The long strands of
thread have knots tied at intervals and the whole thread

is dipped into a dye. It is not allowed to remain long
enough to penetrate through the knots, thereby giving
a shaded effect to the thread which is very handsome
when woven into cloth.

JEFATURA. The official headquarters for the jefe político
   or governor of the province.

JEFE POLÍTICO. A governor or principal civil officer of
   a department.

JÉREZ. Municipio in the department of Jutiapa in south-
      eastern Guatemala. In the highlands, the cabecera is
      at the southwestern foot of Chingo Volcano, near the
      Salvador line and 16 miles southeast of Jutiapa. Pop-
      ulation: 2908. Crops: corn, beans; livestock.

JESUIT. The most aggressive and self-demanding of the
      Catholic orders, the Jesuits worked in the field of ed-
      ucation. During the colonial period they bitterly con-
      tested the founding of a "public" university (San Carl-
      os). In 1767, Carlos III of Spain ordered the removal
      of Jesuits from Latin America, including Guatemala.
      They returned in 1851 under Carrera, only to be
      ousted again in 1871. In 1937, under Ubico, they were
      permitted to open schools; La Merced in Guatemala
      City is the largest. In 1961 the Universidad de Raf-
      ael Landivar was founded and is controlled primarily
      by the Jesuit order.

JESÚS, FELIPE DE [pseudonym] see CABRAL, MAN-
      UEL.

JICARA. An oblong or long gourd grown on a tree and
      widely used by the Indians as a cup or jug.

JICARO, EL. Municipio located in the department of El
      Progreso in east central Guatemala. The cabecera is
      on the Motagua River, 15 miles east-northeast of El
      Progreso. On railroad. Population: 5345. Crops:
      corn, beans; livestock.

JICOTENGA TECUBALSI, DOÑA LUISA see XICOTENGA
      TECUBALSI, DOÑA LUISA.

JIL, SALOMÉ [pseudonym] see MILLA Y VIDAURRE,
      JOSÉ.

JILOTEPEQUE   see   SAN LUIS JILOTEPEQUE.

JIQUILITE   see   INDIGO.

JIUTEMAL   see   AXOPIL.

JOCOTÁN.   Municipio located in the department of Chiquimula in eastern Guatemala.   The cabecera is on a
branch of the Chiquimula River, 11 miles east of Chiquimula.   Population: 21,318.   Crops: corn, beans;
livestock.

JOCOTENANGO.   Municipio located in the department of
Sacatepequez in south central Guatemala.   The cabecera is two miles northwest of Antigua.   Population:
2231.   Altitude: 5052 ft.   Crop: coffee.

JORNALERO.   A temporary migrant day laborer on a plantation, or finca.   Jornaleros Habilitados were paid in ad-
vance and were required to work until salary paid had
been earned.   This method of securing labor is no
longer legal.   Jornaleros No Habilitados were work-
men employed at a set salary and paid at the end of
the work period.   The phrases no habilitados or habilitados have not been used since debt slavery was made
illegal in 1936.

JOYABAJ.   Municipio in the department of El Quiché in
west central Guatemala.   The cabecera is located on
the southern slope of the Sierra de Chuacus, 23 miles
east of Quiché.   Population: 27,733.   Altitude: 4200
ft.   Crops: corn, beans; livestock.

JUÁREZ, O.S.   [pseudonym]   see   ARZU HERRARTE,
JOSÉ.

JUÁREZ MUÑOZ, JOSÉ FERNANDO, 1877-1952.   A Guatemalan author, journalist, and politician.   He wrote romantic historical fiction.   His works include El grito
de la sangre (1930), El secreto de una celda (1937),
and El hijo del bucanero (1952).   He wrote under the
pseudonym Telesforo Talpetate.

JUÁREZ Y ARAGÓN, JOSÉ FERNANDO, 1905- .   Born in
Antigua, he has served as deputy to the national assembly and magistrate to the supreme court.   He wrote
the novels El milagro (1952) and Mas allá de mis

lentes (1956).

JUARROS, DOMINGO, 1752-1820. A priest and Guatemalan
historian who wrote a two-volume history of Guatemala
entitled Compendio de la historia de la ciudad de Guatemala, published 1808-1818. An abridged form was
translated into English in 1823. Juarros' work follows
closely that of Fuentes y Guzmán. This work has been
heavily drawn upon for early Guatemalan history.

JULIUS [pseudonym] see ESTRADA, DOMINGO.

JUMAITEPEQUE VOLCANO. Altitude: 5938 feet. An extinct volcano located in the department of Santa Rosa
in southern Guatemala. It is five miles north-northeast of Cuilapa. On its north slope is the village of
Jumaitepeque.

JUMAY VOLCANO. Altitude: 7218 feet. Extinct volcano
located in the department of Jalapa in east central
Guatemala. It is three miles north of Jalapa.

JUNTA NACIONAL DE ELECTORAL (J. N. E.). An influential board with which all political parties must register
and receive approval before they can participate in an
election. The primary requirement is to have a minimum number of members (500) and to meet other re-
quirements set forth in the Ley Electorial. The
J. N. E. meets once every four years to certify political parties. Members of the J. N. E. are from political parties that received at least 15 per cent of the
valid votes at the previous national election.

JUTIAPA. 1) Department in southeastern Guatemala on the
Pacific coast and Salvadoran border. Its capital is
Jutiapa. It is in the southeast highlands, which slope
toward the Pacific coastal plain. It is drained by the
Río de la Paz, which makes up its southeast border.
It has three volcanoes, Suchitan and Moyuta, with
Chingo Volcano and Lake Güija on the Salvadoran bor-
der. Crops are corn, beans, fodder grasses and rice.
There is extensive livestock raising. Coffee and sugar
cane are grown on the lower slopes. The main cities
are Jutiapa and Asunción Mita. There are 17 municipios in the department: El Adelanto, Agua Blanca,
Asunción Mita, Atescatempa, Comapa, Conguaco, Jalpatagua, Jérez, Jutiapa, Moyuta, Pasaco, El Progreso,

Quesada, San José Acatempa, Santa Catarina Mita,
Yupiltepeque, Zapotitlán. Population in 1950 was
138,925; in 1964, 194,986; and projected to 1980:
277,700. Area: 1242 square miles.
   2) Municipio in the department of Jutiapa in southeastern Guatemala. The cabecera is in the highlands,
near the Inter-American Highway, 45 miles east-southeast of Guatemala City. A commercial center in a
dairying region. Population: 41,891. Altitude: 2926
ft. Crops: corn, beans; livestock.

-K-

KALPUL. Quiché name for public magistrates, who witness
   contracts, referee dances and negotiate marriages.

KAMINAL-JUYU. An archaeological site in the highlands,
   near Guatemala City, dating from the classic empire
   of the early Mayan period (ca. A.D. 600). It is significant because of the highland architectural examples
   it presents.

KANHOBAL. A linguistic group of the Mamean, located in
   the department of Huehuetenango.

KAPERRAJ. A cloth covering similar to a Tzute or Servilleta, used by women to cover foodstuffs or to wear as
   a headscarf. Sometimes called Perrajes.

KEKCHI. One of the larger Mayan dialects making up the
   Kekchian language group of the Proto-Guatemala-Yucatan linguistic family. The Kekchi are located in Alta
   Verapaz, Baja Verapaz, Petén, Izabel, Zacapa, and
   small groupings in Mexico and Belice.

KEKCHIAN. A linguistic group of the Proto-Guatemala-
   Yucatan language family of the Mayan language. The
   dialects making up the Kekchian group are Kekchi,
   Pokonchi and Pokomam, located in scattered areas in
   the east central Guatemalan highlands.

KIEM see STICK LOOM.

KIN. Mayan for "day."

KOPESKWI PLOT (1877). A society calling itself Homicida

and led by a Colonel Kopeskwi, then commander of the
artillery, planned to arrest or remove in some manner, President Barrios and his ministers, and to take
control of the government. The plan involved forging
orders to disperse loyal troops so they would not be in
a position to come to the government's assistance when
needed. One of the troop commanders, upon receiving
his orders, called on Barrios to clarify a point, and
the forgery was discovered. Barrios had the leaders
arrested as they gathered to execute the plot; 17 of
them were then executed in the main plaza.

KUKULCÁN. An early ruler and founder of Mayapan in the
Yucatan area. (See also QUETZALCOATL.) After
setting up a government in Mayapan, Kukulcán returned
to Mexico. The Mayapan league held control of the
area in present-day Petén but did not penetrate into the
Guatemalan highlands.

-L-

L.D. [pseudonym] see AYCINENA, JUAN FERMÍN.

LA. Phrases and place names beginning with an article are
filed under the following word.

LA CRUZ, RODRIGO DE, 1637-1716. Born into Spanish
nobility as Rodrigo de Arias Maldonado, he went to
Costa Rica as a young man with his father, the governor, and took over the governorship when his father
died. He was later moved so much by the Bethlehemites that he joined their order and took over the leadership when Hermano Pedro de Betencourt died. Through
his efforts, the Bethlehemite order was recognized by
the Church, and its activities were greatly expanded.

LA PAZ, ALONSO DE see PAZ, ALONSO DE.

LABOR OVALLE. An experimental farm near Quezaltenango
financed by the Wheat Growers Cooperative and the Ministry of Agriculture. Their work concerns soil fertil-
ity and crop improvement.

LACANDÓN VOLCANO. Extinct volcano about 16 miles west
of Quezaltenango in the municipio of Ostuncalco. Altitude: 9010 ft.

LACANTÚN RIVER.   Often referred to as the Lacandón, it
has several source branches in the Cuchumatanes.   It
flows about 100 miles northeast before emptying into
the Usumacinta River.   The Jatate River empties into
the Lacantún in Chiapas.

LADINO.   Europeans, negroes, Indians or mestizos, who
have adopted the dress and mannerisms associated with
western culture, fall into this loose distinction.   This
is in opposition to Indios or those natives of Central
America who retain the mannerisms of the pre-Hispanic
culture.   When used in reference to the Indians, to
ladinize is to take on characteristics associated with
the Spanish cultural traits.

LAINFIESTA, FRANCISCO, 1837-1912.   A Guatemalan author
and diplomat, he held several ministerial positions in
the national government.   When J. R. Barrios was killed,
Lainfiesta was instrumental in securing the peace with
Salvador.   In 1890 he helped to plan a union of Central
America.   He ran for president in 1892 and was defeated.   His book, A vista de pajaro (1879), is his best
known work.   He wrote under the pseudonyms: Paulino,
Claro, and I. P.

LANDECHO, JUAN NÚÑEZ DE.   Governor from 1559-1563.
His house arrest arising from a charge of corruption
during his rule was a major consideration in the re-
moval of the seat of the audiencia from Guatemala to
Panama in 1564.   The audiencia was again moved to
Guatemala in 1570, largely through the influence of
Bartolomé de Las Casas in the royal court.

LANDÍVAR, RAFAEL, 1731-1793.   Born in Antigua, he studied at the University of San Carlos.   He joined the Jesuit order and lectured on rhetoric and philosophy.   He
went to Italy in 1767, when the Jesuits were expelled
from the Spanish New World.   His best known work is
entitled Rusticatio mexicana and was originally written
in Latin.   He died in Bologna, Italy.   In 1949, his remains were returned to Guatemala for burial.   The
Universidad Rafael Landívar founded in 1961 was named
in his honor.

LANQUÍN.   Municipio in the department of Alta Verapaz in
central Guatemala.   Its cabecera is located in the east
central part of the department, on the road leading from

Cobán. Population: 9532. Crops: coffee, corn, chile, beans, rice.

LAPARRA, JESÚS, 1820-1887.   Born in Quezaltenango, she was a poet and co-editor with her sister of the newspaper La Voz de la Mujer (1885-1887). Her poetry is collected in Decenario del niño Dios (1880).

LAPARRA DE LA CERDA, VICENTA, 1831-1905. A Guatemalan poet and playwright, she is considered the founder of the National Theatre. Co-editor of the newspaper La Voz de la Mujer with her sister, Jesús Laparra. She wrote Angel Caido (1880), Hija maldita and Los lazos del crimen (1897).

LARA Y MOGROBEJO, ANTONIO DE. Acting governor from 1649 to 1654.

LARIOS, JERÓNIMO, 1555-1622? A Mercedarian Friar of Guatemala, he was "Maestro de novicios" for the monastery when charged in 1620 of heretical mysticism. He was sent to Mexico for his trial.

LARRAZABAL, ANTONIO JOSÉ DE LAS MERCEDES, 1769-1853. Professor at the University of San Carlos. He was elected to represent Guatemala in the Cortes which met in Cadiz, Spain, in 1810, to draw up the constitution of 1812. Best known for his Apuntamientos sobre la agricultura y comercio del Reyno de Guatemala (1811).

LARREYNAGA, MIGUEL, 1771-1847. President of the supreme court during the Federation Period (1823-1839). He wrote Discurso ... de la Independencia (1838) and Memoria sobre el fuego da los volcanos (1843).

LAS. Phrases and place names beginning with an article are filed under the following word.

LAS CASAS, BARTOLOMÉ DE, 1474-1566. A Dominican missionary, bishop and historian, he received the title, "Apostle of the Indians." He made the voyage in 1502 to Hispañiola. He received an encomienda in Cuba, but gave it up to devote his life to protecting the Indians. He attempted to found a model colony in Venezuela in 1520, but it failed. After spending ten years in a monastery, he went to Spain to become the moving

force behind the "New Laws" of 1542, which called for
an end to the encomienda system.   The laws were not
enforced, however, and later were modified to the
point of non-existence.   He spent his last twenty years
in Spain, championing the rights of the Indians, and
writing political tracts and a history of the Indies.

LATIFUNDIO.   Large-sized farms or land holdings.   The
sixth census showed .3 per cent of the farm owners
held 50.3 per cent of the farm land.   These latifundios
averaged 1115 acres.

LEAGUE.   A unit of measurement made up of 5,000 vara
and equivalent to 4.18 kilometers.

LEAL, V. MANUEL [pseudonym] see VALLE, MANUEL.

LEIVA, RAUL, 1916- .   Poet, novelist and critic, he was
born in Guatemala City.   He was director of the national radio network (TGW), and director of publications for the Secretary of Information to the President.
He has written Angustia (1942), Nunca el olvido (1957),
and El deseo (1946) in poetic free verse.   His criticisms include: Imagen de la poesía mexicana con-
temporanea (1959), Danza para Cuauhtemoc (1955), and
Batres Montufar y la poesía (1943).

LEY, SALVADOR, 1907- .   Guatemalan composer and pianist, director of the National Conservatory from 1934 to
1937; later on the faculty at New York University
(1967/68).   He has composed Tres fragmentos (1933),
El mar (1941), Sobre un poema propio en inglés (1940),
and Copla triste (elegy).   Original spelling is Salvador
Levy.

LEY DE REFORMA AGRARIA (Decreto no. 900, 1952).
Provided for expropriation of private land not under
cultivation, from owners of more than 223 acres (two
caballerias).   Land parceled out from government
farms was given for lifetime only (usufructo vitalicio).
From private land, it was given in ownership but could
not be sold within 25 years.   The National Agrarian
Bank was set up to aid small farmers in purchasing,
offering three per cent loans.   The law made the president both executive and judicial authority.   Expropriated land would be paid for at the rate at which it was
assessed for tax purposes before 1952.   Between 1952

and 1954, under the program, a total of 917, 659 acres
was distributed to 87, 569 persons. This was about
10. 5 acres per person and above the national average
for size of individual farms. Much of the land re-
verted back to the original owner after the 1954 revolution. In 1956 the law was rewritten to resettle unused government and private land, giving full ownership
to settlers. About 25, 000 families were settled on
390, 000 acres between 1956 and 1963. Again in 1962,
the law was rewritten (Ley de Transformación Agraria)
to place the resettlement program under I. N. T. A. The
law now calls for a special tax on unused land for five
years at which time, if still unused, it can be used
for resettlement. Most of the present-day projects are
in El Petén and Alta Verapaz.

LEYENDA NEGRA   see   BLACK LEGEND.

LEYES DE LAS INDIAS   see   RECOPILACIÓN DE LAS
    LEYES DE INDIAS.

LIBERATO CAUTO [pseudonym]   see   MOLINA, PEDRO.

LIBERTAD, LA.   1) Municipio in the department of Hue-
    huetenango in western Guatemala. Its cabecera is near
    the Inter-American Highway in Western Huehuetenango.
    Population: 11, 615. Crops: corn, beans, sugar cane,
    coffee, potatoes, tobacco.
        2) Municipio located in the department of El Petén
    in northern Guatemala. The cabecera is 18 miles
    southwest of Flores. Population: 1183. Crops:
    corn, beans, rice, sugar cane.

LIBRETO.   A numbered card issued to workers by the Ubico
    government between 1937 and 1944. The cards carried
    information concerning the worker's name, residence,
    his daily wage, dates of employment, class of work,
    and attesting signature of the person employing the
    worker. The cards were the means whereby govern-
    ment officials would determine whether or not a person
    was a vagrant, and, if so, subject to arrest. The
    "Vagrancy Law" required every male to cultivate a
    specified amount of land or to work for another a cer-
    tain number of days per year, or a combination of
    both. The law was almost universally enforced against
    the "Indios" and infrequently enforced against the "Lad-
    inos. "

LICORNES [pseudonym] see GOICOECHEA, JOSÉ AN-
TONIO.

LIENDO Y GOICOECHEA, JOSÉ ANTONIO see GOICOE-
CHEA, JOSÉ ANTONIO.

LIVINGSTON. Municipio in the department of Izabal in eastern Guatemala. The cabecera is a minor port on the
Bay of Amatique at the mouth of the Río Dulce, 11
miles west-northwest of Puerto Barrios. It serves as
a supply point for the Lake Izabal region. Until the
rise of Puerto Barrios, it was the leading Atlantic port
of Guatemala and the capital of the department of Izabal
until 1920. Boatbuilding, mahogany working, custom-
house. Exports bananas, rubber, sarsaparilla, lumber.
Population: 11,918. Crops: corn, beans, bananas,
potatoes, sugar cane.

LIVINGSTON CODE. A code of laws for Louisiana, drawn
up by Edward Livingston. It was translated into Spanish in 1831 and adopted by the State of Guatemala in
1838 after the liberals had separated Church and State.
The old Spanish judicial system was discarded. The
code introduced the right of habeas corpus and trial by
jury. The Guatemalan state assembly accepted the code
in December, 1835, but it did not go into effect until
January 1, 1838. The code was largely misunderstood
by the people and was repealed when Carrera gained
control of the government in 1839.

LIZARDO DÍAZ O., JOSÉ, 1891- . A Guatemalan historian,
he wrote Estrada Cabrera, Barillas y Regalado ... en
1906 (1962) and De la democracia a la dictadura (1946)
on the failure of the revolution of 1897.

LOOM see STICK LOOM.

LÓPEZ, FRANCISCO. On the conquest with Alvarado, he
later became a member of the government of Doña
Beatriz de la Cueva, in 1541.

LÓPEZ, JOSÉ VENANCIO, 1791-1863. A Guatemalan politician active during the period just prior to the revolution in 1821. He was a strong supporter of José del
Valle.

LORENZANA, RAUL, d. 1968. Leader of the right-wing

political group called "mano blanco" (white hand) who
led the kidnapping of Bishop Mario Casariego in early
1968. Lorenzana was assassinated by the leftist group
of urban terrorists, Fuente Armado Revolucionario
(F. A. R.).

LOS. Phrases and place names beginning with an article
under the following word.

LUCIENTES, FRANCISCO [pseudonym] see MARROQUÍN
ROJAS, CLEMENTE.

-M-

M. L. N. see MOVIMIENTO DE LIBERACIÓN NACIONAL.

M. R. -13. Movimiento Revolucionario de 13 de noviembre
de 1960, a revolutionary group led by Yon Sosa that
formed in an attempt to overthrow Ydígoras and did
aid in his downfall in 1962. The M. R. -13 split off
from F. A. R. in 1964 and began operating as a guerilla
band in the lowland of Lake Izabal and Zacapa. Re-
united in 1968 with the F. A. R.

MACACA. Spanish silver currency dating from the mid-
16th century. Guatemala was the last of the Latin
American countries to outlaw the use of these coins in
the reform era of 1873. Macacas were minted in
Peru and Mexico primarily, also in Guatemala and
Spain. The coins were crudely stamped, having an ir-
regular shape that made clipping comparatively simple.
When taken in large quantities, they were accepted on-
ly by weight, not by their nominal value. See also
CASA DE MONEDA.

MACANA. A pointed planting stick about two meters long,
used primarily in lowland agriculture. The term earlier referred to an Indian wooden sabre, edged with
sharp flint.

MACEHAULES. The Indian working class upon which the
ruling elite of the Spanish colonial empire depended to
do certain services and to pay taxes in kind.

MACHADO JAÚREGUI, RAFAEL, 1834- . A Guatemalan
diplomat and poet. Ambassador to Costa Rica, minis-

ter in the Carrera government. His poetry appears
in the anthologies, Amor, esperanza, y fe (1875) and
Poesías (1887).

MACHETE. A large, heavy knife, usually with a curved
blade 20 to 25 inches long and about three inches wide.
It is used in clearing and harvesting the land. The
most significant innovation in the Indian's method of
farming since the Spanish conquest.

MADRE VIEJA RIVER. In southwestern Guatemala, it arises
west of Tecpán and flows about 90 miles south-southwest into the Pacific Ocean at Tiquisate. It forms the
Chimaltenango-Sololá department boundary in its upper
course.

MADRINA. A godmother in pre-20th-century Guatemala,
held in great respect or reverence. The person was
taught to never stand in the shadow of his madrina and
to kiss the hem of the madrina's skirt if she stopped
to speak.

MAESTRESCUELA. A chancellor with royal and pontifical
authority to validate documents pertinent to higher de-
grees at the University.

MAGDALENA MILPAS ALTAS. Municipio in the department
of Sacatepéquez in south central Guatemala. The cabecera is five miles southeast of Antigua. Population:
2360. Altitude: 6158 ft. Crops: corn, beans, fodder grasses.

MAGEE AFFAIR. In September of 1874, the commander of
San José, Colonial González, had a dispute with the
British vice-consul, John Magee. González ordered
Magee whipped and placed in prison. The British Minister protested to Barrios, who had Colonel González
punished severely. An indemnity of 50,000 dollars
was paid and an official salute was made to the British
in the port of San José.

MAGICAL REALISM. A combination of realism and fantasy
with the emphasis on style which transforms the everyday happenings into the awesome and the unreal. A
contemporary literary movement springing from Latin
America. The leading writer in the movement is Miguel Ángel Asturias.

MALACATÁN. Municipio in the department of San Marcos
in southwestern Guatemala in the Pacific Piedmont.
The cabecera is located on the Inter-American Highway, near the Mexican border and 17 miles west-
southwest of San Marcos. Market center. Population:
27,349. Crops: coffee, sugar cane, grain; livestock.

MALACATANCITO. Municipio located in the department of
Huehuetenango in western Guatemala. The cabecera
is situated on the headstream of the Chixoy River, five
miles south-southwest of Huehuetenango. Population:
6348. Altitude: 5203 ft. Crops: corn, wheat, beans.

MALDONADO, ALONSO DE, d. 1560. Governor of Guatemala, 1542-1548. He was responsible for moving the
capital to Antigua after the destruction of Almolonga.
He was governor when the New Laws were announced
and was reluctant to enforce the laws. First sent to
Guatemala in 1536 from Mexico by the Audiencia to investigate Alvarado's venture to Quito. He was unsuccessful because Alvarado had left for Spain.

MALDONADO, FRANCISCO. A 17th-century Guatemalan
Franciscan friar, noted for his linguistic ability. He
left many manuscripts which were used by the Church
in its teachings. The most noteworthy is his Theologia
Indorum.

MALDONADO Y PAS, JUANA DE, 1598-1666? A 17th-cen-
tury nun of the convent La Concepción. Reportedly
very beautiful, very wealthy and intelligent, she created considerable scandal by living in an extremely
elaborate apartment in the convent, and by entertain-
ing too often the bishop and other high church officials
with her poetry and music.

MAM. A language group making up part of the Mamean
linguistic stock of the Proto-Guatemala-Yucatan language family. Located in Huehuetenango, Quezaltenango, San Marcos and in Mexico. One of the earliest
highland settlements, it centered about present-day
Zaculeu. Chinabajul was the early name of the capital, until the 13th or 14th century. Gonzalo Alvarado
conquered the Mames in 1525 after much fierce fighting.

MAMEAN. One of the major linguistic stock of the Maya

language, made up of the following dialects: Mam,
Aguacatec, Ixil, Jacaltec, Kanhobal, Solomec. These
groups are located in Mexico, Huehuetenango, Quezaltenango, Quiché and San Marcos.

MANATI (Sea cow). An quatic mammal found in tropical
waters and at one time common in Lake Izabal. It is
approximately ten feet long, with a snout resembling
that of a cow. It has small, pea-sized eyes and a
thick, heavy tail, and often weighs more than 400
pounds. The manati is sought for its meat and hide
but has become more and more scarce since the 1930's.

MANDAMIENTO. A system of work regulations quite similar to the Repartamiento. It became the dominant
method of extracting services from the Indians after
the encomienda system was forbidden in 1720. Men
from certain areas were required to work on designated plantations in return for a salary. This soon
degenerated into the debt peonage which lasted in Guatemala until the vagrancy laws were passed in 1934.

MANIFIESTO DEL FRENTE UNIDO DE PARTIDOS POLÍTI-
COS Y ASSOCIONES CÍVICAS. The first truly "nation-
alistic" pronunciamento from Guatemalans, published in
1944 by students at the University of San Carlos. It
called for the overthrow of the Ponce government.

MANO. A cylindrical stone grinder used when mashing
maize on the metate. The mano is worked back and
forth in the metate, the motion similar to that of using
a rolling pin.

MANO (Movimiento anticomunista de nacional organización).
More frequently called Mano Blanco, it came publicly
into existence in 1966. It is a right-wing terror group
backed by the leaders of the Guatemalan military,
formed by Colonel Enrique Trinidad Oliva who was assassinated in 1967. Mano Blanco kidnapped Bishop
Casariego in March 1968 in an effort to embarrass the
President. Mano was led by Raul Lorenzana until his
death in 1968. The symbol of Mano Blanco is a white
hand over a red circle framed in black.

MANZANA. A land measurement used to measure smaller
farm areas. It is equal to 100 square vara (1.72
acres). One square mile is equal to 372.09 manzanas.

MARAVEDI.   A unit of money used in the colonial period.
Eight and one-half maravedi was equivalent to one
silver cuartillo, which equaled one-fourth of a real.
See also CASA DE MONEDA.

MARGIL DE JESÚS, ANTONIO, 1657-1726.   A Spanish Franciscan monk who went to Guatemala in 1684 and was
one of the important figures in restoring peace among
rebelling Indians of Verapaz.   He founded the monastery Recoleccion in Antigua.   He died in Mexico.

MARÍA LINDA RIVER   see   MICHATOYA RIVER.

MARIMBA.   A musical instrument consisting of a series of
parallel wooden keys supported by a wooden framework
which allows the struck keys to vibrate over resonance
chambers that hang beneath the keys.   The musicians,
or marimberos, can range in number from seven on a
Marimba Doble to a single player on a Marimba con
Tecomates.   The earliest reference to a marimba in
Guatemala came from Domingo Juarros, who wrote of
one in Antigua in 1680.   This leads authorities to believe that the Guatemalan marimba is an adaptation of
the African instrument bearing a similar name.

MARKET DAYS.   Every day in: Guatemala City, Quezalte-
nango, Santiago Atitlán, Huehuetenango.
Sunday: Chichicastenango, San Pedro Sacatepequez,
    Momostenango, Quiché, Nahuala, Panajachel,
    Comalapa, San Martín Jilotepeque, San Cristobal
    Totonicapán.
Monday: Antigua, Chimaltenango.
Tuesday: Sololá, San Pedro Jocopilas, San Lucas
    Tolimán.
Wednesday: Palín.
Thursday: Chichicastenango, San Pedro Sacatepequez,
    Antigua, Tecpán, Sacapulas, Chimaltenango, Nebaj.
Friday: Sololá, Palín, San Francisco El Altos, Chi-
    maltenango, San Pedro Jocopilas, San Lucas Toli-
    mán.
Saturday: Antigua, Chiche.

MARQUI, SANTIAGO, 1767-1820.   Spanish architect, went
to Guatemala in 1804 to oversee the completion of the
cathedral, which was not quite done when he died.   He
also supervised the construction of the school Educa-
torio de Indias in 1810.

MARROQUÍN, BARTOLOMÉ. Brother of Francisco, he went
to Guatemala in 1530 as Regidor of the capital. He
was Second Alcalde of Guatemala in 1545 and 1550.

MARROQUÍN, FRANCISCO, 1499?-1563. Left Spain for
Guatemala in 1530; he became the first Bishop of
Guatemala in 1534. He was responsible for bringing
Bartolomé de Las Casas to Guatemala in 1535. He
raised money to help build the cathedral in Antigua
by selling the ruined cathedral at Almolonga. The Antigua cathedral was begun in 1543 and completed in
1669, but was destroyed in 1773. Marroquín acted
as joint governor in 1541-42 with Francisco de la
Cueva. He left his estate for the foundation of a university, the provisions for which were not carried out
until 1678. His body, interred in the cathedral at
Antigua, was covered and buried by the earthquake of
1773.

MARROQUÍN ROJAS, CLEMENTE, 1897- . Born in Jalapa, a journalist, writer and politician, he is founder
and director of the newspapers "La Hora" and "El
Impacto." He was a critic of Ubico in exile and since
the revolution of 1944, he has been active in politics
as Mayor of Guatemala City and vice-president under
Méndez Montenegro. He has written Ecco homo
(1926), La bomba (1930), En el coragón de la montaña, Cronicos de la constituyente del 45 (1955), La
derrote de una batalla (1957), and Los Cadetes
(1960).   Pseudonyms: Canuto Ocana, Francisco
Lucientes.

MARSICOETERE Y DURÁN, MIGUEL ÁNGEL, 1912- . A
poet and novelist noted for futuristic short stories and
dramatic productions, such as El evangelio de Odolán,
Cada quien con su fontasma, El espejo roto, La mujer,
El robot and others. Founder of the literary society
known as Los Tepeus, considered one of the outstanding poets of Guatemala.

MARTÍNEZ, CARLOS H , 1885-1945. A Guatemalan poet
of the modernistic movement, he held the rank of
colonel in the army. He was imprisoned in the late
1930's for political reasons. His best known poems
are De Rembrandt and La mujer soñada.

MARTÍNEZ, JOSÉ VICENTE, 1863-1922. A Guatemalan au-

thor and politician, he was elected provisional president of the abortive Federación de Centro América,
in 1921. Pseudonym: Javier Z. Montes.

MARTÍNEZ, JUAN ANTONIO. A wealthy merchant, Martínez was named president in August of 1848 after Carrera went into voluntary exile. He held the office until November 28, 1848.

MARTÍNEZ DURÁN, CARLOS, 1906- . Born in Guatemala
City, a physician and surgeon, minister to Italy (1950-
51) and rector of the University of San Carlos (1945-
50), he has written numerous books on medicine.
They include El arte farmacéutico colonial (1938), Las
ciencias médicas en Guatemala (1941), La epidemias
de tifo en Guatemala (1940), Locos de la colonia (1941),
and Bases humanísticas de la ensenanzas médica (1946).

MARTÍNEZ MONT, LUIS, 1901-1955. A Guatemalan educator, he held several governmental offices in the Ubico
government; his writings include Le jugement moral
chez l'enfant.

MARTÍNEZ NOLASCO, GUSTAVO, 1892- . A Guatemalan
novelist, many years in Mexico, his works include
Le señora es asi (1918), Recatados amores (1921),
La comedianta (1922), and El amigo de la metropoli
(1922). Pseudonyms: El Bachiller Grijalva, Ramiro
Cordova, G. Ramírez Clostán.

MARTÍNEZ SOBRAL, ENRIQUE, 1875-1950. A Guatemalan
novelist and economist, his writings would be classed
as naturalistic, and include Inutil combate, Los de
Peralta, Su matrimonio and Alcohol. He wrote under
the pseudonym Juan de Mata. He later gave up writing and became a leading economist. See his Artículos relativos a la reforma monetaria (1925) and Compendio de economia (1939).

MARURE, ALEJANDRO, 1809-1851. A Guatemalan historian, his best known monographs are Bosquejo historico
de las revoluciones de Centro-América and Efemerides
de los hechos notables acaedidos en la Republica de
Centro-America (1844). He assisted in writing the
"proyecto de constitución" of 1847, which became the
basis of the constitution of 1853.

MARURE, MATEO ANTONIO, d. 1814. The primary leader
of the Belén Conspiracy, he had earlier participated
in the revolt of 1811 in San Salvador. He was exiled
and died in a hospital in Havana. He was the father
of the historian Alejandro Marure.

MASAGUA. Municipio in the department of Escuintla in
southern Guatemala. The cabecera is located on the
Guacalate River, six miles south-southwest of Escuintla, on the railroad. Population: 17,311. Crops:
grain, fruit, livestock, lumbering.

MASION. A lodging house for transient Indians, many of
which are located near the market areas in Guatemala
City.

MATA, JUAN DE [pseudonym] see MARTÍNEZ SOBRAL,
ENRIQUE.

MATAQUESCUINTLA. Municipio located in the department
of Jalapa in east central Guatemala. In the highlands,
the cabecera is at the western foot of Alzatate Volcano,
24 miles east-southeast of Guatemala City. On a road
junction; copper mines nearby. Until 1935, it was in
the department of Santa Rosa. Population: 13,169.
Altitude: 5300 ft. Crops: corn, beans, coffee, livestock.

MATATE. A small net bag, very much like a shopping bag,
with two short handles. Usually carried by men, it is
made of rush pith. Sometimes called a morral, chim,
guangochos, bolsas or redes.

MATOS, JOSÉ, 1875- . Lawyer and diplomat, born in
Guatemala and minister to Chile, Brazil, Uruguay,
Argentina, France and delegate to the League of Na-
tions, 1927-33, where he was council president in 1933.
He wrote numerous works on international law, includ-
ing Estudio del derecho internacional en los paises
americanos (1915) and Le droit international prive de
Guatemala (1930).

MAXENO. An Indian inhabitant of the municipio of Santo
Tomas Chichicastenango. It is a corruption of the
longer word, Tomaseno.

MAYA. A highly developed civilization that predated the

Christian era.   The word Maya (Maia) was first used
in print by Peter Martyr in 1516, who took it from a
manuscript of Bartholomew Columbus, brother of Chris-
topher.   The Mayan civilization was centered in lowland Yucatan and Guatemala.   The peak of the classic
period A.D. 600-800, was marked by development of
sculpture, hieroglyphic writing, astronomy and advanced arithmetic.   The culture collapsed between A.D.
800 and 925 and the people moved out of the area to
the upper Yucatan Peninsula.   A "new empire" period
developed under the Mexican Mayapan between 1000 and
1400.   During the 1400's the Quiché broke away from
the Mayapan and there began a period of civil war
among petty chieftains.   This state of war lasted until
the arrival of the Spanish.   The more impressive architecture is found today at Chichén Itzá (Mexico),
Tikal (Guatemala), and Copán (Honduras).   The predominant languages and customs in the area today are
derived more from the ancient Maya than from the con-
quering Spanish.

MAYORA, EDUARDO, 1891-1960.   A journalist and diplomat; editor of the newspapers, El Unionista and later,
Diario de Centro América.   He headed the diplomatic mission to Mexico and other countries of Central America.

MAYORDOMO.   The mayordomo is appointed by principales,
or elders of the community.   The leading member of a
'cofradia,' or group devoted to the worship of a saint.

MAYORGA, JUAN DE [pseudonym] see HERNÁNDEZ DE
LEÓN, FEDERICO.

MAYORGA, MARTÍN DE, d. 1783.   Governor, 1773 to 1779.
The last of the governors to rule at Antigua.   The
earthquake destroyed the city a few weeks after his arrival.   He established the new capital in the Valle de
las Vacas.   Mayorga was made viceroy of New Spain.

MAZATENANGO.   Municipio in the department of Suchitepequez in southwestern Guatemala.   The cabecera is on
a railroad and on the Sis River (a Pacific coastal
stream), 21 miles south of Quezaltenango.   Crops are
cotton, coffee, sugar cane and livestock.   Manufacture
in the area consists of cotton ginning and milling, cot-
tonseed oil extraction, and other light manufacture.
Population: 32,710.   Altitude: 1250 ft.

MECAPÁL. The broad leather strap for the forehead with
attached ropes, used in carrying the Cacaste, redes,
or other goods on the back. Often referred to as a
tumpline, it is made of ox-hide.

MECATE. A maguey cord. Also refers to a field or square
of land, 65 feet to the side. Land cleared for planting
was generally measured into mecates. The Mayan
farmer measured with a rope about 65 feet (20 meters)
in length and marked corners with piles of stone.

MEJÍA, JOSÉ VICTOR, 1877-1945. An army general, he
wrote Geografía medicomilitar (1928) and El Petén,
datos, geográficos e históricos (1904).

MEJÍA GONZÁLEZ, RAUL, 1891-1919. A poet of the modernistic school, best remembered for his poem Ya no
vuelve.

MELCHOR DE MENCOS. A newly formed (1960) municipio
in Petén whose primary industry is chicle. Named
after the leader of a successful 1754 effort against the
pirates in Belice. The cabecera is Cuidad Melchor
de Mencos, formerly called Fallsbon. Altitude: 348
ft. Population: 2002.

MEMORIAL OF TECPÁN ATITLÁN see ANNALS OF THE
CAKCHIQUELES.

MENCOS, ALBERTO, 1863-1922. Born in Guatemala City,
he was a poet and diplomat. Representative to El
Salvador, Spain, and Honduras. Best known for his
poem El Lago.

MENCOS, MARTÍN CARLOS DE. Governor from 1659 to
1667. Completed the fortifications on Río Dulce at
San Felipe in 1663.

MENCOS FRANCO, AGUSTÍN, 1862-1902. A Guatemalan
author and historian, his chief works are Ragos bio-
gráficos de Francisco Morazán, Chrónicas de la Antigua Guatemala (1894), Don Juan Núñez García, and
Literatura guatemalteca en el periodo de la colonial.

MÉNDEZ, FRANCISCO, 1908-1962. A Guatemalan author
and poet, he worked for many years as an editor for
the newspaper, El Imparcial. His works include

Romances de la tierra verde (1938), Los dedos en el barro, and Trasmundo.

MÉNDEZ, GONZALO, 1505-1582. One of the five Franciscan monks who established the first monastery in Guatemala in 1540. As a missionary, he encouraged the Indians to learn to read and write, and then to write their histories and legends.

MÉNDEZ, JOAQUÍN, 1862-1943. A Guatemalan poet and critic, he was minister to the U.S., Guatemalan representative at the Paris Peace Conference. He wrote Colección de artículos y composisiones poéticas de autores centro-americanos, 3 vols. (1896) and Guatemala de fiesta (1904).

MÉNDEZ MONTENEGRO, JULIO CÉSAR, 1915- . Former head of the Law School at the Universidad de San Carlos, he was president 1966-1970 (as the candidate of the Partido Revolucionario). He attempted to balance the military against the guerilla activity which left the country in a state of unrest.

MENDOZA, BALTESAR DE. On the conquest, he was alcalde of Guatemala in 1524.

MENESES, AUGUSTO, 1910-1955. A Guatemalan poet and regional writer, his best effort was La muerte del potro prieto. Considered a leading poet at the time of his death, his works were published as: Prosa y poesía de ... (1961).

MENGALA. Usually refers to Ladinos who have learned the local Indian dialect and have taken up some of the ways of the Indians. The mengalas are almost always poorer rural Ladinos, living in areas populated by Indians.

MÉRIDA, CARLOS, 1893- . Born in Quezaltenango, one of the leading artists of Latin America. He studied in Europe and Mexico where he has lived most of his life. He is a cubist; his work can be seen in the National Palace. He wrote: Modern Mexican Artist (1936), Orozco's frescos in Guadalajara (1939), and Trajes regionales mexicanos (1944).

MERLO, TOMÁS DE, 1649-1739. An artist from Portugal who spent his life in Guatemala. One of the better

examples of his work hangs in the colonial museum at
Antigua, Saint Nicholas received by Emperor Constan-
tine. Also in the museum is his painting entitled,
Apoteosis de San Ignacio de Loyola.

METATE. A curved, concave volcanic stone used for grinding corn. Often it had short legs, but could be a slab
that rested on the ground or table. See also PIEDRA
DE MOLER.

MEXICAN BOUNDARY DISPUTE. During the colonial period,
the boundary between Guatemala and Mexico was never
defined. In 1823, Chiapas elected to remain with Mexico when the Federation dissolved and a general boundary was then outlined, with details to be worked out at
a later date. Mexico, under Santa Ana, kept pushing
her claims further south. In 1882, when Barrios was
in Washington, D.C., he negotiated with the Mexican
ambassador. Although unfavorable to Guatemala, the
treaty was signed and ratified in September, 1882.
Barrios felt that the only way Guatemala could stop
Mexico from further extending her claims would be to
sign a treaty defining the limits.

MEXICAN CONFEDERATION. The confederation lasted between September, 1821 and July, 1823. Guatemala withdrew from the Mexican union at the downfall of Emperor
Agustín Iturbide. Iturbide had kept an army in Guatemala, commanded by General Vicente Filisofia, to encourage Guatemala to take up closer ties with Mexico.
See also PLAN DE IGUALA.

MICHATOYA RIVER. In southern Guatemala, it drains Lake
Amatitlán and flows about 55 miles south, between the
volcanoes Agua and Pacaya, and past Palín, where
there is a power station. It flows into the Pacific at
Iztapa. Called Río María Linda in its lower course.

MICHES. A handful of red beans carried in a bag of magic
objects by a shaman. The beans are read in the pres-
ence of people needing help; through the beans the shaman is able to foretell the future and thereby assist
the needy.

MILITARY REGENCY. Since 1954 and particularly since
1962 the military has moved to an increasingly dominant position in the government. While over half the

years since 1900 have seen a military person in the
Presidency, the large amount of U.S. technical and
material aid has permitted the Guatemalan military to
effectively control the area outside Guatemala City also. In earlier times, the country was regionally controlled; there now appears to be total control from
Guatemala City. The earlier attempts to arm segments of the population as a counter-balance to the
military and the more recent guerrilla movement has
contributed to the centralization and strengthening of
the military.

MILLA Y VIDAURRE, JOSÉ, 1822-1882. Son of a military
leader, he was educated in military academies. He
edited several newspapers and was exiled in 1848. He
returned in 1849 and became active in the Carrera
government. In the 1860's he began to publish novels
in his paper, Semana, under the pseudonym, Salomé
Jil. Milla again went into exile in 1871 for three
years. On his return to Guatemala he was commissioned to write Historia de la America Central, of
which two volumes appeared before his death. Among
his better known novels are: Don Bonifacio, El visitador, La hija del adelantado, and Los Nazarenos.

MILPA. Refers to a cornfield, often with other crops inter-
planted. The term milpitas may be used in connection
with individual plants. In the broadest sense, a milpa
can refer to a plot of ground cultivated by a single
farmer.

MINIFUNDIO. On the opposite end of the scale from latifundio. It refers to a tiny plot of land of less than
3.5 acres in size. The minifundios are occupied by
47.6 per cent of the farm operators, according to the
Guatemalan sixth census (1950).

MINPOKOM see RABINAL.

MINT see CASA DE MONEDA.

MIRON ALVAREZ, OSCAR, 1911-1938. A Guatemalan poet,
his works are collected in the anthologies, El canto de
la sangre (1933) and Amanecida (1936).

MISTELA. A drink consisting of wine, water, cinnamon
and sugar.

MITA.   A system of rotation of labor, of Indian origin.
The Indians were selected by drawing lots to work by
the day for the Spanish.   Artisans and those tilling
their own land were exempt.

MIXCO.   Municipio located in the department of Guatemala
in south central Guatemala.   The cabecera is on the
Inter-American Highway, four miles west of Guatemala
City.   Pottery making; market center.   Population:
36,917.   Altitude: 5551 ft.   Crops: truck produce,
corn; livestock.

MIXCO VIEJO.   A Pokoman fortress that had its start as a
buffer state between the warring nations of Sacatepequez and Cakchiquel.   Founded shortly before the conquest, Mixco allied with the Sacatepequez against the
Cakchiqueles.   When Alvarado arrived, he, with the
aid of the Cakchiqueles, took the fortress only after
all the allies of the Mixco had left them.   The fortress
was destroyed and the people moved to present-day
Mixco.   Mixco Viejo is located in the northwest corner
of the department of Chimaltenango.

MO.   Quiché for Ladino; also refers to "crazy one."

MODERNISMO.   A literary movement beginning at the turn
of the 20th century.   It was a reaction to naturalism
in literature, to conformity, and to the accepted literary standards of the day.   The leading modernistic
writer was Rubén Darío of Nicaragua; the earliest
Guatemalan writer was Domingo Estrada.   Made up of
free verse and internal rhythms, it stressed creativity,
individualism and subjectivity.

MOLINA, MARCELO, 1800-1879.   President of the Republic
of Los Altos, 1839-40.   When the state was annexed
by Carrera, he went to Mexico until 1847.   He served
on the Supreme Court of Justice for two years.   See
also ALTOS, LOS.

MOLINA, PEDRO, 1777-1854.   A Guatemalan medical doctor,
professor at the University of San Carlos Medical
School, a revolutionary precursor, governor of Guatemala, 1829-1830, and candidate for president against
Morazán in 1830.   He wrote revolutionary articles under the pseudonym, Liberato Cauto.

MOLINA BEDOYA, FELIPE, 1812-1855. Guatemalan diplomat, he was an advisor to Rafael Carrera. His works
include Costa Rica y Nueva-Granada, examen de la
cuestión de límites (1852).

MOLOJ. Nightly rounds made by members of the cofradias
and their families at Chichicastenango and other Indian
pueblos, just before Holy Week. The primary purpose
of the rounds is to collect money or edibles to pay for
fireworks and liquor used during the celebrations. Often called Zarabanda.

MOLOTE. A spool of wool yarn as it comes from the spinning wheel. It is often marketed in this form.

MOMOSTENANGO. Municipio located in the department of
Totonicapan in west central Guatemala. Its cabecera
is on the headstream of the Chixoy River, 11 miles
north of Totonicapan. Wool and market center. Population: 33,078. Altitude: 7546 ft. Crops: corn,
wheat, beans; sheep raising.

MONDONOVISMO. A poetic movement which arose in con-
trast to the cosmopolitan theme of modernismo. Its
basis was the local Latin American theme, reflecting
colonial history and Indian life. It was the first true
Spanish American literary movement. The leading
Guatemalan poet of this movement was Osmundo Arriola.

MONJA BLANCA. The national flower, White Nun (Lycaste
skinneri, var. Alba). A white orchid, grown primarily in Alta Verapaz.

MONJAS. Municipio in the department of Jalapa in east central Guatemala. Its cabecera is located in the highlands, 12 miles southeast of Jalapa. Population: 8377.
Crops: corn, wheat, cotton, beans; livestock.

MONTAOS Y SOTOMAYOR, JOSÉ VÁSQUEZ PREGO, d.
1753. Governor from 1752 to 1753.

MONTE. Sacred place in a rural area.

MONTE OSCURO see UNIÓN, LA.

MONTECRISTO. The peak or mountain on which the com-

mon boundary marker for Guatemala, El Salvador and
Honduras is located. In Chiquimula, altitude is 8131
ft.

MONTEFORTE TOLEDO, MARIO, 1911- . A popular novelist and writer of social protests, he has written serious monographs but is best known for his novels. He
aided in the drafting of the 1952 agrarian law. His
novels include Anaite (1940), La cueva sin quietud
(1949), Entre la piedra y la cruz (1948), Donde acabon
los caminos (1953), and Una manera de morir (1957).
His more serious works include Guatemala, monografía sociológica (1959), and Portidos políticos de
Iberamérica (1961).

MONTENEGRO, DOLORES, 1857-1933. Guatemalan poetess,
best known for her lyric poetry: Al General Barrios
(1885), Flores y espinas (1887), Versos de Lola Montenegro (1895) and others.

MONTERREY see PANAJACHEL.

MONTES, JAVIER Z. [pseudonym] see MARTÍNEZ, JOSÉ
VICENTE.

MONTÚFAR, ANTONIO DE, 1627-1668. A Guatemalan
painter noted for his concentration on facial expressions. He painted a series of murals for El Calvario,
the church at Esquipulas. He went blind at the peak
of his career; his works can be seen at the National
Museum in Guatemala City.

MONTÚFAR, LORENZO, 1823-1898. A Guatemalan historian, he spent his early years in exile in protest against
the Carrera government. He returned to Guatemala in
1872 and was elected to the national legislature. He
ran unsuccessfully for president in 1891. He is best
known for his historical writing, primarily the seven-
volume work, Reseña histórica de Centro-América.

MONTÚFAR, MANUEL, 1859-1896. A Guatemalan poet and
diplomat, he was born in San José, Costa Rica, while
his parents (Lorenzo Montúfar) were in exile.

MONTÚFAR, RAFAEL, 1857-1929. Guatemalan journalist
and politician, he wrote Deslinde de los partidos (1925),
La cuestión económica (1922) and Estudios económicos

(1899).

MONTÚFAR ALFARO, MANUEL, 1809-1857. A Guatemalan
author, he was first to make use of the historical novel in Guatemala with his El alferez real (1858) first
published in serial form.

MONTÚFAR Y CORONADO, MANUEL, 1791-1844. A leader
in the independence movement, he wrote articles for
the newspaper, El Editor Constitucional under the
pseudonym, "Un Guatemalteco." He was one of the
authors of the state constitution and president of the
state assembly. After the civil war, he went into exile in Mexico, where he remained until his death.

MORA, CARLOS FEDERICO, 1889- . Physician and diplomat, born in Quezaltenango, he taught at the University of San Carlos, was minister to Germany, and
wrote El médico y la escuela (1926) and Tratado de
higiene mental.

MORALES. Municipio located in the department of Izabal
in eastern Guatemala. Its cabecera is on the Motagua
River and on a railroad, 22 miles southwest of Puerto
Barrios. Banana area; gold placers nearby. Population: 36,106.

MORALES, GABINO [pseudonym] see VELA, DAVID.

MORALES NADLER, ANTONIO, 1914- . Diplomat and poet, lecturer on literature at the Universities of Havana
and Mexico, Ambassador to the U.S., U.N., Mexico,
France and Ecuador. He has written Romances de
tierra verde and Dionisio y el mar (1954).

MORÁN, PEDRO. An 18th-century Dominican priest, he
wrote several Pokoman dictionaries, which include
Bocabulario de solo los nombres de la lengua Pokoman
and Vidas de santos en forma de homilias en Pokoman
y Castellano.

MORAZÁN. Municipio in the department of El Progreso in
east central Guatemala. Its cabecera is located on a
short branch of the upper Motagua River, seven miles
northwest of El Progreso. Population: 6684. Crops:
corn, wheat, sugar cane; livestock.

MORAZÁN, FRANCISCO, 1792-1842. President of Central
America, 1830-1839. Born in Tegucigalpa, Honduras,
he became active in politics after the union with Mexico broke up. Morazán took Guatemala City in 1829,
resigned as general, ran for President, and won.
The country was continually in revolt against his liberal reforms. He was defeated in the election of
1834 by José del Valle, but retained the Presidency
when Valle died before taking office. The capital was
moved to Sonsonate, Salvador, in 1834 and later to El
Salvador. The Church worked to arouse the people
against Morazán's reform movement. In 1837, Rafael
Carrera led a revolt against the "destroyers of religion." Morazán was unable to capture Carrera and
was later defeated by Carrera in 1839 at Guatemala
City. The Federation ended with the defeat of Morazán. Escaping to Salvador, he was forced into exile
and went to Peru. In 1842 he returned to Costa Rica
and was elected President, but was later captured by
a mob, taken to Cartago, Costa Rica, and was shot
without trial to prevent the union movement from gaining strength and supporters.

MORDIDA. A form of tipping which is paid to a public official, to ensure that any business transacted with the
government does not run into lengthy delays. A government official will at times refuse to legalize documents requiring approval until he has received something "extra" for his efforts.

MORENOS. Also called Caribs. A people, located along
the Caribbean coast, having as ancestors the Carib Indians of the Islands. They were transplanted by the
Spanish. The early Negro slaves who escaped to hide
among the villages of the coastal plains mixed with the
Caribs. These people are not to be confused with the
purer Negroes who were later brought in from the English colonies to work the banana plantations.

MOROS, LOS. Dance of the Moors. First performed in
Spain, it depicts the struggle of the Spanish in the re-
conquest of Spain. There is no dialogue. The dance
is extended through several hours of struggle between
the two factions and is finally ended when the Christian
king stabs the Moorish chieftain (Solomon) in the heart.

MORRAL see MATATE.

MOTAGUA RIVER. The longest and most important river
in Guatemala, it has its origin in the department of
El Quiché and flows in a generally northeasterly direction to empty into the Gulf of Honduras. It is almost
250 miles in length. Known as the Río Grande in its
upper course, the Chiquimula River is a main tribu-
tary. Trade on the river consists of bananas, coffee,
fruit and hides. Some gold placers are along its
course.

MOVIMIENTO DE LIBERACIÓN NACIONAL (MLN). The
party of Castillo Armas in the 1954 "liberation" movement. After his death and since losing the close election of 1958, the party has become militant, very anti-
Communist and has many supporters among church
leaders and from the larger land-holders. Its candidate, Carlos Arana Osorio, won the election in 1970
and took the office of President.

MOYUTA. Municipio in the department of Jutiapa in southeastern Guatemala. Its cabecera is located at the
eastern foot of Moyuta Volcano, 20 miles southwest of
Jutiapa. Population: 20,485. Altitude: 4675 ft.
Crops: corn, beans, coffee, sugar cane; livestock.

MOYUTA VOLCANO. Altitude: 5525 feet. Located in the
department of Jutiapa in southeastern Guatemala, 20
miles southwest of Jutiapa. At its eastern foot is the
town of the same name.

MULUA see SANTA CRUZ MULUA.

MUNICIPALIDAD. The municipal offices for governing the
affairs of the municipio, always located in the cabecera of the municipio.

MUNICIPIO. The smallest political unit, usually consisting
of a cabecera with the same name and one or more
aldeas or rural settlements. Its size varies from
about 30 square miles in the more populous area to
1000 square miles in the less populated jungle area.
Since 1944, the municipio has elected its own officials.
There are 324 municipios in Guatemala, not counting
Belice.

MUÑOZ MEANY, ENRIQUE, 1907-1951. A journalist and
teacher, he became a leading Marxist, active in the

late 1940's, in the Arévalo government as Minister of
Foreign Affairs. His writings include El hombre y la
encrucijada and Preceptora literaria. He was head of
the U.N. delegation at his death.

-N-

NACAOME CONVENTION (1847). A convention held in Nicaragua in an attempt on the part of Salvador, Honduras
and Nicaragua to form a union or federation. Guatemala and Costa Rica were invited but declined. A
pact was signed in 1848; however, numerous reserva-
tions on the part of those signing made the pact worth-
less from the start.

NAHUAL. A Mayan belief is that a person's fate is closely
linked to the well-being of some animal or "nahual."
The nahual accompanies the person throughout his life
and helps to protect him from danger. The type of
animal is determined in various ways, often by the
proximity or action of an animal on the person's day
of birth. Another method of determining one's nahual
concerns the Quiché calendar, which has animal designations for each day of the year. The animal designated for the day following the birth of a male child is
that person's nahual.

NAHUALA. Municipio in the department of Solola in southwest central Guatemala. Its cabecera is located ten
miles northwest of Sololá, near the head of the Nahualate River (here called the Nahuala). Woolen blankets
produced, also corn-grinding stones. Population:
22,145. Altitude: 8199 ft. Crops: corn, black
beans.

NAHUALATE RIVER. In southwestern Guatemala, it begins
in the western highlands and flows about 100 miles
south to the Pacific, southeast of Tahuesco.

NARANJO RIVER. In southwestern Guatemala, just north of
San Marcos. It flows about 60 miles southward, then
west and south into the Pacific Ocean.

NATIONAL AGRARIAN BANK see BANCO NACIONAL
AGRARIO.

NATURAL.   A word frequently used interchangeably with the
term Indian (Indio).

NATURALISMO.   A literary movement of the 19th century
that developed from realism, in opposition to romanticism.   It required documentation or detailed description in novels and left little room for individual creativity.   The movement began late in Guatemala, with
Enrique Martínez Sobral as the leading proponent.

NAVARRO, JOSÉ MARÍA.   Archbishop of Guatemala, he
wrote Memoria del estado actual de la parroquia de
San Martín Xilotepeque (1861), a statistical and geographical account of the municipio, and another work
entitled Memoria del estado de la parroquia de concepción de Villa Nueva (1868).

NEBAJ.   Municipio in the department of El Quiché in west
central Guatemala.   Its cabecera is located at the
east end of the Cuchumatanes Mountains, eight miles
northwest of Sacapulas.   Population: 23,378.   Altitude: 6660 ft.   Crops: corn, beans.

NEGRO RIVER   see   CHIXOY RIVER.

NENTÓN.   Municipio in the department of Huehuetenango in
western Guatemala.   Its cabecera is located on the
western slopes of the Cuchumatanes Mountains, 38
miles north-northwest of Huehuetenango.   Population:
10,322.   Altitude: 2671 ft.   Crops: sugar cane, bananas, tropical fruit; some livestock.

NEW LAWS (1542).   Issued in Barcelona.   Strongly influenced by Bartholomé de Las Casas, the basic thought
behind the New Laws was that no one could legally use
the services of the Indian against his will.   The protest against the Laws was so strong that they were
never actually enforced.   As a result of the protest,
the crown repealed the sections making illegal the in-
heritance of an encomienda and restricting the establishment of new encomiendas.   This took the heart out
of the New Laws and the encomienda lasted until the
18th century.

NIXTAMAL.   Softened grains of corn.   The process entails
boiling the corn in lime water so that it can be ground
into paste to make tortillas.

NOEL [pseudonym] see GORRIZ DE MORALES, NATALIA.

NOVELISTS. Leading literary novelists since the colonial
    era are: 19th Century -- Antonio José de Irisarri
    (1786-1868) and José Milla y Vidaurre (1822-1882);
    20th Century -- Early: Enrique Martínez Sobral
    (1875-1950), Máximo Soto Hall (1871-1944), and En-
    rique Gómez Carrillo (1873-1927); Pre-1944: Rafael
    Arévalo Martínez (1884-), Flavio Herrera (1895-),
    Elsa Hall de Asturias (1900-), and Carlos Wyld Os-
    pina (1891-1956); Post-1944: Miguel Ángel Asturias
    (1899-) and Mario Monteforte Toledo (1911-).

NUESTRA SEÑORA DEL SOCORRO. A sculptured figurine,
    earlier known as the Virgen de la Piedad. It was
    brought from Spain by Francisco de Garay, and to
    Guatemala by Padre Godínez in 1524. Its special prov-
    ince is to ward off public disasters. It is now located
    in the Cathedral of Guatemala City.

NUEVA ESPAÑA (Viceroyalty). A Spanish colonial political
    unit for administrative purposes. It included the area
    north of Panama (Central America, Mexico, western
    and southeastern U. S.), the West Indies and the Philip-
    pines. The viceroy had little power over the more
    distant areas.

NUEVA SANTA ROSA. Municipio in the department of Santa
    Rosa in southern Guatemala. Its cabecera is one mile
    east-southeast of Santa Rosa and eight miles north of
    Cuilapa. Population: 14,346. Crops: coffee, corn,
    beans.

NUEVO PROGRESO. Municipio in the department of San
    Marcos in southwestern Guatemala. Its cabecera is
    located five miles north-northwest of Coatepeque. Pop-
    ulation: 15,949. Crops: coffee, sugar cane, grain.

NUEVO SAN CARLOS. Municipio in the department of Re-
    talhuleu in southwestern Guatemala. Its cabecera is
    on a branch of the Tilapa River, four miles north of
    Retalhuleu. Population: 15,026. Crops: sugar cane,
    corn, rice.

NÚÑEZ, AGUSTÍN. Architect, sculptor and builder, he was
    the principal instructor in sculpture and architecture
    in the late 17th century. He did the figures for the

church "La Concepción" in Antigua.

-O-

O. D. E. C. A. see ORGANIZACIÓN DE LOS ESTADOS CENTRO AMERICANOS.

O. R. I. T. see ORGANIZACIÓN REGIONAL INTERAMERICANA DE TRABAJO.

OCANA, CANUTO [pseudonym] see MARROQUÍN ROJAS, CLEMENTE.

OCARINA. A cylindrical flute of pre-Columbian times, made of baked clay.

OCOS. Municipio in the department of San Marcos in southwestern Guatemala. Its cabecera is a port on the Pacific coast at the mouth of the Naranjo River, 25 miles southwest of Coatepeque. Rail terminus located here; saltworks nearby. Flourished in the 19th century in the indigo and cochineal trade, but this declined after the rise of Puerto Barrios. Population: 7881. Crops: corn, cotton, beans, platanos.

OCOSETO RIVER (Ocosito) see TILAPA RIVER.

OCOTE. Pitch pine splints from Okote Pine, used for torches or for starting fires.

OCTUBRE. June 21, 1950-March 12, 1953. A radical political newspaper for the labor movement. Although suppressed several times under President Arévalo, it became the leading labor spokesman under President Arbenz. It was replaced by the Tribuna Popular as the labor party spokesman of the P. G. T.

OFFICIALES DE HACIENDA (Oficiales Reales). Royal colonial officials in charge of the collection and disposition of royal funds. They had to be present when all deposits of money or bullion were made and had to countersign all treasury reports. They often disagreed with various governors who outranked them. The New Laws (1542) directed the officials to make an annual report of receipts and expenditures to the Council of the Indies.

OIDORES.   Judicial officials of the colonial period who were
members of the audiencia.   Their duties included vis -
its to the encomiendas, mines, etc. to investigate the
treatment of the Indians, and serving as visitadores,
as well as their primary duties in holding court, for
which they were appointed.

OJO.   Evil eye.   An Indian folk medicinal belief that a person can unintentionally infect another with illness or
harm by merely staring at him.   Persons in one of
the following listed conditions are thought to be more
likely to cause the infection: overexhausted, hysteri-
cal, feeble-minded or insane; also women who are
pregnant or menstruating.   Mothers outfit their small
babies with a tight knit stocking hat to ward off the
evil eye.

OJO POR OJO.   A terrorist group organized in opposition
to the Mano Blanco.   Primarily the urban arm of the
F.A.R., it was behind the assassination of the U.S.
military advisors in Guatemala and the assassination
of the U.S. Ambassador in 1968.   Its avowed purpose
is to react to political assassinations done by the Mano
Blanco through equal acts of terror.

OLINTEPEQUE.   Municipio in the department of Quezaltenango in southwestern Guatemala.   Its cabecera is located on the headstream of the Samala River, three
miles north of Quezaltenango.   Cotton weaving.   Population: 8299.   Altitude: 8051 ft.   Crops: corn,
wheat, fodder grasses; livestock.   Sometimes spelled
Olimtepeque.

OLIVA, ENRIQUE TRINIDAD, d. 1967.   Army colonel and
leader of the terrorist group "Mano Blanco."   His assassination led to a civil war among the two extrem-
ist urban terror groups.

OLMEDO, BARTOLOMÉ DE.   Priest who accompanied
Cortés, and later, Alvarado, on the conquest.   He
carried the image of Nuestra Señora de las Mercedes,
which was placed in the Convent of the Redeemers in
Guatemala City.

OLOPA.   Municipio in the department of Chiquimula in eastern Guatemala.   Its cabecera is located near the Honduran border.   Population: 8688.   Crops: coffee,

tobacco, bananas, beans, corn.

OLOTE. Quiché for corncob.

OPUS DEI. An international Catholic religious organization
    made up of priests and laymen. Beginning in Guate-
    mala in 1953, it is supported by the wealthy portion
    of the population. It is regarded with suspicion in
    Guatemala because it appears to be powerful as well
    as being a secret conservative organization.

ORANTES, JOSÉ MARÍA. Acting president (June 23, 1882
    to January 5, 1883) while President Barrios was trav-
    eling in Europe and the United States.

ORATORIO, EL. Municipio in the department of Santa
    Rosa in southern Guatemala. Its cabecera is located
    near the Inter-American Highway, eight miles east-
    southeast of Cuilapa. Population: 11,073. Crops:
    coffee, sugar cane; livestock.

ORDÓÑEZ SOLÍS, RAFAEL, 1878- . Born in San Cristó-
    bal, Verapaz, he was a lawyer and professor at San
    Carlos, Minister of Public Education, Minister to
    Honduras (1928-33), and President of the Supreme
    Court, 1936-40.

ORDUÑA, FRANCISCO DE. On the conquest, he later be-
    came a member of the first Audiencia of Guatemala.
    He was appointed captain-general while Alvarado was
    in Spain in 1529. During this time a colonizing ex-
    pedition was sent to El Salvador from Panama under
    Martin de Estete. Orduña sent Francisco López, who
    managed to escort the Panamanians back out of Cen-
    tral America.

ORELLANA, JOSÉ MARÍA, 1872-1926. President of Guate-
    mala, he first served as provisional president from
    1921-1922 and was later elected to serve from 1922-
    1926. He died of a heart attack in September, 1926.
    He enacted a sweeping currency reform based upon a
    study made in 1920.

ORELLANA, MANUEL. Became President when Palma was
    forced to resign in late 1930. He held office until
    José María Reyna Andrade was appointed provisional
    president by the legislature in early 1931.

ORGANIZACIÓN DE LOS ESTADOS CENTRO AMERICANOS
(O. D. E. C. A.). An economic union formed in 1951
through the efforts of Foreign Minister Manuel Galich.
At that time, Guatemala averted conferences when
communism was proposed as one of the subjects for
discussion. In 1953 Guatemala withdrew, and the
O. D. E. C. A. did not really begin to function until 1955
when Guatemala rejoined. Since then, considerable
progress in economic cooperation has taken place.
Tariff barriers have been lowered, travel among the
member countries is less restricted, and native industry is encouraged.

ORGANIZACIÓN REGIONAL INTERAMERICANA DE TRA-
BAJO (O. R. I. T.). Labor organization affiliated with
the Organization of American States, to assist in the
development of local free labor unions.

ORNATO. A head tax paid to the municipalidad.

ORTIZ, GONZALO. An early settler of Guatemala, he was
elected alcalde in 1541.

OSEGUEDA, RAUL, 1907- . An educator and diplomat, he
was born in Guatemala City. He was a professor at
San Carlos, Minister to Honduras, Mexico, Haiti and
Cuba. Foreign Minister for Arbenz in 1952-53, he
led Guatemala out of O. D. E. C. A. when they threatened to censure the Guatemalan government. He has
written El problema de la libertad (1949) and Opera-
ción centroamerica £$ O K £$ (1957).

OSSAYE GALLARDO, ROBERTO, 1927-1954. A Guatemalan artist, his works are represented in the Museo
Nacional de Historia y Belles Artes.

OSTUA RIVER. In the municipio of Asunción Mita in Juti-
apa, it begins in Jalapa, receives the Tamasulapa
River near Asuncion Mita and empties into Lake Güija.
About 62 miles in length, it is known in part as Río
Grande de Monjas and Río Grande de Mita.

OSTUNCALCO see SAN JUAN OSTUNCALCO.

OVALLE, GONZALO DE see DOVALLE, GONZALO.

-P-

P. A. R.   see   PARTIDO ACCIÓN REVOLUCIONARIA.

P. C. G.   see   PARTIDO COMUNISTA DE GUATEMALA.

P. G. T.   see   PARTIDO GUATEMALTECO DEL TRABAJO.

P. I. A. C.   see   PARTIDO INDEPENDIENTE ANTICOMUN-
ISTA OCCIDENTAL.

P. I. N.   see   PARTIDO INTEGRIDAD NACIONAL.

P. P.   see   PARTIDO DEL PUEBLO.

P. R.   see   PARTIDO REVOLUCIONARIO.

P. R. A.   see   PARTIDO REVOLUCIONARIO AUTÉNTICO.

P. R. G.   see   PARTIDO DE LA REVOLUCIÓN GUATEMAL-
TECA.

P. R. O. G.   see   PARTIDO REVOLUCIONARIO OBRERO DE
GUATEMALA.

P. S.   see   PARTIDO SOCIALISTA.

P. S. D.   see   PARTIDO SOCIAL DEMOCRÁTICO.

P. U. A.   see   PARTIDO UNIFICACIÓN ANTICOMUNISTA.

PACAYA VOLCANO.   Altitude: 8346 feet.   A volcano located in south central Guatemala on the Esquintla-
Guatemala departmental border, and six miles south-
southeast of Amatitlán.   Last erupted in 1775, minor
disturbances in 1967.

PACHECO HERRARTE, MARIANO, 1878- .   An agricul-
turalist born in Quezaltenango, active in the Ministry
of Interior and Ministry of Agriculture for many years.
He wrote Agriculture in Guatemala (1939).

PACORO, D.   [pseudonym]   see   VILLA URRUTIA, JACOBO
DE.

PACT OF CHINANDEGA (1842).   A unity pact signed by all

the republics except Costa Rica. The unified republics called themselves Confederación Centroamérica.
The pact was a reaction against the return of Francisco Morazán to Costa Rica. At his death, later in
1842, the unifying element was gone from the pact; it
officially ceased in 1845.

PADILLA, MARIANO, 1810-1869. A Guatemalan medical
doctor, he wrote Ensayo histórico sobre el origen de
la enfermedad venerea (1861) as well as other medical
handbooks.

PADRINO. Often called compadre; state of compadrazco.
A godparent, chosen by parents for their newly born
children. The padrinos act in behalf of the children
if something happens to the parents. They also serve
to give advice concerning major problems the children
might have. If a child is taken into the home of his
compadres, because of the death of his natural parents,
the child then becomes an hijo de casa.

PAJAPITA. Municipio in the department of San Marcos in
southwestern Guatemala. Its cabecera is located on
the Naranjo River, 12 miles west-northwest of Coatepeque; on railroad. Population: 7711. Crops: cotton, grain, sugar cane; livestock.

PALENCIA. Municipio in the department of Guatemala in
south central Guatemala. Its cabecera is ten miles
east of Guatemala City. Population: 14,329. Altitude: 4690 ft. Crops: coffee, sugar cane; livestock.

PALESTINA. Municipio in the department of Quezaltenango
in southwestern Guatemala. Its cabecera is on the
Inter-American Highway, 13 miles west-northwest of
Quezaltenango. Sometimes called Palestina de los Altos. Population: 4625. Altitude: 8500 ft. Crops:
corn, wheat, fodder grasses; livestock.

PALÍN. Municipio in the department of Escuintla in southern Guatemala. Its cabecera is located on the Michatoya River, nine miles northeast of Escuintla. On
railroad; market center. Just south are falls 200
feet high, and the hydroelectric station of San Pedro
Martir. Population: 7372. Altitude: 3724 ft. Crops:
kapok, coffee, sugar, pineapples.

PALMA, BAUDILLIO, 1884-1946. President of Guatemala
    for 100 hours in 1930. As second designate, the
    Council of Ministers appointed him to control the gov-
    ernment when President Chacón resigned. President
    Palma was forced to resign by General Manuel Orell-
    ana. Señor Palma died in San Salvador.

PALMA, JOSÉ JOAQUÍN, 1844-1911. A poet, born in Cuba,
    he spent many years in Guatemala. He wrote the
    Hymno nacional de Guatemala.

PALMÁR, EL. Municipio in the department of Quezalte-
    nango in southwestern Guatemala. In the Pacific pied-
    mont, the cabecera is located 13 miles south-south-
    west of Quezaltenango. Manac grows here; the leaves
    are prized for raincoats and umbrellas. Sulphur
    springs nearby. Population: 12,181. Crops: coffee,
    sugar cane; livestock.

PALO VOLADOR. Flying pole dance. An Aztec dance per-
    formed to give thanks for a good corn crop. If there has
    been a bad year, more effort is put into the festivities.
    With much ceremony, a tree is selected to provide a 25-
    to 30-yard pole, taken to the village, and raised. A
    number of ropes, usually four, are coiled about the top of
    the pole and fixed to a small frame to stabilize the unwind-
    ing process. Then four men, one to each rope, seat them-
    selves in loops at the end of the ropes. Their weight causes
    the ropes to unwind, lowering the men in ever-widening
    circles to the ground.

PALOMO, JOSÉ IGNACIO. An early 19th-century politician, he
    was on the Audiencia at the time of the revolution. In 1809
    and 1812, he wrote a "memoria" upon the opening of the
    Real Consulado, and in 1803, 1804, and 1806, another on
    the opening of the Junta de Gobierno. He was also the
    joint author with Alejandro Ramírez, of Memoria sobre la
    navegación del Río Motagua (1799).

PANAJACHEL. Municipio in the department of Sololá in
    southwest central Guatemala. Its cabecera is located
    on the Inter-American Highway, three miles southeast
    of Sololá. It is near the northern shore of Lake Atit-
    lán. Just southwest are the lake ports and summer
    resorts of Tzunjuyu and Monterrey. The town is a
    major market center for the area. Population: 3268.
    Altitude: 5184 ft. Crops: coffee, vegetables, sugar

cane, corn, wheat.

PANAJACHEL RIVER. A short river which empties into
Lake Atitlán.

PANCHOY. "Valley of the lakes"; it was the site chosen by
the Cabildo in 1541, for the new (third) capital of
Guatemala. It was renamed Santiago de los Caballeros
de Guatemala, now known as Antigua.

PANELA. A block of brown sugar, molded from heated
cane juice.

PANIAGUA, RAUL, 1897-1953. Guatemalan composer and
pianist, professor at the Conservatorio de Guatemala
(1931-39), director of the National Conservatory of
San Salvador (1939-42). Much of his musical compositions were of a popular nature, best remembered for
"The Mayan Legend," a symphonic poem.

PANIAGUA MARTÍNEZ, JULIÁN, 1856-1908. A music con-
ductor and composer; many of his compositions are
variations of classical music for marching bands.

PANTALEÓN. A village of the department of Escuintla, in
southern Guatemala. It is on the railroad and is situated two miles east-southeast of Santa Lucía. Sugar
milling center.

PANZOS. Municipio in the department of Alta Verapaz in
central Guatemala. The cabecera is a port on the
Polochic River, 37 miles east of Cobán. Eastern
terminus of Verapaz railroad and transfer point for
Polochic River-Lake Izabal water route. Population:
17,252. Crops: coffee, grain, beans, cocoa.

PAPAYA. A tree-melon from the papayo tree.

PARDO. Used in the 18th century to refer to a racial mixture of Spanish-Indian and Negro. By then the caste
mestizo (Spanish-Indian) and mulatto (Spanish-Negro)
were so intermixed, there was no separating them.

PARDO, JOSÉ JOAQUÍN, 1905-1964. Director of the National Archives, responsible for the physical plant and
the excellent facilities for research. He edited the
Memorias del General García Granados, 4 vols.,

Prontuario de reales credulas, 1529-1599 (1941), and
Efemerides para escribir la historia de ... Guatemala
(1944).

PAREDES, MARIANO. An army colonel, he held the office
of president between January 1, 1849 and November,
1851. He attempted to prevent Carrera from returning to Guatemala from Mexico, but when this failed,
he reinstated Carrera as commander-in-chief of the
army to eradicate the rebels who had kept the country
in turmoil since 1847.

PARRAMOS. Municipio in the department of Chimaltenango
in south central Guatemala. The cabecera is on the
Guacalate River, three miles south-southwest of Chimaltenango. Population: 3032. Altitude: 5610.
Crops: corn, wheat, beans.

PARTIDO ACCIÓN REVOLUCIONARIA (P.A.R.). The major
pre-governmental political party of the late 1940's.
It was formed in 1946 with the merger of the Frente
Popular Libertador and the Renovación Nacional. It
had the most extensive electoral support, although it
continually lost the support of splinter groups, which
left to form their own parties. By 1955, it had become ineffectual.

PARTIDO COMUNISTA DE GUATEMALA (P.C.G.). A party
that had operated secretly from 1946 to 1949 as the
Vanguardia Democrática Guatemalteca. The P.C.G.
was active in the campaign for President Arbenz.
When Arbenz was overthrown in 1954, the P.C.G. was
broken up.

PARTIDO DE LA REVOLUCIÓN GUATEMALTECA (P.R.G.).
Political party formed in 1952 by the union of several
parties, to support the agrarian reform bill. Once
the bill passed, the party began to split. It was
formed by a merger of the Frente Popular Libertador,
the leading party in 1948, Partido Integridad Nacional,
Revolucionario de Unidad Nacional and Partido Socialista.

PARTIDO DEL PUEBLO (P.P.). A liberal political party
that supported Jorge García Granados for president in
1950.

PARTIDO DEMOCRÁCIA CRISTIANA GUATEMALTECO.
The political party closest to the Church, it has been
allied with the M.D.N. in most elections. It has usually managed to carry several assembly seats. Rene
León Schlotter, an economics lecturer at the University of San Carlos was nominated to be the party's
presidential candidate for the 1974 election.

PARTIDO GUATEMALTECO DEL TRABAJO (P.G.T.).
Formed in 1952, the political party in support of President Arbenz, it was most active in the rural areas until 1954.

PARTIDO INDEPENDIENTE ANTICOMUNISTA OCCIDENTAL
(P.I.A.C.). Active in the late 1940's and early
1950's, it was a regional, anti-governmental, political
party located in Quezaltenango. It had a loose affiliation with the Partido Unificación Anticomunista in the
election of 1950.

PARTIDO INTEGRIDAD NACIONAL (P.I.N.). A political
party of Quezaltenango, formed to support favorite son
Jacobo Arbenz in the 1950 election. After the election, it merged with the Partido de la Revolución
Guatemalteca.

PARTIDO REVOLUCIONARIO (P.R.). A liberal political
party when formed in 1957 by Mario Méndez Montenegro for the election following Armas' death. The
P.R. was not permitted to put up a candidate. Since
1960 it has become more moderate. The assassination of Mario Méndez Montenegro in 1965 placed his
brother, Julio César, as the candidate. He won the
election and was successful in completing a four-year
term.

PARTIDO REVOLUCIONARIO OBRERO DE GUATEMALA
(P.R.O.G.). A political action group formed in 1950
to support labor and agrarian legislation.

PARTIDO SOCIALISTA (P.S.). A political party formed in
1951 to bring back to Guatemalan politics those leaders
of the 1944 revolution who had abandoned political activities.

PARTIDO DE TRABAJADORES (P.T.). A labor political
party formed shortly after the fall of Ubico. It later

became part of the R. N.

PARTIDO UNIFICACIÓN ANTICOMUNISTA (P. U. A.).   Political party formed in 1947, conservative in nature, that
was most actively in opposition to the election of Jacobo
Arbenz in 1950.

PASACO.   Municipio in the department of Jutiapa in southeastern Guatemala.   The cabecera is located in the
southern part of the department, southwest of Moyuta.
Population: 5089.   Crops: corn, beans, rice, chile,
tobacco, sesame, peanuts.

PASAQUINA, BATTLE OF (1876).   Last of a series of battles between Salvador and Guatemala.   It resulted in
the defeat of El Salvador and in the formation of a pro-
Guatemalan government in Salvador led by Rafael Zal-
dívar.   See CHALCHUAPA, TREATY OF.

PASIÓN RIVER.   It begins in northern Guatemala in the department of Petén, near San Luis.   Known as the Santa
Isabel River here, it flows about 220 miles west, then
northward and again westward past Sayaxche, where it
joins the Salinas River at the Mexican border to form
the Usumacinta River.   It drains the Concuén River.

PASTORES.   Municipio in the department of Sacatepequez in
south central Guatemala.   The cabecera is on the Guacalate River, three miles northwest of Antigua.   Population: 3461.   Altitude: 5118 ft.   Crops: coffee,
grain.

PATAXTE.   A tree closely related to cacao, the fruit of
which is often used as an ingredient in beverages.   It
is an inferior substitute for cacao.

PATULUL.   Municipio in the department of Suchitepequez in
southwestern Guatemala, in the Pacific piedmont.   The
cabecera is located 24 miles eat-southeast of Mazatenango.   Population: 14,511.   Crops: coffee, sugar
cane, grain, fodder grasses; livestock.

PATZICIA.   Municipio in the department of Chimaltenango
in south central Guatemala.   The cabecera is located
on the Inter-American Highway, seven miles west of
Chimaltenango.   Market center; flour milling at La
Sierra, three miles west-northwest.   Here, in 1871,

Justo Rufino Barrios and Miguel García Granados proclaimed the Acta de Patzicia. Population: 8833.
Altitude: 6998 ft. Crops: corn, wheat.

PATZITE. Municipio in the department of El Quiché in
west central Guatemala. The cabecera is located in
the southern part of the department, southwest of Santa
Cruz del Quiché, and close to the Totonicapan border.
Population: 1770. Crops: corn, wheat, beans.

PATZÚN. Municipio in the department of Chimaltenango in
south central Guatemala. The cabecera is located on
the Inter-American Highway, 12 miles west of Chimaltenango. Market center: saw milling nearby. Has a
16th-century church. Formerly spelled Patzum.
Population: 14,501. Altitude: 7300 ft. Crops:
grain, coffee.

PAULINO [pseudonym] see LAINFIESTA, FRANCISCO.

PAVÓN, MANUAL FRANCISCO, d. 1855. Editor of the official Gazeta until 1848, when he was appointed to the
Consejo Consultativo, set up by Rafael Carrera as an
advisory group. Pavón became the most influential
person with Carrera in matters of policy formation.

PAZ, ALONSO DE, 1605-1676. A Guatemalan wood sculptor whose work is found in many churches and muse-
ums. Best known examples are his María Magdalena
in Guatemala City, and El Nazareno in Antigua.

PAZ RIVER. Río de la Paz. It begins on the slope of the
volcano Chingo in the Sierra Madres, and flows about
60 miles southwest to form the Salvadoran border before emptying into the Pacific Ocean.

PAZ Y SALGADO, ANTONIO DE, d. 1757. A Guatemalan
essayist who wrote satirical anecdotes about the legal
profession. Best known for his Instrucción de liti-
gantes (1742) and El Mosqueador (1742).

PECCADO ARBAL. A taboo tree to which yearly rites are
performed, usually in connection with abundant cacao
crops.

PEÑALVER Y CÁRDENAS, LUIS IGNATIUS, 1749-1810.
Born in Havana, Cuba, he was appointed Bishop of

Tricca and Administrator of Louisiana and Florida in
1793. In 1800 he was named Archbishop of Guatemala,
although he did not take possession until 1802. In 1806
he resigned and returned to Havana.

PENINSULARES. A term used during the colonial period to
designate a native born Spaniard. The highest offices
were always reserved for the peninsulares.

PENSATIVO RIVER. A short river bordering the city of
Antigua which flows into the Guacalate River. It was
made famous by Rafael de Landivar in a description
from his epic poem Rusticatio mexicana.

PEONIA. A measurement of land used when the conquistadores split up Central America. The Caballería was
the amount of land given to the cavalrymen and the
Peonia was bestowed on the foot-soldier, or "peon."
A peonia was about 82 acres, or approximately half
the size of a caballeria. Also called peonería.

PEPE GRIS [pseudonym] see VALLE, JOSÉ.

PEPINO. A small, yellowish melon with dark purple stripes,
shaped like a large pointed egg.

PEPITORIA. A brittle candy made from squash seeds.

PERALTA AZURDIA, ALFREDO ENRIQUE, 1908- . Born
in Guatemala City, he was Director of the Escuela
Politecnica in 1943 and Minister of Defense under
Ydígoras. He took control of the government in 1963
when Arévalo's return threatened the government. He
permitted considerable latitude in the election of 1966,
which resulted in the assumption of power by the party
least desirable to the military government.

PERAZA AYALA CASTILLA Y ROJAS, ANTONIO (Conde de
la Gómera). Governor of Guatemala from 1611 to 1626.
He was suspended on charges of extortion and was in-
vestigated by a royal visitador who reinstated Peraza.
This episode was the basis for the historical novel by
José Milla entitled El visitador.

PERCHA. A teasel, for raising nap on wool cloth. It is
made up of 12 to 15 dried teasel flowers tied together,
with the stems forming the handle.

PÉREZ DARDÓN, JUAN, d. 1573. On the conquest, he
  served as Alcalde Ordinario in Guatemala on nine different occasions between 1529 and 1573. He was a
  leading supporter of Doña Beatriz for governor in
  1541.

PÉREZ DE LEÓN, RAFAEL, 1896- . An architect and
  engineer, he designed the present-day National Palace,
  which was built in the late 1930's in classical 16th-
  century Spanish style.

PERRAJES see KAPERRAJ.

PESO. The obsolete monetary unit used officially until
  1924, when the Quetzal was introduced. The peso was
  valued at 60 to the Quetzal in exchange, and was made
  up of eight reales or 100 centavos. The peso was
  still used in the rural areas in the middle 1930's and
  even later as a verbal unit of currency in Indian markets. See also CASA DE MONEDA.

PETAPA see SAN MIGUEL PETAPA.

PETÉN, EL. Department located in northern Guatemala.
  It is bordered on the north and west by Mexico and on
  the east by Belice. It is a low, humid expanse of
  tropical hardwood forest, crossed by savannas and
  ranges of low hills of less than 1,000 feet. It is
  drained by the San Pedro and Pasion Rivers, with the
  Usumacinta River on the western border and the Río
  Azul on the northeast. Lake Petén is the largest of
  several lakes; 70-inch rains in the north, to 150-inch
  rains annually in the south cause many temporary
  lakes. The capital is Flores. Main industries are
  hardwood lumbering and chicle gathering, with some
  agriculture near Lake Petén of sugar cane, rubber,
  cacao and tropical fruit. Very sparsely settled area.
  The department has ten municipios: Dolores, Flores,
  La Libertad, San Andrés, San Benito, San Francisco,
  San José, San Luis, Santa Ana, Sayaxche. Population
  in 1950 was 15,880; in 1964, 26,277, and projected to
  1980 at 61,600. Area: 13,843 square miles.

PETÉN LAKE (Lake Petén-Itzá). Located 160 miles north-
  northeast of Guatemala City, it is 15 miles long, two
  miles wide and about 165 feet deep. Flores, the capital of Petén, is located on one of several islands.

San Benito is on the south shore and San Andrés on
the west shore. Called Hatunnah by the Indians; often
called Lake Flores.

PEYÓN. A shaggy wool rug. It has three-inch ends, made
by pulling loops in the woven yarn and cutting the loops
in half.

PIEDRA DE MOLER. A metate or tripod grinding stone
made of lava. It is used most often for grinding co-
mestibles.

PIEDRAS NEGRAS. Ruins located in the lowlands of Petén
near the Usumacinta River. They date back to the
late classic period of the Mayan era. The site is
noted for the sophisticated sculpture of the stelae and
the consistency with which the stelae were erected,
every five years between A.D. 608 and 810.

PILA. A stone or concrete fountain, trough, or large ba-
sin, used as a watering place.

PINEDA, FERNANDO. A Guatemalan author, best known
for his novel, Luis, memorias de un amigo (1878).

PINEDA IBARRA, ANTONIO DE, 1661-1721. Second printer
in Guatemala and son of the first printer. He was appointed printer in 1681 and held that office until his
death.

PINEDA IBARRA, JOSE DE, 1629-1680. Born in Mexico,
he went to Guatemala in 1660 as the first printer in
Central America. His major printing works include
Explicatio by Payo de Ribera (1663) and Thomasiada
by Diego Sáenz Ovecuri (1667).

PINOLE. A sweet drink made of ground toasted maize and
flavored and seasoned with cacao, panela or white
sugar, aniseed, ginger, cinnamon, and other condi-
ments. Also Pinol.

PIPIL. A non-Mayan tribe of Indians in the southern highlands of Guatemala, more closely akin to the Aztecs.

PIRATES. Piracy reached its peak in the 16th and early
17th centuries. The famous English "privateers" made
numerous attacks on the Caribbean coast and carried

on illegal trade throughout the Spanish Main.   The
pirates were particularly active in the period between
the 1630's and 1670's.   It was at this time that the
English established a foothold on the Central American
mainland with their log cutting activities in present-
day Belice.   Some of the most serious raids occurred
in 1639 and 1640 when English pirates landed at Puerto
Caballos, Omoa, Roatán, Trujillo, and Punto Castilla.
Most of the towns were plundered and burned.   In
1642, pirates settled on the bay islands off Honduras,
but were driven out by Guatemalan-Cuban forces.
François L'Olonnois, between 1660 and 1665, led a
series of raids against the Caribbean coast.   Once the
English and Spanish settled their disputes, around 1670,
raids became infrequent.

PISO DE PLAZA.   A tax imposed on market vendors who
have no fixed or rented stall.   The amount varies,
but is usually a flat rate determined by the location
and type of goods being sold.

PITAFLOJA.   A fine, durable, grass fiber used in the Pacific lowlands to make rain capes, nets and cords.

PLAN DE IGUALA.   The plan presented by Emperor of
Mexico Iturbide in 1821, by which Mexico and Central
America would combine to make up the empire under
his rule.   Guatemala refused at first, but joined when
it was voted upon.   Only El Salvador remained outside
the empire, and it joined on February 9, 1823, upon
the arrival of General Filísola.   The union ended when
Iturbide fell from power.   See also MEXICAN CON-
FEDERATION.

POCHUTA.   Municipio in the department of Chimaltenango
in south central Guatemala.   The cabecera is near the
Madre Vieja River, 22 miles southwest of Chimaltenango.   Sometimes called San Miguel Pochuta.   Population: 10, 548.   Crops: coffee, sugar cane.

POKOMAM.   One of the three Mayan linguistic stocks in
Guatemala, making up the Kekchian linguistic group of
the Proto-Guatemala-Yucatan language family.   Located in the departments of Guatemala, Jalapa and Chiquimula.

POKONCHI.   One of the language groupings, based on the

larger Kekchi language stock, which is part of the
Proto-Guatemala-Yucatan linguistic group. The Po-
konchi are located in parts of Alta Verapaz and Baja
Verapaz.

POLOCHIC RIVER. Located in the Alta Verapaz and Izabal
departments of central Guatemala, it begins east of
Tactic and flows 150 miles east to form the delta south
of El Estór. The upper valley is used by the Verapaz
Railroad. It receives the Cahabón River. Coffee and
lumber are the main crops transported on the river to
the outside market.

POM. A copal incense, usually in the form of a small disk.

PONCE VAIDÉS, FEDERICO, 1889-1956. President of
Guatemala, July-October, 1944. Military governor of
several departments, he was chosen by Ubico to take
control of the government in 1944. He was ousted
when he attempted to retain power.

POPUL-VUH. The Maya-Quiché Bible which tells the story
of the origin of the nation and traditions concerning
its mythology. It presents the legendary history of
the Quichés down to 1550. It is thought to have been
written by a converted Indian named Diego Reynos,
shortly after the conquest. The manuscript lay undis-
covered until Father Francisco Ximénez found it in his
parish at Chichicastenango, in the early 18th century.
Father Ximénez transcribed the manuscript into Latin
and this transcription is now in the Newberry Library
in Chicago. The original Quiché text was lost.

PORTA Y ARELLAÑOS, ALFREDO, 1863-1925. Born in
Barcelona, Spain, he became a Guatemalan citizen and
a successful finquero. He held several diplomatic
posts in Europe.

PORTOCARRERO, PEDRO, d. 1547. Count of Medellín, he
was on the conquest as Alvarado's chief lieutenant.
He married Alvarado's illegitimate daughter, Doña
Leonor. He was Alcalde of Guatemala while Alvarado
was in Mexico in 1526. When the revolt led by Sinacam broke out at Sacatepéquez, Portocarrero led the
forces in putting it down.

POSOLE. A cold drink made from ground, boiled corn,

mixed with water and seasoned. Often the primary sustenance of Indians on their trips to and from markets. Also spelled Posol.

PRESIDENTS OF CENTRAL AMERICA. (Dates indicate terms of office.) See also GOVERNORS ...
   Gainza, Gabino, 1821-1822 (Spanish governor, 1821).
   Filísola, Vicente, 1822-1823.
   Supremo Poder Ejecutivo, Julio, 1823-Abril 1825.
   Arce, Manuel José, 1825-1828.
   Beltranena, Mariano, 1828-1829.
   Barrundia, José Francisco, 1829-1830.
   Morazán, Francisco, 1830-1839.

PRESIDENTS OF GUATEMALA. (Dates indicate terms of office.) See also GOVERNORS ...
   Rivera Paz, Mariano, 1839-1844 (Governor, 1838-39).
   Carrera, José Rafael, 1844-1848.
   Martínez, Juan Antonio, 1848.
   Escobar, José Bernardo, 1848.
   Paredes, Mariano, 1849-1851.
   Carrera, José Rafael, 1852-1865.
   Aycinena, Pedro de, 1865.
   Cerna, Vicente, 1865-1871.
   García Granados, Miguel, 1871-1872.
   Barrios, Justo Rufino, 1873-1885.
   Sinibaldi, Alejandro, 1885.
   Barillas, Manuel Lisandro, 1885-1892.
   Reyna Barrios, José María, 1892-1898.
   Estrada Cabrera, Manual, 1898-1920.
   Herrera, Carlos, 1920-1921.
   Orellana, José María, 1921-1926.
   Chacón, Lazaro, 1926-1930.
   Palma, Baudillio, 1930.
   Orellana, Manuel, 1930-1931.
   Reyna Andrada, José María, 1931.
   Ubico y Castañeda, Jorge, 1931-1944.
   Ponce Vaides, Federico, 1944.
   Triumvirate: Francisco Arana, Jacobo Arbenz, Jorge Toriello Garrido, 1944-1945.
   Arévalo Bermejo, Juan José, 1945-1951.
   Arbenz Guzmán, Jacobo, 1951-1954.
   Castillo Armas, Carlos, 1954-1957.
   González, Luis Arturo, 1957.
   Flores Avendano, Guillermo, 1957-1958.
   Ydígoras Fuentes, Miguel, 1958-1963.

Peralta Azurdia, Alfredo Enrique, 1963-1966.
Méndez Montenegro, Julio César, 1966-1970.
Arana Osorio, Carlos, 1970- .

PRINCIPALES. Elders or leading members of an Indian
   community, who exercise civil and religious authority.
   They make decisions concerning the community, settle
   disputes, and appoint mayordomos to the local cofradias.

PRINCIPE FÉLIZ, EL [pseudonym] see ACEÑA DURÁN,
   RAMÓN.

PRIVATEERS see PIRATES.

PROGRESO, EL. 1) A department located in east central
   Guatemala. It lies in the upper Motagua River valley
   between the Sierra de Chuacus and the Sierra de las
   Minas on the north and highlands on the south. The
   climate is warm and dry. The department was formed
   in 1935 when the boundaries were adjusted. Its capital is El Progreso. Chief centers are El Progreso
   and Sanarate, on the Guatemala to Puerto Barrios
   railroad. Main crops are: corn, beans, sugar cane,
   fodder grasses, with some livestock raised. Eight
   municipios: El Jicaro, Morazán, El Progreso, San
   Agustín Acasaguastlán, San Antonio la Paz, San Cristóbal Acasaguastlán, Sanarate, Sansare. Population
   in 1950 was 47,872. In 1964 the population was 65,365
   and projected to 1980 at 100,900. Area: 742 square
   miles.
      2) Municipio in the department of Jutiapa in south-
   eastern Guatemala. In the highlands, its cabecera is
   six miles northeast of Jutiapa. Road center. Population: 8676. Altitude: 3652 ft. Crops: corn,
   beans; livestock.
      3) Municipio in the department of El Progreso in
   east central Guatemala. The cabecera is the capital
   of the department of El Progreso and is located on the
   Guastatoya River, 35 miles east-northeast of Guatemala City. On railroad; commercial center. The
   town became the department capital in 1935 when the
   departmental boundaries were adjusted. Until 1920, it
   was called Guastatoya or Huastatoya. Here, Serapio
   Cruz began the insurrection that led to the revolution
   of 1871. Population: 9380. Altitude: 1696 ft.
   Crops: corn, beans; livestock, dairying.

PRONUNCIAMIENTO DE CARRERA (1837). Rafael Carrera, with the support of the conservative elements at Antigua, issued a declaration to eliminate the liberal influence in the government. The declaration was the first of Carrera's programs to be announced. Prior to this, his party's actions had been without direction. The Pronunciamiento decreed: 1) the abolishment of the Livingston Code, 2) guaranteed protection of life and property, 3) discontinuance of the Indian capitation tax, 4) general amnesty, 5) reinstatement of the Archbishop and the religious orders.

PROPAGANDA FIDEI see RECOLECCIÓN, LA.

PROVINCIAS UNIDAS DEL CENTRO DE AMÉRICA. A federation of the states of Guatemala, San Salvador, Nicaragua, Honduras, and Costa Rica, proclaimed after secession from Mexico by a constituent assembly in Guatemala City on July 1, 1823. The new nation set up a federal constitution and elected Manuel Jose Arce as president; Guatemala City was made the seat of the federal government. Dissensions over a variety of questions and a growing antagonism between liberals and conservatives led to civil war. The liberals were victorious and their leader, Francisco Morazán, became president (1830). His administration put through a liberal program, which included control of the Church, religious freedom, and the promotion of industry and commerce. The seat of government was moved to San Salvador in 1835. Morazán's government aroused the opposition of the conservative forces. Morazán was defeated and the Confederation collapsed in 1839. The states then assumed the status of independent nations. Since then, several attempts have been made to again unite the countries of Central America, but all have failed. The Organizacion de los Estados Centro Americanos, established in 1951, is currently striving toward unification, and is effective in the economic areas of common tariff barriers, cooperative planning, etc.

PUEBLO. A village which is a cabecera of a municipio, but is of less importance or of smaller size than a villa.

PUEBLO NUEVO. Municipio in the department of Suchitepequez in southwestern Guatemala. Its cabecera is located near the Samala River, 12 miles northeast of

Retalhuleu. The municipio was transferred in 1944
from the department of Retalhuleu. Population: 2317.
Crops: coffee, sugar cane.

PUEBLO NUEVO VIÑAS. Municipio in the department of
Santa Rosa in southern Guatemala, in the Pacific pied-
mont. The cabecera is 13 miles west-southwest of
Cuilapa. Population: 12,396. Altitude: 4430 ft.
Crops: coffee; livestock.

PUEBLO VIEJO see VILLA CANALES.

PUERTO BARRIOS. Municipio in the department of Izabal
in eastern Guatemala. The cabecera is located on the
Bay of Amatique, 150 miles northeast of Guatemala
City. It is the major Caribbean port; rail terminus.
Exports bananas, chicle, coffee, fruit, wood. It was
developed in the 20th century after the completion of
the railroad to Guatemala City, and after expansion of
banana plantations in the lower Motagua valley. Population: 32,474.

PUERTO DE IZTAPA see IZTAPA.

PUERTO SAN JOSÉ see SAN JOSE, def. 2.

PULIQ. A special Quiché sauce for meat seasoning.

PURULHA. Municipio in the department of Baja Verapaz in
central Guatemala. The cabecera is located 12 miles
north-northeast of Salama. Population: 14,247. Altitude: 5699 ft. Crops: coffee, sugar cane, grain;
livestock.

-Q-

QUAHTEMALLÁN. Sometimes spelled Quauhitemallán. A
Cakchiquel word for "full of trees"; from this came
the name, Guatemala.

QUEMADOR. An altar at which rites are observed.

QUESADA. Often spelled Quezada. Municipio in the department of Jutiapa in southeastern Guatemala. Its cabecera is in the highlands, ten miles west of Jutiapa,
near the Inter-American Highway. Population: 7983.

Crops: corn, cotton, beans; livestock.

QUESADA, ANTONIO RODRÍGUEZ DE, d. 1558. Governor
from 1555 to 1558, he further assisted in the establishment of the municipio system and improved treatment of the Indians by sending Audiencia judges throughout the country to check and enforce reforms.

QUETZAL. The national bird of Guatemala, a trogan. The
male is noted for its long, green tail coverts. The
Quetzal bird is called the "bird of freedom," a mis-
nomer based on the legend that it cannot live in cap-
tivity. Also, the monetary unit adopted by Guatemala
in 1924, on a par with the U.S. dollar, is called the
Quetzal.

QUETZAL, EL. Municipio in the department of San Marcos
in southwestern Guatemala. In the Pacific piedmont,
the cabecera is located nine miles northeast of Coatepeque. Population: 12,272. Crops: coffee, sugar
cane, grain; livestock.

QUETZALCOATL. Derived from Quetzalli (bird) and Co-
huatl (snake). Worshipped by the Aztecs as a god-hero
and by the Mayas as Kukulcan. Quetzalcoatl was a
white man with a long beard, who wore a red cross
on his clothing. He taught the people agriculture and
architecture and invented the calendar. When he left,
he stated that he would return from the East, and em-
barked on a raft made of serpents. When Cortés
landed in Mexico, he was thought to be the returning
Quetzalcoatl. The Aztec leaders were divided between
greeting him as the returning god, or as an invader.
This indecision enabled the Spanish to conquer Mexico
with considerable ease. Some scholars have thought
that the legend may have rested on the personage of an
early Christian or perhaps a Viking, who reached Mexico in an unknown manner. The feathered serpent on
which Quetzalcoatl departed is thought to have been one
of the early ships used by the Westerners, with a
dragon's head on the bow. Others claim the Quetzalcoatl legend to be a story symbolic of the movement of
the sun.

QUEZADA see QUESADA.

QUEZALTENANGO. 1) A department in southwestern Guate-

mala. Its capital is Quezaltenango. In the western
highlands, it slopes south into the coastal plains. It
is bounded on the southwest by the Naranjo River and
on the southeast by the Tilapa River. It is drained
by the Samala River in the eastern part. The prominent volcanoes are Santa María, Zunil, and Cerro Quemado. Crops are corn, wheat, beans, fodder grasses.
Considerable livestock is raised on the northern highlands, with coffee, sugar cane and tropical fruit raised
in the southwest coastal plains. The capital is the
main industrial center with textile milling, flour milling and ceramics. The main centers are Quezaltenango, Salcaja, San Juan Ostuncalco and Coatepeque.
There are 24 municipios in the department: Almolonga,
Cabricán, Cajola, Cantel, Coatepeque, Colomba, Concepción Chiquirichapa, La Esperanza, Flores Costa
Cuca, Genova, Huitán, Olintepeque, Palestina, El Palmar, Quezaltenango, Salcaja, San Carlos Sija, San
Francisco la Unión, San Juan Ostuncalco, San Martín
Sacatepequez, San Mateo, San Miguel Sigüila, Sibilia,
Zunil. Population in 1950 was 184,213; in 1964,
271,184; the projection for 1980 is 413,500. Area:
753 square miles. See also ALTOS, LOS.
    2) Municipio in the department of Quezaltenango
in southwestern Guatemala. The cabecera is in the
western highlands, 70 miles west-northwest of Guatemala City. It is the commercial and industrial center
of the western highlands. Industries include textile
milling, flour milling, brewing, and the manufacture
of shoes and cigarettes. Hydroelectric station at Santa
María. Trading center for grain, coffee, sugar cane
and tropical fruit. The city was destroyed in 1902 by
an eruption of the volcano Santa María. Rebuilt, it
never regained its 19th-century semi-independent commerical status. Population: 56,602. Altitude: 7657
ft.

QUEZALTEPEQUE. Municipio in the department of Chiqui-
    mula in eastern Guatemala. The cabecera is located
    in the highlands, 13 miles southeast of Chiquimula.
    Extinct volcano Quezaltepeque is five miles east of the
    town. Manufacturing of mats, baskets, fish nets.
    Population: 14,291. Crops: corn, wheat; livestock.

QUEZALTEPEQUE VOLCANO. Altitude: 3940 feet. An
    extinct volcano, located five miles east of Quezalte-
    peque in the department of Chiquimula.

QUICHÉ.   One of the major linguistic stocks of the Quichean
language groups making up the Proto-Guatemala-Yucatan
language family of the Mayan language.   The Quiché
Indians are located in Huehuetenango, Chimaltenango,
Quezaltenango, Totonicapan, Quiché, Baja Verapaz,
Retalhuleu, Suchitepequez, Sololá and Escuintla.   The
Quiché government and culture were unusually well developed.   Their writing was a form of hieroglyphics.
Utatlán, the capital, was near present-day Santa Cruz
del Quiché and was leveled by the Spanish.   Their
holy book, Popul Vuh, was preserved when a converted
Indian wrote the history and legends in a manuscript,
later discovered in the 18th century.   Under their last
great leader, Tecum-Uman, they first fought the invading Spanish and were defeated.   In 1815, they revolted
under Anastasio Txul and were again defeated.

QUICHÉ   see   SANTA CRUZ DEL QUICHÉ.

QUICHÉ, EL.   Department located in west central Guatemala.   Its capital is Quiché.   The highland Sierra de
Chuacus and Cuchumatanes Mountains slope north into
the lowlands along the Mexican border.   It is bounded
on the east by the Chixoy River and drained by the
Chixoy and Motagua Rivers in the south.   Some lumbering is done in the north; livestock raising.   Crops
are corn, beans, coffee, sugar cane, tobacco and potatoes.   The main centers are Quiché and Chichicastenango.   The department has 18 municipios: Canilla,
Chajul, Chiche, Chinique, Cunén, Joyabaj, Nebaj,
Patzite, Sacapulas, San Andrés Sajcabaja, San Antonio
Ilotenango, San Bartolomé Jocotenango, San Juan Cotzal, San Miguel Uspantan, San Pedro Jocopilas, Santa
Cruz del Quiché, Santo Tomás Chichicastenango, Zacualpa.   Population in 1950 was 174,911; in 1964,
249,704 and the projection to 1980 is 412,400.   Area:
3234 square miles.

QUICHEAN.   Largest of the five linguistic strains--the dia-
lects of Quiché, Cakchiquel, Tzutuhil, Uspantec, and
Rabinal--which are a part of the Proto-Guatemala-
Yucatan language family of the Maya linguistic stock.
The Quichean linguistic groups are located primarily
in highland Central America.

QUINCE DE SEPTIEMBRE DE 1821.   The independence day
of Guatemala; it marks the date on which separation

from Spain was proclaimed in the "Acta de Independencia." See also INDEPENDENCE.

QUIÑONES Y OSORIO, ALVARO DE, d. 1642. Governor
from 1634 to 1642. He permitted gambling only in his
own home and gave out government favors to those
frequenting his tables. He was lost at sea en route
to Peru.

QUINTAL. A unit of measurement equal to four arrobas
(100 libra) and equivalent to 46 kilograms or 101.5
pounds.

QUINTO. The royal fifth, or one-fifth of all products, which
was paid to the crown as a form of taxation.

QUIRIGUA. Ruins situated in the lowlands, on the Motagua
River's northern shore. The site developed briefly in
the classic period of the early Mayan era. It is significant because of the numerous and unusual stelae
found here.

-R-

R. N. see RENOVACIÓN NACIONAL.

RABINAL. 1) A language group making up part of the Quichean
linguistic stock of the Proto-Guatemala-Yucatan language family. Located in Baja Verapaz, their precon-
quest capital was at Minpokom. The area was so well
fortified that Alvarado gave up trying to conquer them
after being driven back several times. Under the direction of Bartolomé de Las Casas, the territory was
peacefully converted to Christianity in less than five
years. Rabinal, the present capital, was founded by
Las Casas in 1538, to relocate the scattered Indians
and to make the teaching of the faith easier.
    2) Municipio in the department of Baja Verapaz
in central Guatemala. The cabecera is located in the
northern highlands, 11 miles west of Salama. Market
center; production of mats, pottery, gourds. Population: 17,696. Crops: rice, corn, beans, fruit.

RABINAL ACHI. A Rabinal dance drama described by Brasseur de Bourbourg in which the defeated Quiché prince

(Queche Achi) was sacrificed to the Rabinal gods.

RAILROAD see ALTOS RAILWAY, LOS; INTERNATIONAL RAILWAY ...; VERAPAZ RAILROAD.

RAMÍREZ, ALEJANDRO, 1774-1821. One of the early editors of the Gazeta de Guatemala; he has been considered one of the two great men in the "enlightened era" of Guatemala history. He helped to compile a Resumen general de las familias de españoles y ladinos domiciliades en el Reyno de Guatemala (1804).

RAMÍREZ, BERNARDO, 1741-1803? Architect and builder, he constructed the water supply system for Guatemala City and drew up the plans for the convents: Las Capuchinas, La Recolección, Santa Catalina, Beaterio de Santa Rosa and Santa Teresa. In 1782, he formulated new regulations for the Brickmasons' Guild.

RAMÍREZ CLOSTÁN, G. [pseudonym] see MARTÍNEZ NOLASCO, GUSTAVO.

RAMÍREZ DE QUIÑONES, PEDRO. Acting governor, 1558-1559. He sent an unsuccessful expedition of conquest against the Lacandones.

RANCHITO. A small, rustic or rural hut.

RAZUMIKIN [pseudonym] see GANDARA DURÁN, CARLOS.

REAL. A unit of colonial money used until 1924, equal to one-eighth of a peso.

REALISMO. A literary movement of the 19th century following romanticism. Most of the writings contained some humor and optimism and were noted for descriptive regionalism. In Guatemala, the movement was never fully developed. Ramón Salazar's book, Conflictos, is the best example of Realismo in Guatemala.

REALISMO MAGICO see MAGICAL REALISM.

RECASENS SICHES, LUIS, 1903- . A Guatemalan jurist on the faculty of law at the University of La Habana, he wrote Filosofía del derecho (1940), Vida humana (1940), ... Derecho de Francisco Suárez (1947), Latin American Legal Philosophy (1948), Tratado general de sociología (1956), and <u>Tratado general de filosofía del derecho</u> (1959).

RECINOS, ADRIÁN, 1886-1962. A Guatemalan historian and diplomat, he held several ministerial positions in Europe and the U.S. (Foreign Minister in 1922-23, Representative to the U.N. in 1954-55) but is best known for his writings. Most widely recognized are <u>Monografía del Departamento de Huehuetenango</u> (1913), <u>Popol Vuh</u> (1947), <u>Memorial de Sololá</u> (1950), and <u>Poesías de J.B. Montúfar</u> (1924).

RECOLECCIÓN, LA. A monastery of Franciscans founded in Antigua in 1700 by Fray Antonio Margil and Fray Melchor López. The monastery was founded to give aid and comfort to the poor and afflicted. The original, simple, thatched-roofed monastery was replaced by an impressive stone edifice, the ruins of which can be seen today in Antigua. The monks were often referred to as the "Propaganda Fidei" because of their zeal for helping the poor. Also called Recoletos.

RECOPILACIÓN DE LEYES DE INDIES. The collection of laws and regulations relating to the Spanish colonies, first published in 1563. Revisions were brought out in 1596, 1628 and 1681. The Spanish government published a definitive edition in 1681 which was not revised until 1805. The Leyes covered all aspects of colonial life, including the Church, finances, the Indians and slavery. It contained many humanitarian regulations, but was so detailed that it could not be effectively enforced.

REDES. A large bag or net made of thin rope, usually open mesh. The two carrying ropes are often fastened to the mecapal for carrying on the back. See also MATATE.

REDUCCIÓN. In the years following the conquest, reducciones or communities of Indians, were formed by moving the natives from their scattered rural dwellings. The purpose was to aid the Spanish in controlling the Indians and to provide greater ease in religious conversion. Also, the encomenderos could gather needed laborers more easily from the settlements. See CONGREGA.

REFAJOS.   Skirts of two types worn by Indian women.   En-
vueltos, wrap-around skirts, usually ankle-length,
which consist of about five and a half yards of material, tightly wrapped.   The other style is a pleated
skirt called a plegado, requiring about eight yards of
cloth.   It is worn either as a short skirt, to the knee,
or in some areas, extends to the ankle.

REFORMA, LA.   Municipio in the department of San Marcos
in southwestern Guatemala.   The cabecera is located
about ten miles south of San Marcos.   Population:
9913.   Altitude: 3800 ft.   Crops: grain, coffee,
sugar cane; livestock.

REGIDOR.   An alderman on the municipal council.   In the
early colonial period, the regidor was elected by the
inhabitants of a community, but later the post was
sold by the crown and often became hereditary.   The
position became and remains little more than an honorary title.

REINA BARRIOS, JOSÉ MARÍA   see   REYNA BARRIOS,
JOSÉ MARÍA.

REMESAL, ANTONIO DE, 1570-1627?   A Dominican priest
who wrote a history of Guatemala while in the country
from 1613 to 1616.   The book was published in Madrid
in 1619 under the title Historia de la provincia de S.
Vicente de Chyapa y Guatemala, not, however, before
its publication was fought by many citizens of Guatemala because of its severe condemnation of Alvarado
and the settlers' treatment of the native Indians.   A
review of this work appears in H. H. Bancroft's
Works, vol. 7, p. 339-40.

REMICHEROS.   A rebellious group in eastern Guatemala
which opposed Barrios shortly after the revolution of
1871.   The name is derived from their use of Sheres
(oak clubs) instead of the Remington rifles used by
Barrios' men.   The two words were combined to form
Remicheros.   The group had some success, but was
defeated by a force led by Barrios.

RENOVACIÓN NACIONAL (R. N.).   One of the major political parties in the 1944 movement to support President
Arévalo.   Internal disputes weakened the party to make
it the least effective of the three government parties

by the end of the Arévalo regime. The party merged
several times, but withdrew from the mergers with
considerable loss of support each time, until it was
largely ineffectual by the end of the Arbenz regime.

REPARTIMIENTO.   The allotment of Indians for a specific
task, usually to carry out public works. The system
was given only quasi-legal status through occasional
credulas prohibiting malpractices, until 1609, when
the Council of Indies set up a detailed code. The Indians were to be paid regularly and were not to suffer
abuses. However, in the mines the Indians continued
to suffer because of the nature of the work. The royal appointees most often took advantage of the Indians
because of their short-term appointments. The appointees looked on the repartimiento as a means to en-
rich themselves as quickly as possible. The system
is not to be confused with the encomienda.

RESIDENCIA.   In colonial Spanish America, an investigation
of the outgoing governor's term of office by the incom-
ing governor. Charges and a defense were heard to
determine the fairness of the government. Prosecu-
tion of the outgoing governor was seldom carried out.

RETALHULEU. 1) A department in southwestern Guatemala.
The capital is Retalhuleu. Located on the Pacific
coast, it is bounded on the northwest by the Tilapa
River. It extends from the Pacific piedmont in the
north to the coastal plain in the south. It is drained
by the Samala River and a few small coastal streams.
Crops are coffee, sugar cane, cotton, rice, cacao, on
the northern slope; corn, beans, and livestock raising
on the coastal plain. Hardwood milling in the north;
salt extraction on the coast. Main cities are Retalhuleu, San Felipe, and Champerico, the Pacific port.
The department has nine municipios: El Asintal,
Champerico, Nuevo San Carlos, Retalhuleu, San Andrés Villa Seca, San Felipe, San Martín Zapotitlán,
San Sebastián, Santa Cruz Mulua. Population in
1950 was 66,861; in 1964, 117,328; projected in 1980
to be 217,300. Area: 716 square miles.
2) Municipio in the department of Retalhuleu in
southwestern Guatemala. Its cabecera is located 23
miles south-southwest of Quezaltenango. It is a market center with lumbering nearby. Customs houses

for the port of Champerico are located here. Population: 35,454. Crops: coffee, cotton, sugar cane,
grain; livestock and beekeeping.

REYES MONROY, JOSÉ LUIS, 1900- . Bibliographer interested in historical geography, he was born in Guatemala City. He has compiled: Catálogo razonado de
las leyes de Guatemala (1945), Bibliografía de los
estudios geográficos ... (1960), Acotaciones para la
historia de un libro (1960), and Corono funebre sobre
Carlos Wyld Ospina (1963).

REYNA ANDRADE, JOSÉ MARÍA, 1860-1947. Provisional
president in 1931, he was elected by the legislature to
fill the office after Manuel Orellana resigned. Reyna
held office until an election could be carried out and
the new president, Jorge Ubico, sworn in. Former
Chief Justice of the Supreme Court, he attended the
constitutional convention of 1877 to begin his political
career.

REYNA BARRIOS, JOSÉ MARÍA, 1856-1898. President of
Guatemala, 1892-1898; he was elected in a comparatively free election. In an effort to see the country
through a period of economic upheaval, Reyna attempted
to have his term of office extended for five years. He
was assassinated during a period of turmoil resulting
from restrictive controls inaugurated by his government.

RIBERA, PAYO DE see ENRÍQUEZ DE RIBERA, PAYO.

RICONCITO, TREATY OF (1838). Treaty drawn up when
Carrera surrendered to General Augustin Guzman.
They agreed that Carrera would respect the Morazán
government and would give up his arms in exchange
for the position of military head in Mitla, near Jutiapa.
The treaty was not enforced, however, and Carrera
was soon back in the field against Morazán.

RIEPELE PRETTO, PIO M., 1872-1948. Born in Italy, but
was raised and lived in Guatemala. He was a journalist and author. He translated El proceso de Jesus
(1906) and wrote Nociones de filosofía del lenguaje.

RÍO BLANCO. Municipio in the department of San Marcos
in southwestern Guatemala. Its cabecera is located

east of San Lorenzo near the Quezaltenango border.
Population: 1923. Crops: corn, wheat, vegetables.

RÍO BRAVO. Municipio in the department of Suchitepequez
in southwestern Guatemala. Its cabecera is located at
the junction of the I. R. C. A. and the U. F. Co. spur line
to Tiquisate. Population: 8352. Crops: corn, beans,
rice, cotton.

RÍO DE LA PAZ   see   PAZ RIVER.

RÍO GRANDE DE ZACAPA   see   CHIQUIMULA RIVER.

RÍO HONDO. Municipio in the department of Zacapa in
eastern Guatemala. Its cabecera is on the Motagua
River, six miles north-northwest of Zacapa. Population: 9046. Crops: corn, beans, sugar cane; livestock.

RÍO NEGRO   see   CHIXOY RIVER.

RISCOS. Crags; in Guatemala it refers to the pinnacled
eroded formations at Momostenango.

RIVAS, FRANCISCO RODRÍGUEZ DE. Governor from 1716
to 1724. While governor, the earthquake of 1717 almost destroyed the capital city of Antigua. Much of
the population wanted to move the capital, and a petition for such a move was sent to the king. Rivas opposed this, however, and had the destroyed buildings
rebuilt. By the time the petition was approved, the
populace had decided to remain.

RIVERA CABEZAS, ANTONIO, 1784-1851. Governor of
Guatemala from 1830-31, while the country was a member of the Central American Federation. He was a
candidate against Morazán for the presidency of Central
America in 1830.

RIVERA MAESTRE, FRANCISCO. Born in Guatemala City,
he became a lawyer and moved to Madrid after the revolution in 1821. There he became a judge in the Spanish court. He wrote poetry having nostalgic undertones;
the best known is Epístola a Guatemala. He died in
Madrid at a very advanced age.

RIVERA PAZ, MARIANO. Was made governor of Guatemala

in July, 1838, to appease Carrera and to end the liberal reforms. Rivera was ousted from office for a short while in 1839 but was reinstated by Carrera and remained in office as President of the New Republic until 1844.

RIVERA Y SANTA CRUZ, TOMÁS DE, d. 1765. Governor from 1742 to 1748.

RIVERA Y VILLALÓN, PEDRO DE. Governor from 1733 to 1742. While on an extensive trip through the Spanish colonies between 1724 and 1728, he compiled Diario y derrotero de la caminando visto ... (1736).

ROBLES, RODOLFO, 1878-1939. A Guatemalan physician and surgeon, he was awarded the Jules Brault prize in 1929 for outstanding work in medicine.

RODAS CORZO, OVIDIO, 1906-1955. Artist and journalist from Chichicastenango, he edited El Imparcial from 1923 to the late 1940's, taught art, and wrote several books on Indian art and legends, including Simbolismos Maya Quiche (1938), Xucut, Origin of the Quiché Cross (1940), and Chichicastenango (1940).

RODAS NORIEGA, FLAVIO, 1882- . Ethnologist from Chichicastenango, he was an inspector of national ruins and monuments in the 1920's. With Rodas Corzo, he wrote Simbolismos Maya Quichés (1938) and made an early translation of Popol Buj (1917).

RODEO, EL see SAN JOSÉ EL RODEO.

RODILLERA. Woolen, knee-length skirts worn by the Indian men of some municipios; at times, they are worn by young girls also.

RODRÍGUEZ, JOSE N., 1861-1939. A general of the army, he wrote Estudios de historia militar de Centroamérica (1930).

RODRÍGUEZ, JUAN FRANCISCO, 1848-1887. A poet and calligrapher from Quezaltenango, he wrote El Azacuán, a novel.

RODRÍGUEZ, JUAN JOSÉ, 1840-1916. A biologist who wrote Apuntamientos sobre los estudios de biología en

Guatemala (1893) and Memoria sobre la fauna de
Guatemala (1894).

RODRÍGUEZ BETETA, VIRGILIO, 1885- . A journalist and
diplomat, he was born in Guatemala City. He directed
Diario de la América Central (1910-20), was Minister
to Honduras, Spain, League of Nations and Chile. He
wrote Evolución de las ideas en el antiguo reino de
Guatemala (1925), El libro de Guatemala Grande (1951),
Evolución de la imprente ... (1962), Solidarity and Re-
sponsibilities of the United States in the Belize Case
(1965), and many others.

RODRÍGUEZ CABRILLO, JUAN see CABRILLO, JUAN
RODRÍGUEZ.

RODRÍGUEZ CERNA, CARLOS, 1894-1961. A Guatemalan
poet, his works are collected in Caravana lirica.
Pseudonym: El Abate Causerie.

RODRÍGUEZ CERNA, JOSÉ, 1884-1952. The first true
Guatemalan modernistic novelist and poet, his works
include Interiores, el poema de la Antigua, Tierras de
sol y de Montaña (1930), and El hermano Pedro (1956)
and several historical works. He wrote under the
pseudonyms Hermani, Casa Roja and Mariano Sandoval.

ROGACIÓN (Prayer for rain). During a dry period, a pro-
cession is held. The image of the patron saint is pa-
raded through the village during the hottest part of the
day. The saint is then taken to the fields to see how
much rain is needed, before being returned to the
church. The ritual is to encourage the saint to use
his influence in bringing rain to the village.

ROJAS, DIEGO DE. On the conquest, he was named Alcalde by Alvarado in 1524 and held the position until
Alvarado went to Mexico in 1526. At that time Portocarrero was appointed Alcalde. Rojas went to Peru in
1534, where he took part in the conquest of Peru.

ROJAS, ULISES, 1881-1959. A botanist born in La Union,
he wrote several works on botany, including Elementos
de botánica general (3 vols.) and Manuel de horticul-
ture. He also held several governmental positions.

ROLZ BENETT, JOSÉ, 1918- . From Quezaltenango, a

lawyer and diplomat, he was sent to Cyprus in 1967
by U Thant as a special U.N. ambassador to serve as
an official observer during an invasion threat.

ROMANTICISM.   A literary movement arising in Spain in
the mid-19th century; it spread to Latin America in
the latter part of the century.   It is characterized by
more individualism and freedom from the established
forms.   The Guatemalan novelist, Antonio José de
Irisarri, was a leader in this movement, with his autobiographical novel, El cristiano errante (1846-47).

ROMERIA.   A pilgrimage to visit saints.

ROZA.   The process of clearing a field for cultivation.   It
usually involves the cutting and burning of trees,
bushes, and weeds in the area.

RUEDA, PEDRO MALLÉN DE.   Governor from 1589 to
1592.   During his administration, several new buildings
were completed and a bridge was built across the Río
de Los Esclavos River to improve communications.

RUIATCOT.   In Quiché mythology, the god of rain who
causes seed grain to germinate.

RUINA, LA.   Refers to the devastating earthquake of 1773.

RUIZ, TOMAS.   An Indian, born in Nicaragua, he attended
the University of San Carlos.   He was one of the pre-
cursors arrested in the Belén Conspiracy (1813).

-S-

S. A. M. F.   see   SINDICATO DE ACCIÓN Y MEJOREMIENTO
DE LOS FERROCARRILEROS.

S. C. I. C. A. S.   see   SERVICIO COOPERATIVO INTERAMER-
ICANO DE CRÉDITO AGRÍCOLA SUPERVISADO.

S. C. I. D. A.   see   SERVICIO COOPERATIVO INTERAMERI-
CANO DE AGRICULTURA.

S. E. T. -C. A. G.   see   SINDICATO DE EMPRESA DE TRA-
BAJADORES DE LA COMPAÑÍA AGRÍCOLA DE
GUATEMALA.

S.G.P.   see   SINDICATO GENERAL DE PANIFACADORES.

S.I.E.C.A.   see   SECRETARIA DE INTEGRACIÓN ECO-
NÓMICA DEL CENTROAMÉRICA.

S.I.G.   see   SERVICIO DE INTELLIGENCIA GUATEMAL-
TECA.

S.T.E.G.   see   SINDICATO DE TRABAJADORES EDUCA-
CIONES DE GUATEMALA.

S.T.E.T.   see   SINDICATO DE EMPRESA DE TRABAJA-
DORES DE LA COMPAÑÍA AGRÍCOLA DE GUATE-
MALA.

SACACHIAN.   The small, dark purple berries of a pokeweed,
used for soap.   Also called Tzichipac.

SACAPULAS.   Municipio in the department of El Quiché in
west central Guatemala.   The cabecera is located on
the upper Chixoy River, 20 miles north-northeast of
Quiché.   Market center; silversmithing and salt production.   Population: 13,874.   Altitude: 4035 feet.
Crops: fruit, sugar cane.

SACATEPEQUEZ.   Department located in south central Guatemala.   The capital is Antigua.   In the central highlands,
the southern part is drained by the Guacalate River.
Agua Volcano in the southeast and Fuego, in the southwest, are its most prominent peaks.   Main crops are
corn, coffee, black beans, fodder grasses, with some
cattle and hog raising.   Its home industrial products
are pottery, metalware, cotton and textiles.   The chief
cities are Antigua, Sumpango, Ciudad Vieja and Santa
María.   Sixteen municipios: Antigua Guatemala, Ciudad
Vieja, Jocotenango, Magdalena Milpas Altas, Pastores,
San Antonio Aguas Calientes, San Bartolomé Milpas
Altas, San Juan Alotenango, San Lucas Sacatepequez,
San Miguel Dueñas, Santa Catarina Barahona, Santa
Lucía Milpas Altas, Santa María de Jesús, Santiago
Sacatepequez, Santo Domingo Xenacoj, Sumpango.   The
population in 1950 was 60,124; in 1964 it was 80,877;
and projected to 1980 to be 114,700.   Area: 179 square
miles.

SACATEPEQUEZ (Nation).   A Pokoman nation started as a
buffer state between the main body of Sacatepequez and

the Cakchiqueles. A very strong fortress was built
near present-day Mixco. The Spanish were able to
conquer the fort after hard fighting and with the assistance of the Cakchiqueles.

SACATINTA. Sometimes called Cuajatinta, it is a plant
from which the fresh leaves are used to make a bluing
dye. Indigo and aniline dye are added and allowed to
ferment.

SÁENZ, BENEDICTO, d. 1831. A musician and composer,
he was the son of Vicente Sáenz. He wrote music
having a military theme or beat, which began a new
era of music in Guatemala. He became organist at
the Cathedral in Guatemala City in 1803.

SÁENZ, BENEDICTO (hijo), 1815-1857. Musician and composer, he was choir master at the Cathedral. He directed several operas and wrote: Invitatorio al sa-
grado corazón de Jesús; Duetto a la Santísima Virgen;
Parce Miki; Niño Dios. He died a victim of cholera.

SÁENZ, FRANCISCO ISAAC, 1816-1880. Composer and musician, he taught at the Colegio Seminario and wrote
Misa en mi bemol and Lamentación.

SÁENZ, VICENTE, 1757-1841. An early composer, best
known for his Christmas carol, Villancicos de pascua.

SÁENZ DE MAÑOSCA Y MURILLO, JUAN DE SANTO
MATÍA, d. 1675. Acting governor from 1670 to 1672,
while Governor Alvarez was under suspension. He
went to Guatemala as Bishop in 1668. In 1672, he was
appointed Bishop of Puebla in Mexico.

SÁENZ DE TEJADA, FEDERICO see TEJADA, FEDERICO
SÁENZ DE.

SÁENZ POGGIO, JOSÉ. Historian and composer, he composed for military bands. He used and studied various
Indian instruments and wrote Historia de la música
guatemalteca (1878). He was the son of Benedicto
Sáenz (hijo).

SAGELLIU Y GIEBLAS, BAÑOGER DE [pseudonym] see
BERGAÑO Y VILLEGAS, SIMÓN.

SAKER-TI. A literary group of the late 1940's concerned with social injustices and associated with the revolutionary political reformers.

SALAMA. Municipio in the department of Baja Verapaz in central Guatemala. In the northern highlands, the cabecera is on the Salama River, 37 miles north-northeast of Guatemala City. Market center for agricultural crops. Population: 18,671. Altitude: 3018 ft. Crops: coffee, sugar cane, olives; livestock.

SALAZAR, JOSÉ GREGORIO, 1793-1838. Born in El Salvador, he was governor there, then vice president of the Federation under Morazán in 1834. He took control of the government while Morazán was in the field. He was killed in Guatemala City when the Indian army, under Carrera, first captured the city in February, 1838.

SALAZAR, RAMÓN A., 1852-1914. A medical doctor and author. His novels fell into a transitional period between the romantic-historical movement and the naturalistic movement. They are more probably classed in the realistic category, although this movement never fully developed in Guatemala. His best effort is Conflictos, Alma enferma and Stella (1896). More serious works include Desenvolvimiento intelectual de Guatemala (1897).

SALAZAR ARGUMEDO, CARLOS, 1863-1954. A judge, he held several public offices. He was a member of the Honduran-Guatemalan boundary commission and was on the Hague Tribunal from 1909 through the 1920's.

SALAZAR Y HERRERA NÁJERA Y MENDOZA, PEDRO DE, d. 1771. Governor from 1765 until 1771. A riot in 1766 occurred as a result of the establishment of a state monopoly over tobacco. Lower prices on tobacco pacified the rioters.

SALCAJA. Municipio in the department of Quezaltenango in southwestern Guatemala. The cabecera is on the Samala River, five miles northeast of Quezaltenango. On the Inter-American Highway; a distillery nearby. Population: 6749. Altitude: 7641 ft. Crops: corn, wheat, fodder grasses; livestock.

SALCEDO, FRANCISCO, 1540?-1600. A Franciscan linguist, he was the first creole to take the Franciscan
habit in Guatemala. His works include Arte y diccionario de la lengua Mexicana and Documentos cris-
tianos en tres lenguas.

SALINAS RIVER see CHIXOY RIVER.

SALOMÉ JIL [pseudonym] see MILLA Y VIDAURRE,
JOSÉ.

SALTO, EL. Town in southern Guatemala, located on the
Michatoya River. It is in the department of Escuintla,
and is two miles east of Escuintla. Sugar mills located here.

SALVADOR AGREEMENT OF 1844. Ex-president Manual
Arce attempted to invade El Salvador and set himself
up as dictator. President Malespín was able to defeat
Arce, but disregarded orders from the legislature and
crossed into Guatemala while pursuing Arce. President Rivera Paz of Guatemala called on Carrera but
before Carrera arrived, Malespín retreated into El
Salvador. An agreement was signed, restoring the
peace and returning to Guatemala the arms left behind
by Arce and his men.

SALVADOR-GUATEMALA PACT (1945). An agreement between the two countries to merge, with the two Presidents, Arévalo and Castañeda Castro, agreeing to step
down in favor of one president. Local revolts and internal politics prevented anything from developing beyond the planning stage.

SALVADOR WAR OF 1839. The federal army, made up of
Salvadorans and Guatemalan exiles and led by Morazán, invaded Guatemala and captured Guatemala City
on March 18, with the purpose of re-uniting the Central American Union. The Guatemalan aristocrats had
Carrera's army for protection and were able to drive
Morazán from the city on the 19th. Morazán returned
to El Salvador but was unable to raise another army,
so left the country on April 5th. Although not mentioned in the treaty, Francisco Malespín was to remain in Salvador as an advisor and he became the
power working under the direction of Carrera.

SALVADOR WAR OF 1850.   The combined forces of Honduras and El Salvador invaded Guatemala in 1850.
The war grew out of the many border skirmishes
originating from all three states.   The expedition was
repulsed at Arada, Guatemala, on February 2, 1851,
when Carrera won the most brilliant campaign of his
career.   The war ended with Carrera in command of
several key border towns of his adversaries.   The liberal regimes were ousted as a result, and replaced
with conservatives more friendly to Carrera.   Francisco Dueñas was made the President of Salvador and
Santos Guardiola, of Honduras.   The treaty was not
ratified until 1853.

SALVADOR WAR OF 1863.   El Salvador and Honduras
signed a treaty of alliance in 1862, of which Carrera
disapproved.   Later, several border incidents occurred,
in which Guatemala and Nicaragua teamed up against
Salvador and Honduras.   Carrera invaded Salvador and
was defeated at Coatepeque.   He regrouped his forces
and, with the assistance of Nicaragua, won at Santa
Ana.   San Salvador was besieged for four months before the war ended with the fall of the government and
of the city in October, 1863.

SALVADOR WAR OF 1876.   Because of ill feeling in Salvador and Honduras toward President Barrios, strong
exchanges were made among the three presidents.   Relations were severed; Barrios led an army of about
8000 against El Salvador and sent General Gregorio
Solares into Honduras with about 1500 men.   Barrios
met the Salvadoran army on April 15th near Apaneca,
Salvador, and routed them after a long day's battle.
On the 17th to the 19th of April, General Solares
gained control of the departments of La Union and San
Miguel.   The Salvadoran army was then hit hard by
desertions, and peace negotiations began.   A treaty
was concluded in the field on April 25, 1876.   The
president of El Salvador was replaced by one less hos-
tile to Barrios.

SAMALA RIVER.   In southwestern Guatemala, it begins
west of San Francisco Totonicapan and flows about 75
miles south-southwest to the Pacific at Playa Grande.
The Zunil and Santa María power stations are located
on the river.

SAMAYAC. Municipio in the department of Suchitepequez
in southwestern Guatemala. The cabecera is four and
a half miles northeast of Mazatenango. Population:
6556. Crops: coffee, sugar cane, grain; livestock.

SAMAYOA CHINCHILLA, CARLOS, 1898- . A writer born
in Guatemala City, secretary to the President, 1931-
44. He wrote Madre milpa (1934), translated into
English as The Emerald Lizard (1957), La casa de la
muerta (1937), Estampas de la Costra Grande (1954),
El Quetzal no es rojo (1956), and Aproximación al arte
Maya (1964).

SAN AGUSTÍN ACASAGUASTLÁN. Municipio in the department of El Progreso in east central Guatemala. The
cabecera is near the Motagua River, about eight miles
northeast of El Progreso. It is a marketing center.
Mayan ruins nearby. Population: 15,309. Crops:
corn, wheat, sugar cane.

SAN ANDRÉS. Municipio in the department of El Petén in
northern Guatemala. The cabecera is on the western
shore of Lake Petén, three miles north-northwest of
Flores. Population: 1855. Crops: sugar cane,
grain; livestock.

SAN ANDRÉS ISLAND. Island in Lake Petén on which is located Ciudad Flores, the capital of the department of
El Petén. The island, then called Tayasal, was the
last stronghold of the Maya, who resisted the Spanish
there until 1697. The city and island were called
Itzá, or Petén Itzá after the group of Mayans living
there. In 1698, the Spanish turned the island into a
penal colony.

SAN ANDRÉS ITZAPA. Municipio in the department of Chimaltenango in south central Guatemala. The cabecera
is located two and a half miles south-southwest of Chimaltenango. Population: 7109. Altitude: 5971 ft.
Crops: corn, wheat, beans.

SAN ANDRÉS SAJCABAJA. Municipio in the department of
El Quiché in west central Guatemala. The cabecera
is located in the central part of the department. Population: 7978. Crops: corn, beans, sugar cane, tul.

SAN ANDRÉS SEMETABAJ. Municipio in the department of

Solola in southwest central Guatemala. The cabecera
is on the Inter-American Highway, five miles east-
southeast of Sololá. Population: 2911. Altitude:
6384 ft. Crops: grain, vegetables, beans.

SAN ANDRÉS VILLA SECA. Municipio in the department of
Retalhuleu in southwestern Guatemala. The cabecera
is located seven miles east-northeast of Retalhuleu.
It is located on the Guatemala City to Mexico railroad.
Population: 20,292. Crops: coffee, sugar cane, ca-
cao, cotton, grain; livestock.

SAN ANDRÉS XECUL. Municipio in the department of Totonicapán in west central Guatemala. Its cabecera is
eight miles west of Totonicapán. Population: 7517.
Altitude: 6880 ft. Crops: corn, wheat, beans.

SAN ANTONIO AGUAS CALIENTES. Municipio in the department of Sacatepequez in south central Guatemala. The
cabecera is four miles west-southwest of Antigua.
Some huipil weaving. Population: 3243. Altitude:
4741 ft. Crops: coffee, sugar cane, grain.

SAN ANTONIO HUISTA. Municipio in the department of
Huehuetenango in western Guatemala. The cabecera
is located on the west slope of the Cuchumatanes
Mountains, 31 miles northwest of Huehuetenango. Manufacturing of palm hats and rope. Population: 4330.
Altitude: 5315 ft. Crops: corn, sugar cane, coffee,
bananas.

SAN ANTONIO ILOTENANGO. Municipio in the department
of El Quiché in west central Guatemala. Its cabecera
is located near Santa Cruz del Quiché on the road between Totonicapán and Santa Cruz. Population: 6045.
Altitude: 6396 ft. Crops: corn, beans, some wheat.

SAN ANTONIO LA PAZ. Municipio in the department of El
Progreso in east central Guatemala. The cabecera is
located near the Atlantic Highway in the western part
of the department. Population: 5774. Altitude: 3968
ft. Crops: corn, beans, tomatoes, yucca.

SAN ANTONIO PALOPO. Municipio in the department of
Sololá in southwest-central Guatemala. The cabecera
is located on the eastern shore of Lake Atitlán and is
seven miles southeast of Sololá. Lumbering; reed mat

weaving.   Population: 3570.   Altitude: 5200 ft.
Crops: coffee, grain.

SAN ANTONIO SACATEPEQUEZ.   Municipio in the department of San Marcos in southwest Guatemala.   Its cabecera is located near the headwaters of the Naranjo
River, on the Inter-American Highway, and five miles
east of San Marcos.   Market center; lumbering.   Population: 5052.   Altitude: 7668 ft.   Crops: coffee,
grain.

SAN ANTONIO SUCHITEPEQUEZ.   Municipio in the department of Suchitepequez in southwestern Guatemala.   The
cabecera is near the Nahualate River, six miles east
of Mazatenango.   Rail terminus.   Population: 18,345.
Altitude: 4100 ft.   Crops: coffee, cacao, grain; livestock.

SAN BARTOLO.   Municipio in the department of Totonicapán
in west central Guatemala.   The cabecera is located in
the northernmost part of the department.   Sometimes
called San Bartolo Aguas Calientes because of the near-
ness of hot springs.   Population: 7303.   Altitude:
7774 ft.   Crops: corn, beans, oranges, cane for livestock.

SAN BARTOLOMÉ JOCOTENANGO.   Municipio in the department of El Quiché in west central Guatemala.   The
cabecera is located in the center of the department.
Not accessible by road.   Population: 3868.   Altitude:
5084 ft.   Crops: corn, beans, tomatoes, sweet potatoes, watermelon, yucca.

SAN BARTOLOMÉ MILPAS ALTAS.   Municipio in the department of Sacatepequez in south central Guatemala.
The cabecera is on the Inter-American Highway, four
miles northeast of Antigua.   Population: 1291.   Altitude: 7005 ft.   Crops: corn, beans, fruit.

SAN BENITO.   Municipio in the department of El Petén in
northern Guatemala.   Its cabecera is located on the
southern shore of Lake Petén, southwest of Flores.
Terminus of the road from Cobán.   Population: 3044.
Altitude: 377 ft.   Crops: grain, sugar cane; livestock.

SAN BERNARDINO.   Municipio in the department of Suchi-

tepequez in southwestern Guatemala. The cabecera is
three miles east-northeast of Mazatenango. Population:
3402. Altitude: 1378 ft. Crops: coffee, grain; livestock.

SAN CARLOS ALZATATE. Municipio in the department of
Jalapa in east central Guatemala. The cabecera is located at the southeast foot of Alzatate Volcano, 13
miles south-southwest of Jalapa. Population: 3366.
Altitude: 5740 ft. Crops: corn, beans; livestock.

SAN CARLOS SIJA. Municipio in the department of Quezaltenango in southwestern Guatemala. The cabecera is
located at the southern foot of Sija Volcano, and is on
the headstream of the Samala River, nine miles north
of Quezaltenango. Population: 12,725. Altitude:
10,500 ft. Crops: corn, wheat, fodder grasses; livestock.

SAN CARLOS UNIVERSITY see UNIVERSIDAD DE SAN
CARLOS DE GUATEMALA.

SAN CRISTÓBAL ACASAGUASTLAN. Municipio in the department of El Progreso in east central Guatemala.
The cabecera is located on the Motagua River, 11
miles east-northeast of El Progreso. Population:
2559. Altitude: 787 ft. Crops: corn, beans; livestock.

SAN CRISTÓBAL CUCHO. Municipio in the department of
San Marcos in southwestern Guatemala. The cabecera
is located south of the city of San Marcos. Population:
5021. Altitude: 7675 ft. Crops: corn, coffee, wheat,
beans, bananas and other fruits of both warm and cool
climates.

SAN CRISTÓBAL FRONTERA. A village in Jutiapa department, in southeastern Guatemala. In the highlands, it
is 16 miles southeast of Jutiapa on the Salvadoran border. Customs station for the Inter-American Highway.

SAN CRISTÓBAL LAKE. In Alta Verapaz department in the
northern highlands of central Guatemala. The town of
San Cristóbal Verapaz is located on its shore. The
lake is small and significant as a weekend resort for
residents of Cobán.

SAN CRISTÓBAL TOTONICAPÁN. Municipio in the department of Totonicapán in west central Guatemala. Its
cabecera is on the Samala River, five miles west of
Totonicapán. On the Inter-American Highway. Market
and textile center; flour milling. Population: 14,817.
Altitude: 7874 ft. Crops: wheat, corn, beans.

SAN CRISTÓBAL VERAPAZ. Municipio in the department
of Alta Verapaz in central Guatemala. The cabecera
is located in the northern highlands, seven miles southwest of Cobán. It is on the small lake, San Cristóbal.
Market center; leather tanning and manufacture. Population: 19,259. Altitude: 4530 ft. Crops: coffee,
sugar cane; livestock.

SAN DIEGO. Municipio in the department of Zacapa in
eastern Guatemala. Its cabecera is located in the
southernmost portion of the department, not easily accessible by road. Population: 3328. Altitude: 2099
ft. Crops: corn, beans, rice, sugar cane, some
coffee.

SAN FELIPE. Municipio in the department of Retalhuleu in
southwestern Guatemala. The cabecera is on the Samala River, nine miles northeast of Retalhuleu. Rail
terminus; market center. Population: 9886. Altitude:
2014 ft. Crops: fruit, coffee, sugar cane, grain.

SAN FRANCISCO. Municipio in the department of El Petén
in northern Guatemala. The cabecera is located nine
miles south-southwest of Flores. Lumbering; agriculture. Formerly called Chachaclun. Population: 1356.
Altitude: 787 ft. Crops: corn, beans, rice.

SAN FRANCISCO EL ALTO. Municipio in the department of
Totonicapán in west central Guatemala. The cabecera
is located on the Samala River, six miles west-northwest of Totonicapán. Market; wool weaving. Population: 16,557. Altitude: 8812 ft. Crops: corn,
wheat, beans; livestock.

SAN FRANCISCO LA UNIÓN. Municipio in the department
of Quezaltenango in southwestern Guatemala. The cabecera is located in the north central part of the department, about seven miles north of Quezaltenango.
Population: 2906. Altitude: 9086 ft. Crops: corn,
wheat, some vegetables.

SAN FRANCISCO ZAPOTITLÁN. Municipio in the department of Suchitepequez in southwestern Guatemala.
The cabecera, in the Pacific piedmont, is located four
miles north-northwest of Mazatenango. Population:
7884. Altitude: 2099 ft. Crops: coffee, sugar cane,
grain.

SAN GABRIEL. Municipio in the department of Suchitepequez in southwestern Guatemala. The cabecera is two
miles south of Mazatenango. Population: 1518. Altitude: 951 ft. Crops: coffee, cacao, grain, fodder
grasses.

SAN GASPAR IXCHIL. Municipio in the department of Huehuetenango in western Guatemala. The cabecera is
located in the southwestern part of the department, on
the Cuilco River. Population: 2003. Altitude: 5592
ft. Crops: corn, beans, yucca, tomatoes, chile,
sugar cane, sweet potatoes.

SAN ILDEFONSO IXTAHUACÁN. Municipio in the department of Huehuetenango in western Guatemala. Its cabecera is near the Cuilco River, 21 miles west-northwest of Huehuetenango. Population: 11,431. Altitude: 5600 ft. Crops: coffee, sugar cane, fruit,
vegetables.

SAN JACINTO. Municipio in the department of Chiquimula
in eastern Guatemala. Its cabecera is located in the
central part of the department, on the highway between
Chiquimula and Quezaltepeque. Population: 5843.
Altitude: 1607 ft. Crops: corn, beans, sugar cane.

SAN JERÓNIMO. Municipio in the department of Baja Verapaz in central Guatemala. The cabecera, in the northern highlands, is six miles southeast of Salama. Market center; alcohol distilling. It was a wine-producing
center in the 17th century. Population: 6208. Altitude: 3277 ft. Crops: coffee, sugar cane, grain;
livestock.

SAN JOSÉ, FRAY ADRIÁN DE [pseudonym] see IRISARRI,
ANTONIO JOSÉ DE.

SAN JOSÉ. 1) Municipio in the department of El Petén in
northern Guatemala. The cabecera is located on the
western bank of Lake Petén, near San Andrés. The

road to Tikal and Uaxactún begins here. Population:
564. Altitude: 377 ft. Crops: sugar cane, corn,
beans, rice, tomatoes, arum, yams.
   2) Municipio in the department of Escuintla in
southern Guatemala. Its cabecera is the principal
Guatemalan port on the Pacific Ocean for the shipment
of coffee, sugar and lumber. It is located 26 miles
south of Escuintla. Rail terminus; tropical tourist
resort. Also called Puerto de San José. Population:
18,177. Altitude: 6 ft. Crops: cotton.

SAN JOSÉ ACATEMPA. Municipio in the department of
   Jutiapa in southeastern Guatemala. The cabecera is
   in the highlands, and on the Inter-American Highway,
   14 miles west of Jutiapa. Formerly called Azacualpa.
   Population: 6965. Altitude: 4619 ft. Crops: corn,
   beans; livestock.

SAN JOSÉ CHACAYA. Municipio in the department of Sololá in southwest central Guatemala. Its cabecera is
   located near Sololá, on the road to Totonicapán.
   Population: 662. Altitude: 7052 ft. Crops: corn,
   wheat, beans.

SAN JOSÉ DEL GOLFO. Municipio in the department of
   Guatemala in south central Guatemala. Its cabecera
   is located 12 miles northeast of Guatemala City. Population: 2899. Altitude: 4701 ft. Crops: corn,
   black beans; livestock.

SAN JOSÉ EL IDOLO. Municipio in the department of
   Suchitepequez in southwestern Guatemala. Its cabecera
   is located in the central lowland part of the department, near the railroad and near the lowland route of
   the Inter-American Highway. Population: 4026. Altitude: 525 ft. Crops: corn, beans, rice, yucca, peanuts, several species of fruit.

SAN JOSÉ EL RODEO. Municipio in the department of San
   Marcos in southwestern Guatemala. The cabecera is
   located on the Inter-American Highway, 12 miles west-
   southwest of San Marcos. Population: 8576. Crops:
   coffee, sugar, grain; livestock.

SAN JOSÉ LA ARADA. Municipio in the department of Chiquimula in eastern Guatemala. Its cabecera is located in the west central part of the department, near

the railroad to El Salvador. Population: 5188. Altitude: 1423 ft. Crops: corn, beans.

SAN JOSÉ OJETENÁN. Municipio in the department of San Marcos in southwestern Guatemala. The cabecera is located in the north central part of the department, in the highlands of the Sierra Madre Mountain range. A woolen mill is in the aldea of Choanla. Population: 7525. Altitude: 10,004 ft. Crops: potatoes, corn, some wheat.

SAN JOSÉ PINULA. Municipio in the department of Guatemala in south central Guatemala. The cabecera is on the Inter-American Highway, nine miles southeast of Guatemala City. Population: 10,739. Altitude: 5610 ft. Crops: corn, black beans; livestock.

SAN JOSÉ POAQUIL. Municipio in the department of Chimaltenango in south central Guatemala. The cabecera is 15 miles north-northwest of Chimaltenango. Population: 7809. Altitude: 6500 ft. Crops: grain, black beans.

SAN JUAN ALOTENANGO. Municipio in the department of Sacatepéquez in south central Guatemala. The cabecera is located on the Guacalate River, between Fuego and Agua volcanoes, and eight miles south-southwest of Antigua. Fuego Volcano may be ascended from here. Population: 6300. Altitude: 4514 ft. Crops: coffee, sugar cane.

SAN JUAN ATITÁN. Municipio in the department of Huehuetenango in western Guatemala. Its cabecera is located in the south central part of the department, not accessible by road. Near the cabecera are Mayan ruins. Population: 5405. Altitude: 8200 ft. Crops: corn, beans, coffee, potatoes.

SAN JUAN BAUTISTA. Municipio in the department of Suchitepéquez in southwestern Guatemala. Its cabecera is located in the western part of the department, at the intersection of the lowland route of the Inter-American Highway and the highway to the Pacific coast. Local manufacturing of wool yarn. Population: 1953. Altitude: 920 ft. Crop: corn.

SAN JUAN CHAMELCO. Municipio in the department of

Alta Verapaz in central Guatemala. The cabecera is
in the northern highlands of Guatemala, three miles
southeast of Cobán. Market center; net and rope
weaving. Population: 18,082. Altitude: 4530 ft.
Crops: coffee; livestock.

SAN JUAN COMALAPA see COMALAPA.

SAN JUAN COTZAL. Municipio in the department of El
    Quiché in west central Guatemala. The cabecera is
    at the eastern end of the Cuchumatanes Mountains, nine
    miles north-northeast of Sacapulas. Population:
    12,150. Altitude: 5250 ft. Crops: corn, beans,
    coffee, sugar cane; livestock.

SAN JUAN ERMITA. Municipio in the department of Chi-
    quimula in eastern Guatemala. Its cabecera is lo-
    cated in the central part of the department, near Chi-
    quimula. Population: 5500. Altitude: 1783 ft.
    Crops: corn, beans, coffee.

SAN JUAN IXCOY. Municipio in the department of Huehue-
    tenango in western Guatemala. The cabecera is lo-
    cated on the road north from Huehuetenango in the
    east central part of the department. Local manufac-
    ture of woolen shirts and capixayes. Population:
    6511. Altitude: 7203 ft. Crops: corn, wheat, beans,
    potatoes.

SAN JUAN LA LAGUNA. Municipio in the department of
    Sololá in southwest central Guatemala. The cabecera
    is located on the western shore of Lake Atitlán, seven
    and a half miles southwest of Sololá. Population:
    2351. Altitude: 4500 ft. Crops: corn, wheat, beans.

SAN JUAN OSTUNCALCO. Municipio in the department of
    Quezaltenango in southwestern Guatemala. The cabe-
    cera is on the Inter-American Highway, six miles
    west-northwest of Quezaltenango, in the agricultural
    region. Market center. Population: 16,078. Alti-
    tude: 8185 ft. Crops: coffee, sugar cane, grain;
    livestock.

SAN JUAN SACATEPEQUEZ. Municipio in the department
    of Guatemala in south central Guatemala. The cabe-
    cera is located ten miles northwest of Guatemala City.
    Agricultural center; textile weaving. Flower gardens;

zinc and lead mining nearby. Population: 35,588.
Altitude: 5814 ft. Crops: corn, coffee, sugar cane.

SAN JUAN TECUACO. Municipio in the department of Santa
Rosa in southern Guatemala. The cabecera, in the
Pacific Piedmont, is eight miles east of Chiquimulilla.
Population: 3349. Altitude: 1558 ft. Crops: fodder
grasses; livestock.

SAN LORENZO. 1) Municipio in the department of San Marcos
in southwestern Guatemala. The cabecera is seven
miles northeast of San Marcos. Population: 1357.
Altitude: 689 ft. Crops: corn, wheat, vegetables.
     2) Municipio in the department of Suchitepe-
quez in southwestern Guatemala. The cabecera, in the
Pacific piedmont, is four miles south-southwest of
Maztenango. Population: 3091. Altitude: 722 ft.
Crops: grain; livestock.

SAN LUCAS SACATEPEQUEZ. Municipio in the department
of Sacatepequez in south central Guatemala. The cabecera is located on the Inter-American Highway, five
miles east-northeast of Antigua. Population: 3474.
Altitude: 8924 ft. Crops: grain, beans, fruit.

SAN LUCAS TOLIMÁN. Municipio in the department of Sololá in southwest central Guatemala. Its cabecera is
located on the southeastern shore of Lake Atitlán, five
miles east-northeast of the town of Atitlán. Ascent of
Atitlán and Tolimán volcanoes starts here. Population:
6797. Altitude: 4000 ft. Crops: coffee, sugar cane.

SAN LUIS. Municipio in the department of El Petén in
northern Guatemala. The cabecera is located 55 miles
south-southeast of Flores. Agriculture, lumbering.
Population: 9341. Altitude: 1558 ft. Crops: corn,
beans, rice, tropical fruit.

SAN LUIS JILOTEPEQUE. Municipio in the department of
Jalapa in east central Guatemala. In the highlands,
the cabecera is 15 miles east of Jalapa. Population:
12,832. Altitude: 2562 ft. Crops: corn, beans.

SAN MANUEL CHAPARRÓN. Municipio in the department
of Jalapa in east central Guatemala. The cabecera,
located in the highlands, is 17 miles southeast of Ja-

lapa. Population: 4191. Altitude: 3011 ft. Crops: corn, beans; livestock.

SAN MARCOS. 1) Department located in southwestern Guatemala. Its capital is San Marcos. On the Mexican border in the western highlands, it slopes southward to the coastal plain, with a short Pacific coast. It is drained by the Suchiate River on the southwest border, and the Naranjo River in the south. Tacana and Tajumulco are the two main volcanoes. Crops are: coffee, rice, corn, bananas, sugar cane in the coastal plain, with corn, beans, wheat and sheep raising in the highlands. Industries are textile milling and salt working. The main towns are San Marcos, San Pedro, Ocos, and Ayutla, the railroad terminus on the Mexican border. There are 29 municipios in the department: Ayutla, Catarina, Comitancillo, Concepción Tutuapa, Esquipulas Palo Gordo, Ixchiguán, Malacatán, Nuevo Progreso, Ocos, Pajapita, El Quetzal, La Reforma, Río Blanco, San Antonio Sacatepequez, San Cristóbal Cucho, San José el Rodeo, San José Ojetenán, San Lorenzo, San Marcos, San Miguel Ixtahuacán, San Pablo, San Pedro Sacatepequez, San Rafael Pie de la Cuesta, Sibinal, Sipacapa, Tacana, Tajumulco, Tejutla, El Tumbador. Population in 1950 was 232,591; in 1964 it was 337,117; projected to 1980 at 503,600. Area: 1463 square miles.

2) Municipio in the department of San Marcos in southwestern Guatemala. In the western highlands, the cabecera is on the Inter-American Highway, 20 miles west-northwest of Quezaltenango. Important market center in the coffee zone; has an airport, radio station, and a notable government building. Population: 13,705. Altitude: 8136 ft. Crops: coffee, corn, wheat, vegetables.

SAN MARCOS LA LAGUNA. Municipio in the department of Sololá in southwest central Guatemala. The cabecera is located on the northwestern shore of Lake Atitlán, five miles southwest of Sololá. Population: 709. Altitude: 5400 ft. Crops: fruit, grain.

SAN MARTÍN JILOTEPEQUE. Municipio in the department of Chimaltenango in south central Guatemala. The cabecera is 12 miles north of Chimaltenango. Market center; cotton weaving, jug making. Thermal springs (iron sulphate) nearby. Population: 26,822. Altitude:

5900 ft.   Crops: grain, beans, sugar cane; livestock
raising.

SAN MARTÍN SACATEPEQUEZ.   Municipio in the department of Quezaltenango in southwestern Guatemala.   The
cabecera is located eight miles west-southwest of Quezaltenango.   Population: 7357.   Altitude: 7798 ft.
Crops: coffee, sugar cane, grain.

SAN MARTÍN ZAPOTITLÁN.   Municipio in the department
of Retalhuleu in southwestern Guatemala.   In the Pacific piedmont, the cabecera is located on the Samala
River, seven miles northeast of Retalhuleu.   Population: 2551.   Altitude: 1719 ft.   Crops: coffee, sugar
cane, grain.

SAN MATEO.   Municipio in the department of Quezaltenango
in southwestern Guatemala.   The cabecera is located
on the Inter-American Highway, five miles west-northwest of Quezaltenango.   Population: 1095.   Altitude:
8400 ft.   Crops: corn, wheat, fodder grasses; livestock.

SAN MATEO IXTATÁN.   Municipio in the department of Huehuetenango in western Guatemala.   The cabecera is in
the northern Cuchumatanes Mountains, 35 miles north
of Huehuetenango.   Salt production, sheep raising and
wool.   Population: 12,022.   Altitude: 8540 ft.   Crop:
wheat.

SAN MIGUEL ACATÁN.   Municipio in the department of
Huehuetenango in western Guatemala.   The cabecera is
located on the western slope of the Cuchumatanes Mountains, 29 miles north-northwest of Huehuetenango.   Industries: hat and rope making, flour milling, lead
mining nearby.   Population: 12,921.   Altitude: 6020
ft.

SAN MIGUEL CHICAJ.   Municipio in the department of Baja
Verapaz in central Guatemala.   The cabecera, a market center, is in the northern highlands, four miles
west of Salama.   Population: 7253.   Altitude: 3600
ft.   Crops: sugar cane, grain; livestock.

SAN MIGUEL DUEÑAS.   Municipio in the department of
Sacatepequez in south central Guatemala.   Its cabecera
is located at the foot of Acatenango Volcano, five miles

southwest of Antigua. Beekeeping and honey production. Population: 3493. Altitude: 4724 ft. Crops:
coffee, sugar cane, grain.

SAN MIGUEL IXTAHUACAN. Municipio in the department
of San Marcos in southwestern Guatemala. The cabecera is in the Sierra Madra Mountains, 20 miles north
of San Marcos. Population: 9657. Altitude: 6700 ft.
Crops: wheat, corn; livestock.

SAN MIGUEL PANÁN. Municipio in the department of Suchitepequez in southwestern Guatemala. The cabecera is
located in the north central part of the department, 15
miles east of Mazatenango. Population: 2900. Altitude: 1148 ft. Crops: coffee, cacao, sugar cane,
corn, beans, rice.

SAN MIGUEL PETAPA. Municipio in the department of
Guatemala in south central Guatemala. The cabecera
is located ten miles south-southwest of Guatemala City,
near the northern shore of Lake Amatitlan. Population: 3375. Altitude: 3806 ft. Crops: coffee, sugar
cane, fodder grasses; livestock.

SAN MIGUEL POCHUTA see POCHUTA.

SAN MIGUEL SIGÜILA. Municipio in the department of
Quezaltenango in southwestern Guatemala. The cabecera is located in the central part of the department,
nine miles west-northwest of Quezaltenango. Population: 2002. Altitude: 8036 ft. Crops: corn, wheat,
vegetables.

SAN MIGUEL TUCURU see TUCURU.

SAN MIGUEL USPANTÁN. Municipio in the department of
El Quiché in west central Guatemala. The cabecera,
in the east outlier of the Cuchumatanes Mountains, is
17 miles east-northeast of Sacapulas. Population:
29,519. Altitude: 6033 ft. Crops: coffee, sugar
cane, corn; livestock.

SAN PABLO. Municipio in the department of San Marcos in
southwestern Guatemala. Its cabecera is located on the
Inter-American Highway, 14 miles west-southwest of
San Marcos. Population: 15,279. Crops: coffee,
sugar cane, grain.

SAN PABLO JOCOPILAS.   Municipio in the department of
    Suchitepequez in southwestern Guatemala.   The cabe-
    cera is located in the Pacific piedmont, five miles
    northeast of Mazatenango.   Population: 5534.   Alti-
    tude: 2066 ft.   Crops: coffee, sugar cane; livestock.

SAN PABLO LA LAGUNA.   Municipio in the department of
    Sololá in southwest central Guatemala.   The cabecera
    is located on the northwest shore of Lake Atitlán, five
    and a half miles southwest of Sololá.   Center of local
    henequen industry; hammock, net making.   Population:
    1773.   Altitude: 4000 ft.   Crops: oats, corn, beans.

SAN PEDRO AYAMPUC.   Municipio in the department of
    Guatemala in south central Guatemala.   Its cabecera
    is located ten miles north-northeast of Guatemala City.
    Founded in 1549.   Population: 9534.   Altitude: 3999
    ft.   Crops: sugar cane.

SAN PEDRO CARCHA.   Municipio in the department of Alta
    Verapaz in central Guatemala.   The cabecera is in the
    northern highlands, three miles east of Cobán.   Mar-
    ket center; weaving; pottery making.   Population:
    69,748.   Altitude: 4200 ft.   Crops: coffee; livestock.

SAN PEDRO JOCOPILAS.   Municipio in the department of
    El Quiché in west central Guatemala.   Its cabecera is
    located nine miles north of Santa Cruz del Quiché on
    the main highway.   Population: 8935.   Altitude: 7003
    ft.   Crops: corn, beans.

SAN PEDRO LA LAGUNA.   Municipio in the department of
    Sololá in southwest central Guatemala.   Its cabecera
    is located on the western shore of Lake Atitlán, at the
    northern foot of San Pedro Volcano, five miles north-
    west of Atitlán.   Fisheries.   Population: 3713.   Alti-
    tude: 5269 ft.   Crops: grain, beans, tomatoes.

SAN PEDRO NECTA.   Municipio in the department of Hue-
    huetenango in western Guatemala.   The cabecera is on
    the western slope of the Cuchumatanes Mountains, 24
    miles west-northwest of Huehuetenango.   Population:
    8354.   Altitude: 4950 ft.   Crops: sugar cane, corn,
    wheat.

SAN PEDRO PINULA.   Municipio in the department of Ja-
    lapa, in east central Guatemala.   Its cabecera is in

highlands, nine miles east of Jalapa. Population: 20,670. Altitude: 3330 ft. Crops: corn, beans.

SAN PEDRO RIVER. In Peten department, it flows about 200 miles west, then northwest and into the Usumacinta River in Mexico.

SAN PEDRO SACATEPEQUEZ. Municipio in the department of Guatemala in south central Guatemala. A market town, the cabecera is located nine miles west-northwest of Guatemala City. Tile making; textiles. Population: 8720. Altitude: 6890 ft. Crops: corn, black beans.

SAN PEDRO SACATEPEQUEZ. Municipio in the department of San Marcos in southwest Guatemala. The cabecera is located on the Naranjo River and on the Inter-American Highway, just east of San Marcos. Market center; government textile school. Population: 25,189. Altitude: 8136 ft. Crops: grain, fodder grasses; livestock.

SAN PEDRO SOLOMA. Municipio in the department of Huehuetenango in western Guatemala. The cabecera is located on the eastern slope of the Cuchumatanes Mountains, 26 miles north of Huehuetenango. Population: 11,837. Altitude: 7438 ft. Crops: corn, wheat; livestock.

SAN PEDRO VOLCANO. Altitude: 9921 feet. Inactive, it is in southwest central Guatemala near Lake Atitlán, two miles south of San Pedro.

SAN PEDRO YEPOCAPA. Municipio in the department of Chimaltenango in south central Guatemala. The cabecera is 15 miles south-southwest of Chimaltenango. Population: 11,026. Altitude: 3999 ft. Crops: coffee, sugar cane, grain.

SAN RAFAEL LA INDEPENDENCIA. Municipio in the department of Huehuetenango in western Guatemala. The cabecera is located in the central part of the department, at the terminus of the highway north from Huehuetenango. Lead mining nearby. Population: 5067. Altitude: 7796 ft. Crops: corn, wheat, beans.

SAN RAFAEL LAS FLORES. Municipio in the department

of Santa Rosa in southern Guatemala. The cabecera,
in the highlands, is located 15 miles north-northeast
of Cuilapa. Population: 3510. Altitude: 4500 ft.
Crops: corn, cotton, fodder grasses; livestock.

SAN RAFAEL PETZAL. Municipio in the department of
Huehuetenango in western Guatemala. The cabecera
is located in the southern part of the department, eight
miles west of Huehuetenango. Population: 2046. Altitude: 5704 ft. Crops: corn, beans, coffee, sugar
cane.

SAN RAFAEL PIE DE LA CUESTA. Municipio in the de-
partment of San Marcos in southwestern Guatemala.
In the Pacific piedmont, the cabecera is located on the
Inter-American Highway, eight miles west-southwest
of San Marcos. Population: 7882. Altitude: 4405 ft.
Crops: coffee, sugar cane, grain.

SAN RAYMUNDO. Municipio in the department of Guatemala in south central Guatemala. The cabecera is 12
miles north-northwest of Guatemala City. Pottery making (jugs) and textiles. Founded late 16th century.
Sometimes spelled San Raimundo. Population: 8616.
Altitude: 6000 ft. Crops: sugar cane, corn, black
beans.

SAN SEBASTIÁN. Municipio in the department of Retalhuleu
in southwestern Guatemala. In the Pacific piedmont,
the cabecera is on the railroad, two miles northeast
of Retalhuleu. Lumbering. Population: 8564. Altitude: 1020 ft. Crops: coffee, sugar cane, grain,
cacao; livestock.

SAN SEBASTIÁN COATÁN. Municipio in the department of
Huehuetenango in western Guatemala. The cabecera is
located in the north central part of the department and
is inaccessible by road. Some woolen industry. Population: 5909. Altitude: 7708 ft. Crops: wheat,
corn, beans, potatoes.

SAN SEBASTIÁN HUEHUETENANGO. Municipio in the department of Huehuetenango in western Guatemala. The
cabecera is located in the southern part of the department, 12 miles west of Huehuetenango. Population:
6565. Altitude: 5672 ft. Crops: corn, beans.

SAN VICENTE MARTIR   see   SAN VICENTE PACAYA.

SAN VICENTE PACAYA.   Municipio in the department of
    Escuintla in southern Guatemala.   The cabecera is lo-
    cated at the eastern foot of the Pacaya Volcano, 12
    miles east-northeast of Escuintla.   Ascent of the vol-
    cano begins here.   Formerly called San Vicente Mar-
    tir.   Population: 5185.   Altitude: 5052 ft.   Crops:
    coffee, corn, wheat.

SANARATE.   Municipio in the department of El Progreso in
    east central Guatemala.   In the highlands, the cabecera
    is located on a railroad, nine miles west-southwest of
    El Progreso.   Market center.   Population: 13,767.
    Altitude: 2663 ft.   Crops: corn, beans, sugar cane;
    livestock.

SÁNCHEZ, DIEGO.   On the conquest, he later founded a
    woolen mill at Almolonga, and mined metals near
    Quezaltenango.

SÁNCHEZ, SERAPIO.   A member of the faculty of the Uni-
    versity of San Carlos, he was appointed to attend the
    Assembly of September, 1821, to draw up the Acta de
    Independencia.   He wrote many religious tracts, some
    under the name El Hermano Serapio.

SANDE, FRANCISCO DE.   Governor, 1593-1596.   He was
    disliked by the Cabildo of Guatemala because he abol-
    ished one of their more profitable duties, that of "fiel
    ejecutor."   The office had been rotated among the
    members of the Cabildo.   It was made appointive by
    Governor Sande.

SANDOVAL, LISANDRO, 1862-1946.   Engineer and philolo-
    gist, born in San Francisco, he was on the border
    commission to settle the Honduran boundary dispute.
    Active as an educator, he wrote several books, includ-
    ing Monografía filológica (1935), Semántica guatemal-
    ense (1941), and Diccionario de raíces griegas y
    latinas ... (1930-31).

SANDOVAL, MARIANO [pseudonym]   see   RODRÍGUEZ
    CERNA, JOSÉ.

SANSARE.   Municipio in the department of El Progreso in
    east central Guatemala.   In the highlands, the cabecera

is seven miles south-southwest of El Progreso. Population: 6547. Altitude: 2624 ft. Crops: corn, beans, sugar cane; livestock.

SANTA ANA. Municipio in the department of El Petén in northern Guatemala. The cabecera is located on the road between Flores and Río Sarstun. Population: 311. Altitude: 627 ft. Crops: corn, beans, sugar cane.

SANTA ANA HUISTA. Municipio in the department of Huehuetenango in western Guatemala. The cabecera is located near the Mexican border and is inaccessible by road. Population: 3327. Altitude: 2624 ft. Crops: corn, beans, coffee, some sugar cane.

SANTA APOLONIA. Municipio in the department of Chimaltenango in south central Guatemala. The cabecera is located on a branch of the Inter-American Highway, three miles northeast of Tecpán. Population: 3457. Altitude: 7280 ft. Crops: corn, wheat, black beans.

SANTA BÁRBARA. 1) Municipio in the department of Huehuetenango in western Guatemala. The cabecera is located in the south central part of the department, not accessible by road. Population: 6379. Altitude: 7298 ft. Crops: corn, beans
     2) Municipio in the department of Suchitepequez in southwestern Guatemala. In the Pacific piedmont, the cabecera is located 20 miles east-southeast of Mazatenango. Population: 11,457. Altitude: 1371 ft. Crops: coffee, sugar cane, grain; livestock, lumbering.

SANTA CATARINA BARAHONA. Municipio in the department of Sacatepequez in south central Guatemala. The cabecera is located at the northeast foot of Acatenango Volcano, five miles west-southwest of Antigua. Population: 933. Altitude: 4741 ft. Crops: coffee, sugar cane, grain.

SANTA CATARINA IXTAHUACÁN. Municipio in the department of Sololá in southwest central Guatemala. Its cabecera is on the Nahualate River, nine miles west of Sololá. Sometimes called Santa Catalina. Population: 12,628. Altitude: 7610 ft. Crops: corn, beans.

SANTA CATARINA MITA. Municipio in the department of
Jutiapa in southeast Guatemala. The cabecera is located in the highlands on the Ostua River (an inlet of
Lake Güija), 15 miles northeast of Jutiapa. Population: 13,754. Altitude: 2296 ft. Crops: corn,
beans; livestock.

SANTA CATARINA PALOPO. Municipio in the department
of Sololá in southwest central Guatemala. The cabecera is located on the northern shore of Lake Atitlán,
four and a half miles southeast of Sololá. Reed-mat
weaving; fishing; crabbing. Sometimes called Santa
Catalina Palopo. Population: 879. Altitude: 5184 ft.

SANTA CATARINA PINULA. Municipio in the department
of Guatemala in south central Guatemala. The cabecera is five miles south-southeast of Guatemala City.
Sometimes called Santa Catalina. Population: 9950.
Altitude: 5499 ft. Crops: corn; livestock.

SANTA CLARA LA LAGUNA. Municipio in the department
of Sololá in southwest central Guatemala. Its cabecera
is located near the west end of Lake Atitlán, eight
miles west-southwest of Sololá. Basket weaving.
Population: 2263. Altitude: 6234 ft. Crops: corn,
wheat, beans.

SANTA CLARA VOLCANO. Altitude: 9186 ft. Inactive volcano in southwest central Guatemala near Lake Atitlán.
It is four miles southwest of San Pedro.

SANTA CRUZ, ROSENDO, 1915-1945. A Guatemalan author
and newspaperman, he was editor of Nuestro Diario
(1933-36) and of Diario de Centro América (1936-44).
He is best known for his novel, Cuando cae la noche
(1943) and short stories, Tierras de lumbre (1938) and
Ramón Gallardo (1944).

SANTA CRUZ BALANYA. Municipio in the department of
Chimaltenango in south central Guatemala. Its cabecera is five miles northwest of Chimaltenango. Population: 2379. Altitude: 5085 ft. Crops: Corn,
wheat, black beans.

SANTA CRUZ BARILLAS. Municipio in the department of
Huehuetenango in western Guatemala. The cabecera
is on the eastern slope of the Cuchumatanes Mountains,

11 miles east-southeast of San Mateo Ixtatán. Population: 19,149. Altitude: 4800 ft. Crops: coffee, sugar cane, grain; livestock.

SANTA CRUZ DEL QUICHÉ. Municipio in the department of El Quiché in west central Guatemala. In the western highlands, the cabecera (also the capital of the department) is about 50 miles northwest of Guatemala City. Market center. Ruins of Utatlán, ancient capital of the Quiché Indians, are two miles northwest. Population: 30,576. Altitude: 6250 ft. Crops: corn, beans; livestock.

SANTA CRUZ LA LAGUNA. Municipio in the department of Sololá in southwest central Guatemala. The cabecera is located on the northern shore of Lake Atitlán, three miles southwest of Sololá. Population: 1350. Altitude: 4000 ft. Crops: grain, beans.

SANTA CRUZ MULUA. Municipio in the department of Retalhuleu in southwestern Guatemala. In the Pacific piedmont, its cabecera is three miles east-northeast of Retalhuleu. On railroad, junction for rail branch to San Felipe. Population: 4347. Altitude: 1276 ft. Crops: coffee, sugar cane, grain; livestock.

SANTA CRUZ NARANJO. Municipio in the department of Santa Rosa in southern Guatemala. In the Pacific piedmont, the cabecera is eight miles northwest of Cuilapa. Population: 5731. Altitude: 3500 ft. Crops: corn, beans; livestock.

SANTA CRUZ VERAPAZ. Municipio in the department of Alta Verapaz in central Guatemala. The cabecera is located 13 miles south of Cobán, on the main road to Cobán. Population: 5866. Altitude: 4612 ft. Crops: corn, beans, cane, coffee.

SANTA EULALIA. Municipio in the department of Huehuetenango in western Guatemala. The cabecera is located in the north central part of the department, not accessible by road. Population: 10,536. Altitude: 8515 ft. Crops: corn, wheat, beans, potatoes.

SANTA ISABEL RIVER see PASIÓN RIVER.

SANTA LUCÍA COTZUMALGUAPA. Municipio in the depart-

ment of Escuintla in southern Guatemala. The cabecera is on the railroad, 15 miles west of Escuintla.
Road center; sawmilling nearby; sugar mill at El Baul.
Population: 36,731. Altitude: 1164 ft. Crops:
sugar cane, coffee, grain; livestock.

SANTA LUCÍA LA REFORMA. Municipio in the department
of Totonicapán in west central Guatemala. The cabecera is located in the northeastern part of the department, on the El Quiché border. Population: 4530.
Altitude: 6068 ft. Crops: corn, beans.

SANTA LUCÍA MILPAS ALTAS. Municipio in the department of Sacatepequez in south central Guatemala.
The cabecera is located three miles east of Antigua.
Population: 1831. Altitude: 6293 ft. Crops: grain,
beans, fruit.

SANTA LUCÍA UTATLÁN. Municipio in the department of
Sololá in southwest central Guatemala. Its cabecera
is five miles west of Sololá. Population: 6018. Altitude: 8199 ft. Crops: corn, beans.

SANTA MARÍA CAHABÓN. Municipio in the department of
Alta Verapaz in central Guatemala. In the northern
highlands, the cabecera is on the Cahabón River, 30
miles east-northeast of Cobán. Population: 21,456.
Crops: coffee, livestock.

SANTA MARÍA CHIQUIMULA. Municipio in the department
of Totonicapán in west central Guatemala. The cabecera is located eight miles north-northeast of Totonicapán. Market center. Population: 15,313. Altitude: 6601 ft. Crops: corn, wheat, beans.

SANTA MARÍA DE JESÚS. Municipio in the department of
Sacatepequez in south central Guatemala. The cabecera
is located at the northern foot of Agua Volcano, five
miles southeast of Antigua. Ascent of Agua Volcano
starts here. Cotton weaving. Population: 5793. Altitude: 8596 ft. Crops: vegetables, corn, beans.

SANTA MARÍA IXHUATÁN. Municipio in the department of
Santa Rosa in southern Guatemala. In the Pacific pied-
mont, its cabecera is located six miles southeast of
Cuilapa. Population: 11,304. Altitude: 4035 ft.
Crops: coffee, sugar cane; livestock.

SANTA MARÍA VISITACIÓN. Municipio in the department of
Sololá in southwest central Guatemala. The cabecera
is located near the Nahualate River, one and a half
miles northwest of Santa Clara. Basket weaving.
Population: 640. Altitude: 6929 ft. Crops: corn,
beans.

SANTA MARÍA VOLCANO. Altitude: 12,362 ft. Active volcano, located in Quezaltenango department, six miles
south-southwest of Quezaltenango. Last active in 1929,
its eruption of 1902 destroyed Quezaltenango. The village of Santa María is at the southeastern foot of the
volcano.

SANTA ROSA. Department in southern Guatemala; its capital is Cuilapa. On the Pacific piedmont, it slopes
south to the coastal plain. It is drained by the Esclavos River. In the department are located Lake Ayarza
and the volcanoes Tecuamburro and Junaitepeque. In
the highlands the crops are corn, beans. Crops of the
lower areas are coffee, sugar cane, sesame, rice.
Cattle are raised in the fodder grass area. The Chiquimulilla Canal serves the coastal trade with fish and
salt. Main centers are Cuilapa, on the Inter-American Highway, and Chiquimulilla and Guazacapán.
There are 14 municipios in the department: Barberena,
Casillas, Chiquimulilla, Cuilapa, Guazacapán, Nueva
Santa Rosa, El Oratorio, Pueblo Nuevo Viñas, San
Juan Tecuaco, San Rafael las Flores, Santa Cruz Naranjo, Santa María Ixhuatán, Santa Rosa de Lima,
Taxisco. Population in 1950 was 109,836. In 1964 the
population had grown to 157,341 and projected to 1980
is 253,600. Area: 1141 square miles.

SANTA ROSA DE LIMA. Municipio in the department of
Santa Rosa in southern Guatemala. In the Pacific
piedmont, the cabecera is on the Esclavos River, eight
miles north of Cuilapa. Department capital until 1871.
Population: 6791. Altitude: 3103 ft. Crops: coffee,
sugar cane, grain; livestock.

SANTIAGO. The name given to the first capital of Guatemala by Pedro de Alvarado. The capital was founded
on July 25, 1524, in a corn field near Iximche. The
site was changed while Alvarado was in Spain in 1527.
The original location was too high with too cold a climate, and it was too far from the mines and timber.

The new capital site was at Almolonga. See also
TECPÁN GUATEMALA.

SANTIAGO ATITLÁN. Municipio in the department of Sololá in southwest central Guatemala. The cabecera is
located on the southern shore of Lake Atitlán, ten
miles south-southwest of Sololá. Market center. Population: 12,938. Altitude: 4675 ft. Crops: coffee,
grain; beekeeping.

SANTIAGO CHIMALTENANGO. Municipio in the department
of Huehuetenango in western Guatemala. The cabecera
is located in the south central part of the department,
inaccessible by road. Population: 2645. Altitude:
7216 ft. Crops: corn, beans, potatoes, coffee, sugar
cane, bananas.

SANTIAGO SACATEPEQUEZ. Municipio in the department
of Sacatepequez in south central Guatemala. The
cabecera is five miles northeast of Guatemala City.
Population: 6357. Altitude: 7316 ft. Crops: grain,
beans, fruit.

SANTO DOMINGO SUCHITEPÉQUEZ. Municipio in the department of Suchitepéquez in southwestern Guatemala.
In the Pacific piedmont, the cabecera is five miles
south-southeast of Mazatenango. Population: 16,040.
Altitude: 699 ft. Crops: coffee, sugar cane, grain;
livestock, some lumbering.

SANTO DOMINGO XENACOJ. Municipio in the department
of Sacatepequez in south central Guatemala. The cabecera is located nine miles north-northeast of Antigua.
Market center. Population: 2476. Altitude: 8661 ft.
Crops: corn, black beans; livestock.

SANTO TOMÁS. In 1842, a Belgian company (Compagnie
belge de colonisation) obtained the rights to cover a
million acres of land between the Río Motagua, Lake
Izabal, and the Caribbean. For the land, the company
was to: pay ten annual installments of 16,000 pesos;
deliver to the government 2000 muskets and four large
cannon similar to those used at the time in the Belgian
army; assume one-fifth of the expenses of erecting a
port town at Santo Tomás; construct a wagon road from
there to the Motagua River; induce steamboat traffic on
the Motagua; and bring at least 100 families of five

members every year until a thousand families were
settled. The settlers were to immediately take up
Catholicism and were to be made citizens. They could
be governed by their own authorities and according to
their own laws and customs. About 600 settlers were
brought into Santo Tomás and a town started. The
Belgian crown subsidized the company but the project
failed, and in 1854, the state resumed control of the
property. Those settlers who did not die either returned to Europe or moved to more hospitable parts of
Guatemala.

SANTO TOMÁS CHICHICASTENANGO. Municipio in the department of El Quiché, in west central Guatemala. In
the western highlands, the cabecera is seven miles
south-southeast of Quiché. It became the market center of the Quiché Indians following the Spanish capture
of Quiché, and is much visited by tourists today. Cotton and wool weaving. Population: 36,046. Altitude:
6650 ft. Crops: corn, beans.

SANTO TOMÁS LA UNIÓN. Municipio in the department of
Suchitepéquez in southwestern Guatemala. In the Pacific piedmont, its cabecera is located ten miles northeast of Mazatenango. Transferred in 1944 from Quezaltenango department. Population: 3684. Altitude:
2854 ft. Crops: coffee, grain, tobacco; livestock.

SANTO TOMÁS VOLCANO. Altitude: 9793 feet. An inactive volcano, located in southwestern Guatemala on the
Quezaltenango-Retalhuleu-Suchitepéquez departmental
border. It is ten miles south-southeast of Quezaltenango. Hot springs resorts, Aguas Amargas and Fuentes Georginas, are on its northern slope.

SAPUYUL. Large, dark seeds from the Zapote Mamey tree,
used in beverages and in soap.

SARSTUN RIVER. It begins in Alta Verapaz department and
flows 75 miles east along the Guatemala-Belice border
and into the Gulf of Honduras at the village of Sarstoon. Mostly rubber and lumber shipments are transported along the river. Sometimes spelled Sarstoon.

SAULO [pseudonym] see AYCINENA, JUAN FERMÍN.

SAYAXCHE. Municipio in the department of El Petén in

northern Guatemala. The cabecera is on the Pasión
River, 35 miles southwest of Flores. Population:
1341. Altitude: 410 ft. Crops: livestock raising.

SAZ, ANTONIO DEL. A 17th-century Franciscan linguist,
he was educated in Guatemala. His works include
Compuesto en lengue Cakchiquel (1662) and Adiciones
al arte de la lengua de Guatemala ....

SECRETARIA DE INTEGRACIÓN ECONÓMICA DEL CENTRO-
AMÉRICA (S. I. E. C. A.). Founded in 1960 by Guate-
mala, El Salvador, Honduras and Nicaragua, with
Costa Rica joining later. An outgrowth of O. D. E. C. A. ,
it is an effort to further the economic integration of
Central America. The headquarters is in Guatemala
City.

SELEGUA RIVER. Begins near Huehuetenango and flows
northward before entering Mexico and eventually emptying into the Gulf of Mexico. The Inter-American Highway follows the river canyon for several miles. Also
called Río Trapichillo.

SENAHU. Municipio in the department of Alta Verapaz in
central Guatemala. The cabecera is in the northern
highlands, 29 miles east of Cobán. Population:
27,539. Altitude: 3850 ft. Crops: coffee, cacao,
sugar cane; livestock.

SENINLATIU RIVER. Begins near Chahal in Alta Verapaz
and forms part of the boundary between Alta Verapaz
and Petén. The Seninlatiu joins the Chiruchipec to
make up the Sarstún River.

SEÑOR DE PORTALES [pseudonym] see HERNÁNDEZ DE
LEÓN, FEDERICO.

SEROON see ZURRÓN.

SERVICIO COOPERATIVO INTERAMERICANO DE AGRICUL-
TURA (S. C. I. D. A.). Began in 1942 as a part of the
Institute of Inter-American Affairs, and expanded in
1945 into the Instituto Agropecuario Nacional to carry
out research and experimentation in agriculture. Little
was done between 1949 and 1955. In 1955, the institute was reorganized into S. C. I. D. A. and has been active in the agricultural development of Guatemala.

SERVICIO COOPERATIVO INTERAMERICANO DE CRÉDITO
AGRÍCOLA SUPERVISADO (S. C. I. C. A. S.). Beginning
in the post-revolutionary period, it is in competition
with B. N. A. in that it offers credit to small farmers,
primarily in the coastal and altaplano region. Most
of its resources come from loans of the Interamerican
Development Bank.

SERVICIO DE INTELLIGENCIA GUATEMALTECA (S. I. G.).
A partially secret government agency set up in 1955 to
watch over local communistic activities. It served the
purpose of government watchdog over any activities
possibly anti-governmental in nature.

SERVILLETA. A utility cloth used to wrap or cover food;
it differs from the tzut in that the servilleta is less
colorful, usually a basic white.

SHAMAN. The medicine man or witch doctor of the Mayas,
sometimes called Zahroi. He cures, foretells, and
acts as go-between on behalf of man when speaking to
the gods. Most specialize in one area but do practice
in all fields. The skill is usually passed from father
to son. Their counsel is requested for judgment on
all questions, from individual grievances to community
problems. Sometimes called "chiman" in northern
Guatemala. Not to be confused with a "brujo" (q.v.).

SIBILIA. Municipio in the department of Quezaltenango in
southwestern Guatemala. The cabecera is located in
the northern part of the department on the San Marcos
border. Some local industry: weaving, tailoring, car-
pentry. Population: 3654. Altitude: 9184 ft. Crops:
corn, wheat, vegetables, some fruit.

SIBINAL. Municipio in the department of San Marcos in
southwestern Guatemala. In the Sierra Madre, the
cabecera is located near the Mexican border, 19 miles
northwest of San Marcos. Population: 5734. Altitude:
8465 ft. Crops: coffee, sugar cane, grain.

SIERRA, JOSEF DE. Architect and engineer, he revised
plans for the Cathedral in 1788 to include a vaulted
roof, rather than one of wood and tile as was originally planned. He started a gun factory in Antigua in
1798 and attempted to found a school of architecture in
Guatemala City, but returned to Spain (1802) before his

plans could be carried out.

SIERRA DE CHAMA-SANTA CRUZ.   A range of mountains
    located mostly in Alta Verapaz.   Extends to the Carib-
    bean coast and from east to west along the northern
    edge of Lake Izabal and the Polochic River.

SIERRA DE CHUACUS.   A spur of the Sierra Madre Moun-
    tains, extending eastward through the departments of
    Baja Verapaz and Quiché.

SIERRA DE LAS MINAS.   A range of mountains beginning in
    the highlands and extending along an easterly course to
    the Caribbean coast on the south bank of the Polochic
    River and Lake Izabal.

SIERRA DE LOS CUCHUMATANES.   A range of mountains
    in the departments of Huehuetenango and Quiché in
    northwestern Guatemala, extending about 100 miles
    southeast from the Mexican border.

SIERRA MADRE.   The main body of mountains entering from
    Mexico and extending about halfway through Guatemala.
    The range runs from northwest to southeast.   Taju-
    mulco, the highest peak in Central America, is in this
    range.

SIETE OREJAS VOLCANO.   Altitude: 11,054 ft.   Extinct,
    it is in the municipio of San Martín Sacatepequez near
    Quezaltenango.   Known by the Mams as Tuigucxingán.

SIJA   see   SAN CARLOS SIJA.

SILVA, CARMÉN P. DE, 184?-1900.   A Guatemalan journal-
    ist, he founded the journal El ideal and wrote literary
    pieces for other publications of his time.

SILVA, JESÚS, 1858-1928.   A Guatemalan pianist, he also
    conducted and composed for bands.

SINACAM.   A Cachiquel chief at Tecpán, he remained loyal
    to the Spanish until their injustices caused him to lead
    a rebellion in 1526.   The rebellion was put down by
    Portocarrero and Sinacam was imprisoned for 15 years.

SINDICATO CENTRAL DE ARTISTAS TEATRALES Y SIMI-
    LARES.   A non-affiliated union located in Guatemala

City led by Carlos Escobedo Rodríguez. It claimed
350 members in 1962.

SINDICATO DE ACCIÓN Y MEJOREMIENTO DE LOS FERRO-
CARRILEROS (S. A. M. F.).   A union which developed
in 1944 from a pre-revolutionary railway mutual aid
society.   After getting an effective start, the union became embroiled in an internal power struggle in the
early 1950's.   It has since that time been a non-affiliated union claiming in 1964 over 3200 members.   The
union publishes a bulletin called <u>SAMF</u>.

SINDICATO DE EMPRESA DE TRABAJADORES DE LA
COMPAÑÍA AGRÍCOLA DE GUATEMALA (S. E. T. -
C. A. G.) Organized in 1944 at the UFCo. Tiquisate
plantation.   In the revolutionary period, it had as
many as 5700 members and was affiliated with C. G. -
T. G. , although it did take independent action often-
times.   In 1962 its membership was down to 1300 because of restrictive governmental controls.   Also known
under its former title, Sindicato de Trabajadores de
Empresa de Tiquisate (S. T. E. T.).

SINDICATO DE EMPRESA DE TRABAJADORES DE LA
UNITED FRUIT COMPANY (S. E. T. U. F. C. O.).   The
UFCo. Pacific coast plantation (Bananera) labor union
with membership of 2500.   It is not affiliated with national organizations.

SINDICATO DE TRABAJADORES DE LA CERVECERÍA CEN-
TRO AMERICANA.   A non-affiliated brewery union located in Guatemala City which claimed over 500 members in 1964.

SINDICATO DE TRABAJADORES DE LA FÁBRICA DE HI-
LADOS Y TEJIDOS CANTEL.   Affiliated with the
C. S. G. , a factory union located in Quezaltenango,
claiming in 1962 almost 500 members.

SINDICATO DE TRABAJADORES DEL INSTITUTO GUATE-
MALTECA DE SEGURIDAD SOCIAL (S. T. I. G. S. S.).
The I. G. S. S. union located in Guatemala City, affiliated with C. S. G. and claiming in 1963 over 625 members.

SINDICATO DE TRABAJADORES EDUCACIONES DE GUATE-
MALA (S. T. E. G.).   Labor organization of school
teachers, formed in 1944, it became very influential

in the development of left-wing unionism in Guatemala in the early 1950's. It was disbanded in 1954.

SINDICATO GENERAL DE PANIFICADORES (S. G. P.). A bakers' union formed in the 1920's. It later became the F. R. T.

SINDICATO UNICO DE CHICLEROS Y LABORANTES EN MADERAS. A non-affiliated lumber and chicle union located in San Benitos, Petên. In 1962 it claimed over 500 members.

SINDICO MUNICIPAL. Legal adviser to the political leaders of a municipio during the revolutionary period.

SINIBALDI, ALEJANDRO M. President of Guatemala, 1885. At the death of J. R. Barrios, he took office as first designate, from April 3 until April 8, 1885. At the close of the war to unify Central America, El Salvador would not negotiate peace settlements with any of Barrios' ministers and a new government had to be set up to sign the peace settlement.

SIPACAPA. Municipio in the department of San Marcos in southwestern Guatemala. The cabecera is located in the northeastern part of the department; it is not accessible by road. Population: 4296. Altitude: 6462 ft. Crops: beans, corn, wheat, avocados, oranges, lemons.

SIQUINALA. Municipio in the department of Escuintla in southern Guatemala. In the Pacific piedmont, the cabecera is 11 miles west of Escuintla. Sugar cane mill at Pantaleon. Population: 8503. Altitude: 1092 ft. Crops: cacao, coffee, sugar cane, fodder grasses; livestock.

SOCIEDAD ECONÓMICA DE AMIGOS DE GUATEMALA. Founded in 1795, primarily through the efforts of Jacobo de Villa Urrutia. The Society's publication was the Gazeta de Guatemala. The Society became a leading spokesman in the struggle to improve education. To do this, it began an adult night school in 1797. In 1881, the Society and its building was taken over by the Ministerio de Fomento, which was organized to encourage and develop education in Guatemala.

213   Soconusco

SOCONUSCO   see CHIAPAS.

SOLARES, ENRIQUE, 1910- . A composer and pianist, he
    studied in Europe and the U.S. Compositions: Suite-
    miniatura (1938), Sonatina (1940-41), Preludio airos-
    toccata (1943) and a book, Estudio en formia de marcha
    (1947).

SOLÍS, IGNACIO, 1839-1912. Active in the government of
    Estrada Cabrera, he wrote an essay, Sobre el fomento
    de la inmigración y colonización extranjeras (1889).

SOLOLÁ. 1) Department in southwest central Guatemala. The
    capital is Sololá. In the central highlands, it is
    bounded on the west by the Nahualate River and the
    Madre Vieja River on the east. It includes Lake
    Atitlán and the volcanoes, Atitlán, Tolimán and San
    Pedro. Some cattle and hog raising, with crops of
    corn, beans and wheat. Coffee is grown on the south
    shore of the lake. Cotton and woolen milling; fishing
    on the lake. Chief centers are Sololá, Panajachel,
    Atitlán and San Lucas. Nineteen municipios: Concep-
    ción, Nahuala, Panajachel, San Andrés Semetabaj, San
    Antonio Palopa, San José Chacaya, San Juan la Laguna,
    San Lucas Tolimán, San Marcos la Laguna, San Pablo
    la Laguna, San Pedro la Laguna, Santa Catarina Ixta-
    huacán, Santa Catarina Palopo, Santa Clara la Laguna,
    Santa Cruz la Laguna, Santa Lucía Utatlán, Santa
    María Visitación, Santiago Atitlán, Sololá. Population
    in 1950 was 82,921; in 1964 it was 107,852, and pro-
    jected to 1980 is 154,800. Area: 409 square miles.
    See also ALTOS, LOS.
       2) Municipio in the department of Sololá in south-
    west central Guatemala. Near the northern shore of
    Lake Atitlán and on the Inter-American Highway, its
    cabecera is 45 miles west-northwest of Guatemala
    City. Trade center for local agricultural products;
    flour milling nearby. Population: 21,954. Altitude:
    6900 ft. Crops: vegetables, grain, coffee.

SOLOMA see SAN PEDRO SOLOMA.

SOLOMEC. A language group making up part of the Mame-
    an linguistic stock, located in Huehuetenango.

SOLÓRZANO, CARLOS, 1922- . A dramatist, he has

spent much of his life in Mexico. He has written
several plays and has compiled anthologies of plays
in addition to writing critical works. These include
Doña Beatriz (1951), El hechicero (1954), El crucifi-
cado (1957), Las manos de Dios (1957), El Sueño del
angel (1960), Teatro latinoamericano del siglo XX
(1961), Teatro guatemalteco (1964), and El teatro his-
panoamericano contemporaneo, 2 vols. (1964).

SON. The only well-defined Guatemalan dance that is an
authentic piece of folk music. It is a mixture of Indian and Spanish rhythm, having a short, jumpy six-
eighths measure. Variations of the central dance ex-
ist in Son Agarrado, having sad, expressive characteristics, or Son Chapín with the use of a marimba.

SOTO-HALL, MÁXIMO, 1871-1944. A Guatemalan novelist
and poet, he actually spent very little of his life in
Guatemala. His work is in the style of the naturalist
writers, with strong elements of the modernistic influence. He holds the distinction of having written El
problema, the first anti-U.S. novel of the Central American area. His works include Catalina; Don Diego
Portales (1935), La divina reclusa (1938), Los Mayas
(1937), La niña de Guatemala (1943) and many others.

SPINOLA, RAFAEL, 1865-1901. A Guatemalan poet, influenced by Rubén Darío.

STATE OF SIEGE (Estado de sitio). In an emergency, the
president has the power to suspend constitutional guar-
antees, and this, in the past, has provided administra-
tions with a legal means of staying in power. Particularly when organizations or influential persons
openly criticize the government, the state of siege
serves as a means to restrict the words and acts of
such critics.

STELAE. Sculptured monuments of the ancient Maya,
carved from limestone and erected throughout the lowland Maya area, usually every 20 years as ceremonial
time markers. Some are 15 to 20 feet tall, others
only four or five feet. The monuments served as cal-
endars; the earliest is found at Tikal and is dated
A.D. 317, while the most recent is in central Yucatan,
dated A.D. 909. Most Mayan sites have at least one
stelae. Tikal and Uaxactún have the most in number

and their stelae cover the longest time period of activity. Probably the stelae most easily accessible and
most ornamental are located at Quirigua.

STICK LOOM. Made of sticks and a broad strap or mecapal that goes around the hips and against which the
weaver sits or squats to give tension to the strings of
the loom. The end of the loom opposite the weaver is
attached to a tree or post. This is an indigenous loom,
operated usually by Indian women, but never by ladinas.
There are also small belt and head-band looms of this
nature, operated by both men and women. Also called
back-strap loom, telar de mano, or kiem.

SUCHIATE RIVER. It begins south of Ixchiguán and flows
about 100 miles southwest to enter the Pacific three
miles northwest of Ocos. The river forms a portion
of the boundary between Mexico and Guatemala.

SUCHITÁN VOLCANO. Altitude: 6699 feet. An extinct volcano in Jutiapa department in southeastern Guatemala,
11 miles northeast of Jutiapa. Last erupted in 1469.

SUCHITEPÉQUEZ. A department in southwestern Guatemala
on the Pacific coast. The capital is Mazatenango. In
the Pacific piedmont and coastal plain, it is drained
by the Nahualate and Madre Vieja Rivers. Crops are
coffee, sugar cane, cacao, rice and tobacco on the
mountain slopes; corn, beans and bananas on the coastal plains. Industries are sugar milling, lumbering,
textile milling, cotton ginning and oil extraction. The
chief towns are Mazatenango, Cuyotenango and San Antonio. Twenty municipios: Chicacao, Cuyotenango,
Mazatenango, Patulul, Pueblo Nuevo, Rio Bravo, Samayac, San Antonio Suchitepéquez, San Bernardino,
San Francisco Zapotitlán, San Gabriel, San José el
Idolo, San Juan Bautista, San Lorenzo, San Miguel
Panán, San Pablo Jocopilas, Santa Bárbara, Santo
Domingo Suchitepéquez, Santo Tomás la Unión, Zunilito. Population in 1950 was 124,403; in 1964 it was
185,489. The population projected to 1980 is 286,200.
Area: 969 square miles.

SUMPANGO. Municipio in the department of Sacatepequez in
south central Guatemala. On the Inter-American Highway, the cabecera is five miles north of Antigua.
Market center; soap and candle manufacturing. Popu-

lation: 8084. Altitude: 5974 ft. Crops: grain, black beans.

SUPREMO PODER EJECUTIVO. A ruling triumvirate of
   Central America between the time General Filísola left
   and Manual Arce began as President (July, 1823 through
   April, 1825). The SPE went through four changes of
   personnel as follows: First SPE: July-October, 1823
   --Pedro Molina, Juan Vincente Villacorta, Antonio
   Rivera Cabezas. Second SPE: October, 1823-Febru-
   ary, 1824--Juan Vincente Villacorta, José Santiago
   Milla, Tomás Antonio O'Horan. Third SPE: February-
   October, 1824--José del Valle, Tomás A. O'Horan,
   Manual José Arce. Fourth SPE: October, 1824-April,
   1825--José del Valle, Tomás A. O'Horan, José Manuel
   de la Cerda. There was no governor of the area of
   present-day Guatemala until Juan Barrundia took office
   in October, 1824.

SURCO. A furrow in a plowed or hoed field.

SUSTO see ESPANTO.

SUYACAL. A rain cape made from leaf segments of the
   Corozo Palm.

-T-

T.G.W. The Guatemalan National Radio network call letters.

TABLON. A square, terraced garden plot that is well fer-
   tilized and irrigated for intensive cultivation.

TACANA. Municipio in the department of San Marcos in
   southwestern Guatemala. In the Sierra Madre Mountains, the cabecera is located 27 miles northwest of
   San Marcos. Population: 28,030. Altitude: 8996 ft.
   Crops: corn, wheat; livestock.

TACANA VOLCANO. Altitude: 13,333 feet. Volcano on
   the Mexico-Guatemala border, in the Sierra Madres,
   19 miles northeast of Tapachula. Second highest mountain in Central America. Major eruptions occurred in
   1855 and 1878. It emits sulphuric gases.

TACTIC. Municipio in the department of Alta Verapaz, in

central Guatemala. In the northern highlands, the
cabecera is nine miles south of Cobán. Market center;
weaving, soap and candle making. Population: 8529.
Altitude: 4855 ft. Crops: coffee, sugar cane, corn,
beans.

TAHUAL VOLCANO. Altitude: 3476 feet. Extinct volcano
in the southernmost part of the department of Jalapa.

TAJUMULCO. Municipio in the department of San Marcos
in southwestern Guatemala. The cabecera is located
at the northern foot of Tajumulco Volcano, 11 miles
north-northwest of San Marcos. Population: 15,091.
Altitude: 6560 ft. Crops: coffee, sugar cane, grain.

TAJUMULCO VOLCANO. Altitude: 13,816 feet. Extinct
volcano and the highest mountain in Central America.
Located in San Marcos department in southwestern
Guatemala. It is climbed from San Marcos, nine miles
southeast. Sulphur deposits.

TALMIRO [pseudonym] see AYCINENA, JUAN FERMÍN.

TALPETATE, TELESFORO [pseudonym] see JUÁREZ
MUÑOZ, JOSÉ FERNANDO.

TAMAHU. Municipio in the department of Alta Verapaz in
central Guatemala. The cabecera is located in the
south central part of the department, on the road leading to El Estor. Nearby is a soda water plant. Population: 4679. Altitude: 3436 ft. Crops: coffee,
corn, beans, sugar cane.

TAMALE. A small cake of corn softened in lime water,
then ground and wrapped in corn husks and steamed
in a deep jar. The center filling of a tamale is well
seasoned meat and vegetables. Also called Tamal.

TAMENES. Indian carriers. The men who employ the use
of a tumpline to carry heavy weights on their backs
for great distances. This is an early colonial term
that applies to the present-day itinerant merchant.

TAMIRO [pseudonym] see AYCINENA, JUAN FERMÍN.

TAPAOJO. A heavy leather blind that is placed over the
eyes of a pack animal to keep him from bolting while

being loaded.

TAPISQUE. Grain harvest.

TAREA. A basis for judging the day's work of a laborer.
On the coffee finca it is usually an area of about one
cuerda, or 28 vara square, cleared of rubbish, weeds,
and second growth. See also CUADRILLERO.

TARRO. A giant bamboo, used in the construction of lowland house walls.

TATA. The familiar name used in reference to President
Jorge Ubico.

TAXES see ALCABALA.

TAXISCO. Municipio in the department of Santa Rosa in
southern Guatemala. In the coastal plain, the cabecera
is located six miles west of Chiquimulilla. Population:
14,033. Altitude: 702 ft. Crops: coffee, rice,
spices, corn; livestock raising center, dairying.

TAYASAL see SAN ANDRÉS ISLAND.

TEACHUC see TZUTUHIL.

TECPÁM see TECPÁN GUATEMALA.

TECPÁN-ATITLÁN see ANNALS OF THE CAKCHIQUELES.

TECPÁN GUATEMALA. Municipio in the department of
Chimaltenango in south central Guatemala. The cabecera is located 15 miles west-northwest of Chimaltenango. Market center; some cotton weaving; flour milling; saw milling. Site of the first capital of Guatemala
in 1524, called Santiago, built near the ruins of the
Indian capital, Iximche. Formerly called Tecpám.
Population: 20,107. Altitude: 7579 ft. Crops: corn,
beans, wheat, oats.

TECTITÁN. Municipio in the department of Huehuetenango
in western Guatemala. The cabecera is located in the
southwestern part of the department; is inaccessible by
road. Population: 3208. Altitude: 7150 ft. Crops:
corn, beans, sugar cane, bananas.

TECUACO   see   SAN JUAN TECUACO.

TECUAMBURRO VOLCANO.   Altitude: 6384 feet.   Extinct
    volcano located in Santa Rosa department in southern
    Guatemala.   It is 12 miles southwest of Cuilapa.

TECULUTÁN.   Municipio in the department of Zacapa in
    eastern Guatemala.   The cabecera is on the Motagua
    River, 11 miles west of Zacapa.   Several archaeologi-
    cal sites exist in the area.   Population: 4786.   Alti-
    tude: 820 ft.   Crops: sugar cane, corn, tomatoes,
    beans; much livestock raising.

TECUN UMAN, d. 1524.   Son of Kicab Tanub, leader of the
    Quichés.   King Kicab Tanub died while attempting to
    unite the Indians to meet the Spanish.   Tecun Uman
    then led a force of about 90,000 Quiché warriors to
    meet the Spanish under Pedro de Alvarado.   The native
    warriors were defeated in the first encounter on a
    plateau near Utatlán.   When the armies met a second
    time, Tecun Uman sought out and engaged Alvarado
    during the battle.   Tecum Uman was no match for a
    man on horseback and, although he fatally wounded the
    horse, he was slain by Alvarado on February 20, 1524.
    Tecun Uman remains the Indian hero of Guatemalan lit-
    erature because of his leadership.

TEJADA, FEDERICO SÁENZ DE, 1877-1928.   Minister of
    Protocol under Estrada Cabrera, he compiled the three-
    volume work, Colección de tratados de Guatemala and
    wrote Guatemala, agricultura, comercio e industria
    (1909).

TEJAR, EL.   Municipio in the department of Chimaltenango
    in south central Guatemala.   On the Inter-American
    Highway, the cabecera is located two and a half miles
    east-southeast of Chimaltenango.   Population: 2231.
    Altitude: 5600 ft.   Crops: corn, wheat, black beans.

TEJUTLA.   Municipio in the department of San Marcos in
    southwestern Guatemala.   The cabecera is on the head-
    stream of the Cuilco River, 11 miles north of San
    Marcos.   Population: 10,767.   Altitude: 8300 ft.
    Crops: corn, wheat, beans.

TELAR DE MANO   see   STICK LOOM.

TELETOR, CELSO NARCISO, 1891- . A linguist and Catholic priest, he has written Memorial de Tecpán-Atitlán
(1946), Epítome Quiché (1951), Apuntes para una monografía de rabinal (1955), and Diccionario castellano-
quiché (1959).

TEMASCAL. A sweat bath or hot water bath housed in a
low structure constructed from poles, mud and stones.
The foundation is usually excavated with a small opening in one side.

TEMPORADISTA JORNALERO. A migrant day laborer on a
finca or plantation, working on a temporary day-to-day
basis. See also CUADRILLERO.

TENANGO. A native word meaning "place of," i.e., Chimaltenango is the Place of Shields.

TEPEISCUINTE. A small, pestilent animal, valued as food.

TEPEUS, LOS. A literary society of the 1930's, made up
of Guatemalan poets. It comprised a loose circle and
had little impact upon its members or on Guatemalan
literature.

TERRASA Y REJÓN, DIONISIO [pseudonym] see IRISARRI,
ANTONIO JOSÉ DE.

TERRONISTAS. The group opposing the removal of the capital from Antigua to the present site in 1773, after the
destruction of Antigua by the earthquake.

TERTULIAS PATRIOTICAS. Patriotic groups formed in late
1821, to discuss the annexation proposal with Mexico.
Annexation did not occur until January, 1822, and from
these groups proponents of annexation found a basis
from which to work.

TEULES. An early name given the invading Spaniards by the
Indians.

THIRTEENTH OF NOVEMBER REVOLUTIONARY MOVE-
MENT see M.R.-13.

TIERRA CALIENTE. The hot region of Guatemala, below
1000 meters (3280 ft.) elevation. The annual temperature varies only slightly from the mean of 71.6° F.

TIERRA FRÍA.   The cooler region above 2000 meters (6562
ft.) elevation, where the annual temperature varies
little from the annual mean of 60.8° F.

TIERRA TEMPLADA.   The more temperate region between
the two extremes, where the annual mean temperature
ranges from 71.6 to about 60.8° F.

TIKAL.   Ruins located in the lowlands of Petén, near Lake
Petén.   This was the largest and oldest Mayan center
of northern Petén.   It dates from A.D. 292.   It is
noted for its great pyramid-temples, which range in
height from 143 feet to 229 feet, and for the long series of dated stelae.

TILAPA RIVER.   Begins in southwestern Guatemala on the
west slope of Santa María Volcano and flows about 50
miles south, then west, then south.   It forms the border between the departments of Quezaltenango and Retalhuleu, then empties into the Pacific two miles southwest of Ocos.   Called Ocoseto River in its upper
course.

TINAJAS.   Large vessels for transporting water.

TINAMIT.   Sometimes spelled Chinamit, it is the Indian
name for the municipio, as used in many of the more
rural areas.   This is not referring to the geographical region, but to the local political organization.

TIQUISATE.   Municipio in the department of Escuintla in
southern Guatemala.   The cabecera is on the Siquacán
River, 20 miles southeast of Mazatenango.   The center
of the banana growing area, it was developed in the
1940's as headquarters for the Pacific coast division
of U.F.Co. under the title Compañía Agrícola de Guatemala.   Population: 71,161.   Altitude: 326 ft.   Crops:
bananas, corn, beans, platanos, cotton.

TITHE.   In the Spanish colonies, a ten per cent tax levied
on agricultural products for the maintenance of the
Church.   A Papal Bull in 1501 gave the crown the right
to exact tithes for ecclesiastical purposes if the crown
would maintain and build churches.   The crown retained
one-ninth of the amount received.   The Indians were
usually exempt since they worked on an encomienda for
the Church, which took the place of the tax.

TIZATE.   A chalk cone on which to rub the fingers while
spinning cotton.

TOBÓN VOLCANO.   Altitude: 5905 feet.   An extinct volcano
in El Progreso department in east central Guatemala,
nine miles southeast of El Progreso.

TOCAXEPUAL.   The name of the fifth month in the Cakchiquel calendar, referring to the time of seed planting.

TODOS SANTOS CUCHUMATÁN.   Municipio in the department of Huehuetenango in western Guatemala.   The
cabecera is located on the west slope of the Cuchumatanes Mountains, 17 miles north-northwest of Huehuetenango.   Pottery making; textile weaving.   Population:
8514.   Altitude: 8041 ft.   Crops: corn, beans, wheat,
potatoes.

TOLIMÁN VOLCANO.   Altitude: 10,344 feet.   An inactive
volcano in Sololá department in southwestern Guatemala.
It is located near Lake Atitlán, three miles southwest
of San Lucas.   Last erupted in 1852.

TONALAMATL   see   TZOLKÍN.

TONELADA.   A unit of weight equal to 20 quintals or about
one ton.

TONIATIUH.   The Indian name for Pedro de Alvarado, meaning "the sun."   Also spelled Donadiu.

TORIELLO GARRIDO, GUILLERMO, 1911- .   Lawyer and
diplomat, he was a participant of the 1944 revolution
and served as Ambassador to Mexico and the U.S., as
representative to the San Francisco UN conference, the
OAS Caracas conference (1953), as foreign minister
(1953-54).   He wrote the widest known commentary on
the 1954 counter-revolution, entitled La batalla de
Guatemala (1955).

TORIELLO GARRIDO, JORGE.   The only civilian member
of the 1944-45 ruling triumvirate.   As a local business-
man, he was able to act as go-between for the military
and the anti-military students during planning stages.

TOTONICAPÁN.   1)   Department in west Central Guatemala.
Its capital is Totonicapán.   In the western highlands,

it is the highest department of Guatemala. It is
drained by the headstreams of the Chixoy River in the
north, and by the Samala River in the southwest.
Crops are corn, wheat, beans and fodder grasses.
There is some sheep raising. Flour milling is the
main industry; home industries are production of textiles, pottery, and furniture. The main centers are
Totonicapán and San Cristóbal. Eight municipios:
Momostenango, San Andrés Xecul, San Bartolo, San
Cristóbal Totonicapán, San Francisco el Alto, Santa
Lucía la Reforma, Santa María Chiquimula, Totonica-
pán. Population in 1950 was 99,354; in 1964 it was
142,637; and projected to 1980 is 227,100. Area:
409 square miles. Sometimes called Totonicapám.
See also ALTOS, LOS.

    2) Municipio in the department of Totonicapán
in west central Guatemala. Its cabecera is located 12
miles east-northeast of Quezaltenango. Market and
textile center; cotton and woolen mills; home handi-
crafts: pottery, furniture, leather goods. Sulphur
springs. Site of 1817 Indian uprising (see TXUL,
ANASTASIO). Population: 43,522. Altitude: 8215 ft.
Crops: corn, wheat.

TOTOPOSTE. A toasted tortilla, usually salted.

TOYACALES. Women's headgear, often in the form of
    strands of woolen cords, twisted or braided in the hair,
    with the ends falling down the side of the face or down
    the back of the head. Also known as Tuntún or Cintas.

TRADICIÓN. A literary term referring to an anecdote or
    short essay based on history or legend, similar to the
    work of the costumbristas.

TRAPICHILLO RIVER. Located in northwestern Huehuete-
    nango, it flows into Mexico. It is also called Río
    Selegua in part.

TRASLACIONISTAS. The group which favored the removal
    of the capital from Antigua to its present site, in 1773.

TROCOSO, MIGUEL [pseudonym] see CABRAL DE LA
    CERDA, MANUEL.

TRONCOSO MARTÍNEZ DEL RINCÓN, BERNARDO. Governor from 1789 to 1794, he was governor of Vera Cruz (Mexico) before going to Guatemala.

TRONOS. Litters on which images or statues of saints are carried by members of the Cofradias.

TSIJOLACH. Patron saint of the makers of fireworks, probably Santiago. He is represented by a small figure of a man on horseback. Sometimes spelled Tzijolach.

TUCURU. Municipio in the department of Alta Verapaz in central Guatemala. The cabecera is on the Polochic River, 17 miles southwest of Coban. Market center. Population: 13,283. Altitude: 1561 ft. Crops: bananas, coffee. Sometimes called San Miguel Tucuru.

TUL. A rush or reed used primarily for making mats.

TUM. An Indian musical instrument consisting of a section of log used as a drum. Most frequently utilized as part of the ceremony of Palo Volador.

TUMBADOR, EL. Municipio in the department of San Marcos in southwestern Guatemala. Its cabecera is 11 miles north-northwest of Coatepeque. Population: 25,468. Altitude: 3018 ft. Crops: coffee, sugar cane, grain; livestock.

TUMPLINE see MECAPAL.

TUN. The Mayan reference to their 360-day calendar period representing a year. The other four or five days were ceremonial and not counted in the calendar.

TUNTÚN see TOYACALES.

TURCIOS LIMA, LUIS AGOSTO, 1941-1966. A revolutionary guerrilla associated with F. A. R. Trained as a military officer, he took part in an abortive revolt in 1960 against Ydígoras. He and Yon Sosa then took to the mountains to form the MR-13. Turcios was the overall leader and was assassinated in 1966 by La Mano.

TXUL, ANASTASIO, 1790?-1819? Last of the Quiché ruling house, he led an uprising in 1817 at Totonicapán. His defeat and imprisonment ended Indian resistance against the Spanish.

TZENDAL REBELLION. Begun in 1712 with an Indian alliance in Chiapas, the rebellion was led by an Indian
girl, Doña María Angel, who was supposedly inspired
by the Virgin Mary. The Tzendales captured several
towns, completely exterminating all the Spanish men.
The commanding officer of one of the Spanish garri-
sons finally rallied some of the forces to oppose the
Tzendales. The two forces met at Huistlan where the
Spaniards won the battle. Later, under the leadership
of Nicolás de Segovia, the Spanish met and defeated
the Tzendales at Occhuc in Chiapas. The Spanish, under the command of Governor Cosio, defeated the Indians again at Cancuc. The last of the Tzendales were
defeated in 1713, and Doña María Angel escaped. The
expense of putting down the rebellion weakened the
Spanish strength in Chiapas to the point of commercial
decay.

TZICHIPAC see SACACHIAN.

TZIJOLACH see TSIJOLACH.

TZIJOLAJ. A piccolo of cane or reed with three or four
perforations. Used by shepherds and by the Maya
Quiché in ritual music.

TZOLKIN. The sacred year of 260 days in the Mayan calendar. The time period had no subdivision; it was only a count of days determining the pattern of ceremonial life. The tzolkin is thought to have been set up to
measure the time that elapsed between the sun's zenith
over the Mayan area as it moved south in August, and
its zenith in April on its way north. While the sun
was to the north, the rainy season occurred in the area
of the Mayan empire, and therefore marked important
dates in the agricultural society. Sometimes called
Tonalamatl.

TZUNJUYU see PANAJACHEL.

TZUTE see ZUTE.

TZUTUHIL. Located in Sololá, it is a dialect group of the
Quichean linguistic stock of the Mayan language. The
nation was the third strongest in Central America at
the time of the conquest and the strongest defensively.
Their capital, Atziquinahay, was located on a peninsula

in Lake Atitlán. The nation was the most difficult for
the Spanish to conquer and without the aid of the Cakchiqueles, the Tzutuhiles could have delayed the conquest for several years. The semi-island fortress is
now called Teachuc, "Where glory departed."

-U-

U. F.CO. see UNITED FRUIT COMPANY.

U. N. T. E. see UNIÓN NACIONAL DE TRABAJADORES EN
EXILO.

U. N. T. L. see UNIÓN NACIONAL DE TRABAJADORES
LIBRES.

U. O. S. see UNIFICACIÓN OBRERA SOCIALISTA.

UAXACTUN. Ruins in the lowlands of Petén, near Tikal.
The site was a primary center of activity throughout
the classic empire of the Mayan period. It is significant because of the sequence of development of lowland
architecture and ceramic ware.

UBICO Y CASTAÑEDA, JORGE, 1878-1946. President of
Guatemala from 1931-1944. He was a son of Dr. Arturo Ubico, Envoy to the U. S. He was commended for
his efforts in the sanitary campaigns of 1918 to 1920.
He became Chief of Staff in 1920 and took an active
part in the ouster of Herrera in 1921. He was Minister of War in 1922, and candidate for president in 1922
and 1926. He amended the constitution in 1937 to extend his term of office, and extended it again in 1941.
He was overthrown in June, 1944, by the combination
of student strikes and a military junta. He died in
New Orleans.

UINAL. Mayan word for the 20-day month represented on
the Mayan calendar.

UNIFICACIÓN OBRERA SOCIALISTA (U. O. S.). A short-
lived leftist union active in the 1920's, formed by students and governmental arsenal workers. It affiliated
with the communist international in 1924; the organization published the newspaper El Socialista and was suppressed in 1925.

UNIÓN, LA. Municipio in the department of Zacapa in eastern Guatemala. The cabecera is 11 miles south-southeast of Gualán. Until 1920, named Monte Oscuro. Population: 9792. Altitude: 3608 ft. Crops: coffee, sugar cane; livestock.

UNIÓN NACIONAL DE EDUCADORES DE PRIMARÍA. A union of school teachers not affiliated with any federations. Formed in 1959, it claimed over 300 members by 1962.

UNIÓN NACIONAL DE TRABAJADORES EN EXILO (U. N. - T. E.). Formed in Honduras in the early 1950's in opposition to President Arbenz.

UNIÓN NACIONAL DE TRABAJADORES LIBRES (U. N. T. L.). Formed in the early 1950's as an anti-governmental union, in opposition to the regime of President Arbenz.

UNIÓN SINDICAL DE TRABAJADORES DE PUERTO BAR-RIOS. A union of dock workers in Puerto Barrios not affiliated with a federation. The union claimed 463 members in 1962.

UNITED FRUIT COMPANY (U. F. Co.). Formed in 1899 from the Boston Fruit Company and several small tropical fruit companies controlled by Minor C. Keith. The lowland areas in the Caribbean and Central America were developed to produce bananas on a large scale. At the same time, the company developed its own shipping and railroad lines and distribution points in the United States to facilitate moving the crops. The U. F. Co. began its first production in Guatemala in 1908, in the Caribbean Bananera Zone near Quirigua. By the 1930's, Panama disease and sigatoka so imperiled its plantations that the U. F. Co. established new cultivations on the Pacific coast at Tiquisate, under the title Compañía Agrícola de Guatemala. Bananas soon became the second most important export crop in Guatemala, until the rise in cotton export in the 1960's. The U. F. Co. also raises coconuts, abaca, cacao, and oil palms. Its plantations are worked largely by natives, who receive relatively good wages and such benefits as hospitalization, housing, and schools for the children. U. F. Co. often became involved in the politics of the country in which it worked. The company slowly forced out its competitors until al-

most all the banana trade was handled by the U. F. Co.
In the 1950's it became involved in a dispute with the
government of Jacobo Arbenz.   Much of its unused
land was expropriated in order to be turned over to
the landless peasant.   Most of the land was returned
to U. F. Co. when the revolt of June, 1954, overthrew
the Arbenz government.   Since 1954, U. F. Co. has attempted to cut its unused lands through crop diversification and land sales.

UNITED NATIONS.   The Latin American republics were
members of the charter meeting of the U. N. and voted
en bloc to legalize regional blocs.   Until the early
1960's, the Security Council always included at least
two Latin American countries.   The U. N. has not in-
tervened in any Latin American disputes, although
President Arbenz appealed to the U. N. in the revolt of
1954.   It was referred back to the O. A. S.

UNITED PROVINCES OF CENTRAL AMERICA see
PROVINCIAS UNIDAS DEL CENTRO DE AMÉRICA.

UNIVERSIDAD DE SAN CARLOS DE GUATEMALA.   Founded
in 1679, largely through bequests of Bishop Marroquín
and P. Crespo Juárez, its first classes were held in
1681, and the first degree was issued in 1689.   The
university's original title was "Real y Pontificio Universidad de San Carlos de Borromeo."   In 1875, it
was taken over by the government and renamed "La
Universidad Nacional de Guatemala."   It remained as
such until 1945 when it was again given autonomy and
its present title was chosen.   A ciudad universitaria
was constructed south of Guatemala City, where the
eight faculties were brought together on one campus.

UNIVERSIDAD RAFAEL LANDÍVAR.   Founded in 1961 in
Guatemala City, it began with less than 100 students
in 1962.   By 1966, there were almost 1,000 students.
A Catholic Jesuit school, it offers work in law, human-
ities and economics.   It began as a branch of San
Carlos but was granted autonomous status in Article
102 of the constitution of 1965.   Under Ydígoras, a
grant of Q300,000 was made to found the university.

URIARTE, RAMÓN, 1846-1897.   A Guatemalan poet, his
works include an anthology of Central American poets,
entitled Galería poética centro americana (1888), and

La convención de 7 de diciembre de 1877.

URIARTE-BAYARTA AGREEMENT (1877). An agreement
to study a boundary line from the port of Ocos to the
Izbul Mountains. This is the approximate boundary
line of today and the agreement signified that Guatemala would renounce its rights to Chiapas and Soconusco. The agreement was the basis of the treaty
signed by President J. R. Barrios with Mexico.

URRUTIA, CARLOS. Governor from 1818 to 1821. Prior
to going to Guatemala, he was governor of Santo
Domingo. He was a capable, progressive person, but
too old to effectively govern. When the revolutionary
movement became strong, he delegated his powers to
Gabino Gainza, his troop commander. When independence was declared, Urrutia left the country for
Havana.

URRUTIA, CLAUDIO, 1857-1934. A Guatemalan engineer
commissioned by the government to carry out the Honduran boundary survey and to develop a geologic map
of Guatemala.

URRUTIA, MIGUEL ANGEL, 1852-1931. An author and editor of Diario de Guatemala. Best remembered for his
novels Blanca and Los secretos de las familias, as
well as the plays La expiacion (1884), Un conflicto en
el hogar (1903) and Silencio heroico (1924).

URRUTIA Y GUZMÁN, JOSÉ MARÍA. He studied at the
school at San Buenaventura and at the University of
San Carlos. He became well known for his writings
on journalism, literature, education and the military.

USPANTÁN see SAN MIGUEL USPANTÁN.

USPANTEC. A language group making up part of the Quichean linguistic stock of the Proto-Guatemala-Yucatan language family. It is a minor group, located in the department of Quiché.

USUMACINTA RIVER. A river formed at the confluence of
the Pasión and Chixoy rivers, on the Mexican border.
It forms the boundary line that extends northwestward
about 350 miles into Chiapas and Tobasco, then to the
Gulf of Mexico. Its length, including the Chixoy, is

about 600 miles.

USUMATLÁN.   Municipio in the department of Zacapa in
eastern Guatemala.   The cabecera is located in the
western part of the department, between the Atlantic
Highway and the Motagua River.   Population: 3461.
Altitude: 820 ft.   Crops: corn, beans, sugar cane,
platanos, yucca, tomatoes, chile.

UTATLÁN.   Stronghold capital of the Quiché Indians, cap-
tured and destroyed by Pedro de Alvarado in 1524.
The ruins are located two miles northwest of Santa
Cruz del Quiché.

-V-

V.D.G.   see   VANGUARDIA DEMOCRÁTICA GUATEMAL-
TECA.

VAGRANCY LAW.   A law set up to punish idle workers by
accusing them of vagrancy.   Passed by Ubico in 1934,
it continued until the constitution of 1945 went into effect.   It required all able-bodied men to be employed
a minimum of 150 days per year.   The required work
time was scaled down, depending on the amount of
land each milpero worked for himself.   Each male was
required to carry a libreto showing the amount of time
employed.   The 1965 constitution still states that vagrancy is punishable but does not define the term nor
provide for punishment.   See also LIBRETO.

VALENZUELA, GILBERTO, 1866-1955.   Guatemalan bibliographer, he compiled Bibliografía guatemalteca (1933)
which formed the basis for the ten volume set of the
same title covering 1660 to 1960.   He also wrote
Guatemala y sus gobernantes, 1821-1958 (1959).

VALENZUELA, PEDRO JOSÉ.   Governor of Guatemala from
February to July, 1838, while the country was a member of the Federation of Central America.   He took the
post after Mariano Gálvez resigned and held it until
Rivera Paz was elected.   He was a member of the
faculty of San Carlos Universidad prior to the revolution.

VALLADARES MÁRQUEZ, JORGE, 1891-1962.   A Guatemal-

an poet, best known for his poems Madre naturaleza
and Quetzaleida. The theme of his poetry centers
around the Indian and nature, simply expressed.

VALLADARES Y RUBIO, ANTONIO, 1871- . An author and
poet, born in Guatemala City, he held several high
governmental posts and wrote under the pseudonym
Chas-Carrillo. His works include De otros dias (1925),
Diccionario de champinismos--Cosas de mi tierra, and
Detalles de la vida.

VALLE, JOSÉ, 1900-1952. Guatemalan novelist who wrote
many travel articles on Guatemala, including the book
Guatemala para el turista (1929). Pseudonym: Pepe
Gris.

VALLE, JOSÉ CECILIO DÍAZ DEL, 1776-1834. Born in
Honduras, he held several high posts in the colonial
government. He was against breaking with Spain but
later joined the revolutionists in their work toward independence, and was largely responsible for the writing of the declaration of independence. While Central
America was part of Mexico, he held a high post in
the Iturbide government. In Central America, he was
a member of the ruling triumvirate until the first president was elected. He worked as an advisor to Morazán and was elected president of Central America in
1834, but died before taking office.

VALLE, MANUEL, 1861-1913. A Guatemalan poet-drama-
tist and politician. He was a deputy in the legislature
and Minister of Public Instruction. Pseudonym: V.
Manuel Leal.

VALLE, RAFAEL, 1894-1922. A newspaperman and poet.
At the time of his death he was editor of Revista Universitaria. His works include Rayo de Luz and El
retorno (both plays); and La Alegría del producir (poems). Pseudonyms: Ariel and Dorian Gray.

VALLE MATHEU, JORGE DEL, 1906-1956. A sociologist,
he edited the works of José del Valle (1929-30). His
works include Sociología guatemalteca (1932), Chrono-
logía guatemalteca del siglo XVII (1943), Guía socio-
geográfica de Guatemala (1956) and La verdad sobre el
"Caso de Guatemala" (1956).

VALLEDARES, JOSÉ. An 18th-century Guatemalan artist, his best known painting is the Apostles which hangs in the Church of Nuestra Señora de la Merced.

VALVERDE, GARCÍA DE. Governor from 1579-1589. Increased coastal raiding forced Valverde to build up defenses and secure arms for local residents.

VALVERDE, MARIANO, 1884- . Born in Quezaltenango, he wrote popular music and was an accomplished marimba performer, but is remembered for his Noches de luna en las ruinas.

VANGUARDIA DEMOCRÁTICA GUATEMALTECA (V.D.G.). A small leftist-oriented group founded in 1946 to encourage union activity. It broke up in 1950 after a split among the leaders, most of whom joined the Partido Comunista de Guatemala.

VARA. Linear measure of 32 to 33 inches, originating from the early use of the staff of authority carried by village officials in settling land disputes. This practice is still found in regions of the highlands today, where the silver-tipped staff of office is carried by office holders and is called a "vara de autoridad."

VARONA, SANCHO DE. On the conquest, he was First Alcalde of Guatemala in 1535 and 1543, Second Alcalde in 1538.

VÁSQUEZ, FRANCISCO DE ASÍS, 1647-1713. A Guatemalan historian, he was a Franciscan monk who is best known for his Crónica de la provincia del Santisimo Nombre de Jesús de Guatemala (1714-1716). He also wrote Historia nuestra Señora de Loreto (1694).

VÁSQUEZ DE ESPINOSA, ANTONIO, d. 1630. A Carmelite friar, he traveled through America, returning to Spain in 1622. He wrote several works, the most significant being Description of the Indies (1620?), which contains much on the everyday life in Mexico and Central America.

VEDA, VIDAL [pseudonym] see VELA, DAVID.

VELA, CARLOS H., 1885-1912. A poet, born in Quezaltenango.

VELA, DAVID, 1901-   Novelist and journalist, editor of
El Imparcial and author of El hermano pedro (1932),
Geneonomia Maya-Quiché (1935), El mito de Colón
(1935), Nuestro Belice (1938), Literature guatemalteca
(1943), Un personaje sin novela (1958).   Pseudonyms:
Cayamusio, Gabino Morales, Vidal Veda.

VELARDE Y CIENFUEGOS, JUAN.   Acting governor from
1753 to 1754.

VENADO, EL (Dance of the deer).   A 75-foot pole is selected with great ceremony and placed upright in the
plaza.   A line is fastened from the church steeple to
the pole.   A person dressed as a monkey goes to the
top of the church; a shaman climbs to the top of the
pole and tries to encourage the monkey to cross over.
When he does, they embrace, the monkey descends,
and the crowd cheers.   It is symbolic of man winning
over the animals.   The dance in this simple form lasts
from one to 15 days, depending upon the wealth of the
village.

VERANO.   The summer dry season, lasting from November
through April in most of the highlands of Guatemala.
However, it is actually winter in terms of the sun's
position.

VERAPAZ RAILROAD.   A government owned railroad, 32
miles in length, extending from Pancajche to Panzos.
It connects the highland coffee fincas with the Polochic
River, and world trade.   Originally a German built
railway, it was confiscated during World War II by the
Guatemalan government.   The railroad was abandoned
in the mid-1960's.

VERITAS [pseudonym] see AYCINENA, JUAN FERMÍN.

VICEROY (Virrey).   The crown's direct representative in the
colonies and the highest colonial office.   The viceroy
was selected by the crown and the Council of the Indies.
He was usually a member of a high ranking family and
usually held the office from three to five years.   The
viceroyalties of New Spain and Peru were the only two
until the 18th century, when the viceroyalties of La
Plata and New Granada were formed.   Guatemala was
included under the jurisdiction of the Viceroyalty of
New Spain (Mexico City).   Viceroyalty duties were to

enforce law, collect revenue, and convert the Indians.
The viceroy appointed most officials, down to the min-
or posts. He granted the encomiendas in his territory.
At the end of his term of office, his activities were
reviewed by the residencia, who had to approve his
record. He was limited in his actions by the audiencia, which functioned as an advisory council.

VIDAURRE, ADRIÁN, 1860-1937. A journalist who supported Cabrera in his early years but later helped to
bring about his downfall. He wrote Paralelo entre dos
administraciones (1907), Los últimos treinta años ...
(1921), Orientaciones para el porvenir (1922).

VIEJO LICORNES, EL [pseudonym] see GOICOECHEA,
JOSÉ ANTONIO.

VIEJO REPORTER, EL [pseudonym] see DÍAZ, VICTOR
MIGUEL.

VIGIL, ADAN [pseudonym] see CÓRDOBA, ALEJANDRO.

VIGIL, ANDRÉS [pseudonym] see CASANOVA Y ESTRADA,
RICARDO.

VILLA. A large village, usually of greater importance than
the pueblo, but of smaller size and less importance
than a ciudad. The villa is an important seat of the
municipio (cabecera), but not a departmental capital.
A cabecera can be designated a villa or a ciudad, depending on its geopolitical importance.

VILLA CANALES. Municipio in the department of Guatemala in south central Guatemala. The cabecera is located near the eastern shore of Lake Amatitlán, on
the railroad, and 11 miles south of Guatemala City.
Agricultural center. Until 1921, called Pueblo Viejo.
Population: 26,917. Altitude: 3989 ft. Crops:
coffee, sugar cane, grain, fodder grasses; livestock
raising; lumbering.

VILLA LÓPEZ, JAIME [pseudonym] see VILLA URRUTIA,
JACOBO DE.

VILLA NUEVA. Municipio in the department of Guatemala
in south central Guatemala. Its cabecera is located
ten miles southwest of Guatemala City. Population:

17,507. Altitude: 4300 ft. Crops: grain; livestock
and lumbering.

VILLA ROCA, JOSÉ DE [pseudonym] see IRISARRI, AN-
TONIO JOSÉ DE.

VILLA URRUTIA, JACOBO DE, d. 1833. Born in Santo
Domingo, he went to Spain to attend the University of
Salamanca. He was appointed oidor of the Audiencia
of Guatemala in 1793, the highest civil office under the
captain-general. He was the driving force behind the
founding of the Sociedad Económica de Amigos de
Guatemala. He often wrote under the pseudonyms D.
Pacoro and Jaime Villa López, and contributed to the
progressive intellectual movement of the late 18th century. He left Guatemala in 1805.

VILLACORTA CALDERÓN, JOSÉ ANTONIO, 1879- . The
outstanding Guatemalan historian and anthropologist of
the 20th century. He was the editor of the series
Biblioteca goathemala. He is noted for his histories
of Guatemala and for his work in editing the various
Mayan sacred books. His works include Hombres
celebres de América (1927), Monografía del departamento de Guatemala (1926), Arqueología guatemala
(1930), Estudio bio-bibliográfico sobre Rafael Landívar
(1931), Anales de los Cakchiqueles (1937), Pre-historia
e historia antigua de Guatemala (1938), and Bibliografía guatemalteca (1944).

VILLAGRAN AMAYA, VICTOR, 1914-1954. A Guatemalan
poet. His poems were collected under the title
Romances de la tierra Alta (1937); he edited Poetas
de Guatemala (1947).

VILLALOBOS, PEDRO DE, d. 1579. Governor from 1573
to 1578. Serious earthquakes in 1575 and 1578 dis-
rupted an otherwise quiet regime.

VILLALPANDO, FRANCISCO DE. A Guatemalan painter of
the 17th century. He devoted much of his time to
painting the life of Saint Francis de Assisi. His better
works include La confessión and Conversión de los
ladrones, found in the National Museum in Guatemala
City.

VILLAPEDROSA, ROMUALDO [pseudonym] see IRISARRI,

ANTONIO JOSÉ DE.

VIRGEN DE LA PIEDAD   see   NUESTRA SEÑORA DEL
SOCORRO.

VIRREY   see   VICEROY.

VISITA.   In referring to the ecclesiastic, a visit of a priest
to a parish having no regular priest; also the area included in such visits.

VISITACIÓN   see   SANTA MARÍA VISITACIÓN.

VISITADOR.   An official with unlimited power, appointed by
the crown to visit the colonies and to investigate the
viceroy or other officials during their terms of office.
The visitador sent a detailed report to the crown on
the honesty and competence of the official in question.
An unfavorable report could lead to the removal of an
official.

VOLADOR   see   PALO VOLADOR.

VOLCANOES.   Of the 33 volcanoes within the border of
Guatemala, only Fuego and Santa María still erupt, if
infrequently.   The following are the more important
volcanoes; see under the individual names for descrip-
tions.   Acatenango, Agua, Atitlán, Cerro Quemado,
Fuego, Ipala, Pacaya, Quezaltepeque, San Pedro, Santa
Clara, Santa María, Santo Tomás, Suchitán, Tacana,
Tajumulco, Tecuamburro, Tolimán, Zunil.

-W-

WALIS.   A colonial term referring to present-day Belice
(British Honduras).   Probably a corruption of Wallace,
the name of an early English pirate who made his
base of operations there.

WARS   see   under the principal country with which the war
was waged.

WASHINGTON CONFERENCE (1907).   Convened through the
efforts of President Theodore Roosevelt of the U.S.
and President Díaz of Mexico.   The long-range objective of most of the delegates was to develop a basis

for unifying the Republics.   They agreed to one treaty
and six major conventions.   A peace treaty, to last
ten years, was signed and a Central American Court
of Justice was set up to arbitrate disputes.

WASHINGTON CONFERENCE (1923).   Called through the efforts of the U.S. to study a tribunal to replace the
   Court of Justice.   A new treaty of peace was signed.
   The tribunal was set up to arbitrate disputes, but its
   power did not approach that of the Court of Justice of
   1907.

WYLD OSPINA, CARLOS, 1891-1956.   A poet, author, and
   newspaperman.   Editor of El Imparcial (1922-25), he
   was one of the early modernistic social protest authors.
   His works include La autocrata (1929), El solar de los
   Gonzagas (1924), La tierra de las nahuyacas (1933),
   La gringa (1935), and La mala hembra.

-X-

XACA.   A dark bread made from whole wheat and brown
   sugar.

XANCATAL.   Indian residents of Santa Catarina Ixtahuacán.

XBALANKE.   In Quiché mythology, the god of the sun.

XENACOJ   see   SANTO DOMINGO XENACOJ.

XICOTENGA TECUBALSI, DOÑA LUISA.   Daughter of the
   Aztec Indian chief, Tlaxcala Xicotencatl.   She became
   the mistress of Pedro de Alvarado and bore him a
   daughter, Doña Leonor de Alvarado.

XIMÉNEZ, FRANCISCO, 1666-1729.   A Dominican friar and
   the discoverer of the manuscript Popul-Vuh, in Chichicastenango, which he translated into Latin.   He made
   numerous archaeological discoveries and studied native
   languages.   His major work, Tesoro de los lenguas
   Quiché, Cachikel, y Tsutuhil, has partly been lost.   A
   second work was Historia de la provincia de San Vincente de Chiapas y Guatemala.

XIMÉNEZ, XAVIER DE   [pseudonym]   see   AGUILAR, SIN-
   FOROSO.

XIPATE, IXTO [pseudonym]   see   AGUILAR, SINFOROSO.

-Y-

YAXCHILÁN.   Ruins located in the lowlands of the Usumacinta River valley.   A high level of artistic achieve-
ment was reached here in the late classic period of
the Mayas, ca. A.D. 700.   The site is significant for
its outstanding temples, containing 12 sculptured stone
lintels of unequaled aesthetic quality.

YDÍGORAS FUENTES, MIGUEL, 1895- .   President, 1958-
1963.   Born in Pueblo Nuevo, Retalhuleu, he was a
general and served as military governor of Retalhuleu,
Petén, Jalapa, San Marcos (1922-39) and was head of
the highway department (1939-44).   He was candidate
for President in 1950, was elected in 1958.   Under his
term of office the Cuban exiles were trained in Guatemala for the Bay of Pigs invasion.   He was forced
from office when former President Arévalo returned
to Guatemala.   Ydígoras has since served as ambassador to various countries.   He wrote My War with Communism (1963) and Consolidación de la doctrina de
Monroe (1963).

YELA GUNTHER, RAFAEL, 1888-1942.   A Guatemalan
sculptor and the director of the National Academy of
Fine Arts in Guatemala City.   As a teacher, his distinctive subjective form has had a great influence on
local artists.

YEPOCAPA   see   SAN PEDRO YEPOCAPA.

YON SOSA, MARCO ANTONIO, 1932-1970.   Former leader
of MR-13, he took part in a military revolt against
Ydígoras in 1960.   When it failed, he took to the hills,
primarily in Izabal, where he led a group of guerrilla
fighters.   Turcios and Yon Sosa were the leaders of
F.A.R.   Yon Sosa was reported killed by the Mexican
army in Chiapas in 1970.

YUCATEC.   A Maya proper linguistic grouping located in
northeastern Petén.   Most of this group is located in
the Mexican Yucatan area.

YUDICE, JOAQUÍN   see   BELÉN CONSPIRACY.

YUPILTEPEQUE. Municipio in the department of Jutiapa
    in southeastern Guatemala. In the highlands, the
    cabecera is 11 miles southeast of Jutiapa. Population:
    5846. Altitude: 3444 ft. Crops: corn, beans; live-
    stock.

YZABAL LAKE see IZABAL LAKE.

-Z-

ZACAPA. 1) Department in eastern Guatemala. The capital
    is Zacapa. It is situated in the Motagua River valley,
    between the Sierra de las Minas in the north and the
    eastern highlands in the south. It has a warm, dry
    climate. Irrigated crops are corn, beans, tobacco and
    sugar cane. Livestock raising and dairying. Coffee
    is grown on the lower slopes. The main cities are
    Zacapa and Gualán. Nine municipios: Cabañas, Es-
    tanzuela, Gualán, Río Hondo, San Diego, Tuculután,
    La Unión, Usumatlán, Zacapa. Population in 1950 was
    69,536; in 1964 it was 96,715, and projected to 1980
    to be 143,200. Area: 1,038 square miles.
        2) Municipio in the department of Zacapa in eastern
    Guatemala. On the Chiquimula River, the cabecera is
    70 miles east-northeast of Guatemala City. Rail center
    (branch to San Salvador). Developed rapidly after build-
    ing of the railroad in 1896. Population: 31,647. Alti-
    tude: 738 ft. Crops: corn, beans, sugar cane; live-
    stock, dairying.

ZACATE. Hay or cultivated grasses.

ZACUALPA. Municipio in the department of El Quiché in
    west central Guatemala. In the Sierra de Chuacus,
    the cabecera is 20 miles east-northeast of Quiché.
    Local shoe manufacturing. Population: 9819. Alti-
    tude: 7782 ft. Crops: corn, beans, sugar cane,
    tobacco.

ZACULEU. Ruins in the northern highlands of Guatemala,
    near Huehuetenango, noted for the earthenware from
    the early classic period of the Mayas. The site,
    easily accessible from the Inter-American Highway,
    was restored in 1947 at the expense of the U. F. Co.

ZAHROI   see   SHAMAN.

ZAMBO.   A racial cross involving, primarily, the Indian
and Negro races.   This term is not as extensively
used in Guatemala as in other parts of Latin America.

ZAMORA CASTELLANOS, PEDRO, 1879-1954.   A Guatemalan engineer and army officer, he held several high governmental posts.   His writings include Nociones de
fortificación; Vida militar de Centro América (1924),
and El grito de independencia (1935).

ZAPOTITLÁN.   Municipio in the department of Jutiapa in
southeastern Guatemala.   The cabecera is located in
the east central part of the department, and is inaccessible by road.   Population: 4533.   Altitude: 2952
ft.   Crops: corn, rice, beans.

ZARABANDA   see   MOLOJ.

ZARAGOZA.   Municipio in the department of Chimaltenango
in south central Guatemala.   On the Inter-American
Highway, the cabecera is three miles west of Chimaltenango.   Population: 5858.   Altitude: 6630 ft.
Crops: wheat, corn, avocados.

ZEA RUANO, RAFAEL, 1911- .   Journalist and author, he
was born in Chiquimula.   Editor of Diario de Centro
América and author of Cactos (1943), Gurantías soci-
ales (1946), Tierra nuestra (1952), Ñor Julian (1959),
Las Barbas de don Rafay (1960), and Voces de Soledad
(1966).

ZENTENO, MARIANO.   Elected acting governor of Guatemala in late 1828 until April, 1829, when Juan Barrundia returned.   A meeting of the deposed state legislature of 1826 was convened at Antigua by Morazán,
and Zenteno was elected their leader.

ZONTLE.   A measure of cacao beans, with each zontle equal
to about 400 beans.   Used in the colonial period and
earlier as a medium of trade.   Sometimes spelled
Contle.

ZOOMORPH.   Sculptured boulders as the type found at Quirigua and Copán.   Mayan representations of the animal
gods.

ZÚÑIGA, EVARISTO. A Guatemalan religious sculptor of
the late 17th century. Several examples of his works
are found in the Church in Guatemala City, Corazón de
Jesús and in the national museum.

ZUNIL. Municipio in the department of Quezaltenango in
southwestern Guatemala. On the Samala River, the
cabecera is five miles south-southwest of Quezaltenango. It is located at the northwestern foot of Zunil
Volcano. Hydroelectric station on the Samala River.
Market center; flour milling nearby. On the northern
slope of Santo Tomás Volcano, near Zunil, are the
hot-spring resorts of Aguas Amargas (three miles
south) and Fuentes Georginas (five miles southeast).
Population: 4679. Altitude: 7598 ft. Crops: coffee,
grain.

ZUNIL VOLCANO. Altitude: 11,591 feet. Inactive volcano
in southwestern Guatemala, on the Quezaltenango-
Sololá-Suchitepéquez department border. It is nine
miles southeast of Quezaltenango.

ZUNILITO. Municipio in the department of Suchitepéquez in
southwestern Guatemala. In the Pacific piedmont, the
cabecera is on the southern slope of Santo Tomás Volcano. It is nine miles north-northeast of Mazatenango.
Transferred in 1944 from Quezaltenango Department.
Population: 1505. Altitude: 2591 ft. Crops: coffee,
grain, tobacco.

ZURRÓN. A bundle or bale of indigo or cochineal prepared
for export, usually weighing around 150 pounds. Two
bundles make up a mule load. Sometimes spelled
Seroon.

ZUTE. A general utility cloth used by Indians. It can be
folded on the head as protection from the sun, wrapped
around the shoulders, sat upon, used as a baby sling
across the back, or as padding to balance a basket on
the head. Indian men use the Zute to wrap around
their heads, tie around their hats, or to throw across
their shoulders for use as a handkerchief. Similar in
size and style to the servilleta but much more colorful.
Often spelled Tzut or Tzute.

ZUYACALES. Raincoats made from palm leaves. The man-
ac leaves from Palmar, Quezaltenango, are highly

prized for these raincoats. The manaco or corozo
(Cohune Palm) is the largest and most useful of the
lowland plants.

Part II

BIBLIOGRAPHICAL GUIDE*

The intellectual development of Guatemala began with
the pre-conquest Mayans. This earlier period can be covered only by general histories and commentaries, because
there are few sources of accurate, concise information for
reference purposes. The research person is required to use
general histories and compendiums. This section is concerned, therefore, with the availability of sources of information for Pre-Columbian and Colonial Guatemala, periods
in which no guides have been compiled.

The native Mayans produced many codices of pre-
conquest vintage; of those, only three remain, but are yet
to be deciphered from the hieroglyphic form. They are:
the Codex Cortesianus, Madrid; the Codex Peresianus, Paris;
and the Codex Dresdensis, Dresden, Germany. While these
items are not sources for precise information, they do reflect the type of intellectual activity of the pre-conquest Mayan and should be familiar to anyone doing work on the Mayans. A monumental work on the early civilization was done
by Bishop Diego de Landa in 1566. There have been several editions; the seventh, edited by A.M. Tozzer [Landa, Diego de. Landa's relación de las cosas de Yucatán (Cambridge, Harvard University Press, Peabody Museum Papers,
v. XVIII, 1941)] is the most useful in that the notes and ap-
pendices make it a variable encyclopedia of the Mayan culture.

Following these early accounts were the epic histories, written or compiled from Mayan oral histories. Most
significant of the epic histories is Popul Vuh, first discovered in the late 17th century by Father Francisco Ximénez.
This Maya-Quiché bible outlines the history of the Quiché
from their origins to 1550. The manuscript, written in the
Quiché language using the Latin alphabet, is in the Newberry

---

*A subject index to this Guide appears immediately following it.

Library in Chicago and has been translated into several languages, including English [see Popul Vuh, edited by Adrián
Recinos (Norman, University of Oklahoma Press, 1950)].
A second important epic history is the Annals of the Cak-
chiquels, thought to have been written in the 16th century by
Francisco Hernández Arana Xahila, a converted descendant
of one of the last ruling houses. The genealogy of the ruling houses of the Cakchiqueles is traced down to the 16th
century.

From the conquistadores, there are several eyewitness accounts. The best known is the True History of the
Conquest of New Spain by Bernal Díaz del Castillo; the best
transcription of this was done by Genaro García in 1905
[see Bernal Díaz del Castillo, True History of the Conquest
of New Spain, 5 vols. (Cambridge, Haklyut Society publications, 1908-16), recently reprinted by H. P. Kraus]. Although Diaz is concerned primarily with Mexico, he includes
some reports on Guatemala. The most complete manuscript
known is now in the National Archives of Guatemala. The
letters of Hernando Cortés have much information, primarily
the fourth letter written in 1524, describing his trip through
the lowland Mayan area, from Yucatan to Honduras [Five
Letters, 1519-1926 (New York, Norton, 1962)]. Concerning
the main conquest, the two letters of Pedro de Alvarado,
written in 1524-25, describe the conquest of highland Guatemala; these contain the most detailed information on the conquest [An Account of the Conquest of Guatemala in 1524, edited and translated by S. J. Mackie (New York, Cortes Society, 1924)]. Originally there were four letters; two have
been lost in the intervening years. There is also much
about the conquest and the period in the proceedings of Alvarado's trial, where specific charges (34 in all) were an-
swered, each separately, by Alvarado [Ramírez, J. L.,
comp., Proceso de residencia contra Pedro de Alvarado
(Mexico, 1847); translated in part and published in Golden
Conquistadores, edited by H. M. Rosen (Indianapolis, Bobbs-
Merrill, 1960)].

Following the eyewitness accounts of the conquest
came the religious writings of Catholic priests and monks,
who wrote linguistic grammars to assist in translating ser-
mons which were used in the conversion of the Mayans.
Along with the religious authors were a number of friars
who were historians and whose efforts, as a whole, were
formidable. Some wrote little more than travelogues; of the
religious histories, most were partisan, but most factions

were represented.

A number of general 16th-century writers included
Guatemala in their discussions, among them, Oviedo, Gómara, and Las Casas. There were other writers, as Sahagún
and Motolinía, who were concerned with Mexico, mentioning
Guatemala, but not giving full attention to the country.

The earliest important writer to be concerned primarily with Guatemala was Antonio de Remesal, a 17th-cen-
tury Dominican who was critical of the handling of the Indians by the conquistadores and favored the Las Casas method of converting the Indians [Historia general de las indias
occidentales ... 3d. ed. 2 vols. (Madrid, Biblioteca de
autores Españoles, tomos 175 y 189, 1964-66)]. His style
of writing makes the work difficult to use, yet it is an important work. A non-Spanish colonial eyewitness account appeared in 1661 by the Englishman Thomas Gage: A New
Survey of the West Indies [see the later edition, Travels in
the New World (Norman, University of Oklahoma Press,
1958)]. It critically describes the Spanish activities in working with the Indians. Not all that Gage writes is accurate,
but he offers much of interest. The first history by a native Guatemalan, rather than a Spaniard living in Guatemala,
was written by Francisco de Fuentes y Guzmán, in the
1690's. It was not published, however, until 1882, in an
incomplete edition under the title Recordación florida del
reyno de Guatemala [for the complete edition see Historia de
Guatemala, recordación florida, 2 vols. (Guatemala, Tipografía Nacional, 1932-33)]. Fuentes y Guzmán carries on
the tradition of the conquistadores, and has not a few inac-
curacies, but as a whole, his work is one of the better colonial accounts. Francisco de Asís Vásquez compiled his
Crónica de la provincia ... de Guatemala, (1716) [reprinted
in Guatemala in 2 vols. in 1937-38], taking considerable
from the work of Remesal, but differing on points of church
doctrine in that he favored the Franciscan Order. He is
primarily concerned with the history of the church, but outlines the social and political history of Guatemala. Much of
the book is taken up with defending the methods used by the
conquistadores in their handling of the native races.

Written around 1721 but not published until 1929 in
Guatemala, was the Historia de la provincia de San Vicente
de Chiapa y Guatemala (3 vols.) by Francisco Xímenez, who
discovered and transcribed the manuscript, Popul Vuh. The
account presents much concerning the work with the Indians

and lacks only in that it relentlessly promotes the Dominican
cause over that of the Franciscan. Domingo Juarros drew
heavily from Fuentes y Guzmán for his Compendio de la historia de la Ciudad de Guatemala (1808-1818). This work,
basically a history of Central America down to the 19th century, deals with the political, commercial, and geographical
aspects of the area. Although incomplete in many respects,
it is a major source for colonial history and serves as an
atlas for the region. An abridgement was translated into
English by John Baily in 1823 under the title, A statistical
and commercial history of the Kingdom of Guatemala.

Since the revolution in 1821, one can trace the historiography of Guatemala by consulting the article listed below by Lázaro Lamadrid [item 105]. A quick reference
book in English that is available in most libraries is the
History of Central America by H. H. Bancroft [item 17].
This set has a good general index and covers most of the
historical episodes. Some caution should be exercised in ac-
cepting as actual fact, all the theories put forth.

There were no guides published as official directories
of government agencies, or other publications describing government agencies and their organization prior to the brief
guide compiled by Henry V. Besso [item 24] in 1947. Since
then, one can consult annual reports of the various agencies
and available subject bibliographies listed with monographic
studies. There is the notable exception of the Colección
bibliográfica del III centenario de la introducción de la imprenta en Centroamérica [item 82]. This ten-volume set
(in 11 parts) serves as a national bibliography from 1660
through 1960 and is a must for any student doing work in the
area.

ANNOTATED BIBLIOGRAPHY

1. Academia guatemalteca.   Biográfica de literatos na-
    cionales. Guatemala, Tipográfia La Unión, 1889.
    Vol. 1 was only vol. published.
    Brief biographies and excerpts with criticisms of the
    following authors: Rafael García Goyena; Ignacio
    Gómez; Manuel Diéguez Olaverri; José Batres; Juan
    Diéguez Olaverri; and Alejandro Marure.
2. Academia guatemalteca. Publicaciones de la Academia
    guatemalteca. Vols. 1-7 (1932-1940).
    Literary articles and poems, history and criticisms

of Guatemalan literature.
3. Adams, Eleanor B. A Bio-Bibliography of Franciscan
   Authors in Colonial Central America. Washington,
   D.C., Academy of American Franciscan History,
   1953.
   A good bibliography, many unpublished manuscripts
   of Franciscans, but little biographical information.
4. Adams, Richard N. Cultural Surveys of Panama, Nicaragua, Guatemala, El Salvador, Honduras. Washington, D.C., Pan American Sanitary Bureau Scientific Publications, no. 33, 1957.
   A survey of each area conducted by established anthropologists in predesignated communities. Each
   describes various aspects of Indian and Ladino culture, including the living and working conditions, religion, and family relations.
5. Almanaque literario centroamericano, 1937. Guatemala,
   n.p., 1936.
   Only published in 1936, a yearbook of literature and
   criticisms which is basically a general collection of
   short stories and poetry. A directory of literary
   persons is included, with their dates and the dates of
   important literary works.
6. American Geographical Society of New York. A catalogue of maps of Hispanic America, including maps
   in scientific periodicals and books, sheet and atlas
   maps. New York, 1930-1933, 4 vols.
   Volume I, p. 111-194 on Central America. Arranged by type of map, then chronologically. Map
   types are: maps in scientific periodicals, p. 117-
   138; maps in books, p. 139-164; sheet and atlas
   maps, official publications, p. 165-168; sheet and atlas maps, unofficial publications, p. 169-186; historical maps, p. 187-194.
7. Ames, Oakes. Orchids of Guatemala. Chicago, Natural History Museum, 1952.
   Gives descriptions, drawings, locations of all then-
   known orchids, also where the first descriptions appeared. It has a good index.
8. Antropología e historia de Guatemala. Guatemala, Instituto de antropología e historia. vol. 1 (1949)-
   A semi-annual with brief articles, primarily on the
   Mayan civilization. Good format lends to easy reading of scholarly articles. Edited by Carlos Samayos
   Chinchilla.

9. "Anuario bibliográfico guatemalteco, 1960 (por Autores)."
Guatemala. Biblioteca nacional, Revista. vol. 1,
no. 1 (1962) p. 137-170.
A listing of books and periodicals received in 1960
by the Biblioteca Nacional, compiled by Enrique Pol-
onsky Celcer. Not all the books are published in
Guatemala, but, if not, they deal with Guatemala.
Included is a list of periodicals received that were
published in Guatemala and a list of presses (colonial, 19th-century, and current presses with addresses). The list is alphabetical with full bibliographical information given.

10. Aparicio y Aparicio, Edgar Juan. Conquistadores de
Guatemala y fundadores de familias guatemaltecas.
2d. ed. Mexico, Tipografía Guadelajara, 1961.
A genealogical study beginning with the conquest, arranged by the century, with an alphabetical sub-ar-
rangement. Each entry contains: place and date of
birth, spouse, children, and names of ancestors of
importance. An index of royal titles appears at the
end.

11. Arévalo Martínez, Rafael. "Bibliografía guatemalteca."
Guatemala. Boletín de museos y bibliotecas, año 1,
no. 2, 2d epoca (Julio, 1941), p. 63-65.
A brief listing of outstanding bibliographies relating
to Guatemala; includes lengthy bibliographies accompanying monographs.

12. Atlas climatológico de Guatemala. Guatemala, Observ-
atorio nacional, 1964.
Includes a list of weather stations, their altitude,
longitude, latitude, number of years making observa-
tions; monthly and annual maps of precipitation temperature (centigrade), and relative humidity.

13. Atlas preliminar de Guatemala. 3d edición. Guatemala, Instituto geográfico nacional, 1966.
The geographical aspects, population development,
communications and electrical systems, and political
units illustrated by maps. Very little text.

14. Banco de Guatemala. Boletín estadístico. no. 1
(1948)- irreg., usually monthly.
Statistics and charts on money, banking, finance, foreign trade, etc. No text beyond an accompanying
leaflet, "carta mensual." First issued as Boletín.

15. Banco de Guatemala. Carta semanal de cafe. Guatemala. no. 1 (1958)- weekly.
Late market news concerning the coffee market from
the New York Stock Exchange and other international

trade centers. Issued by the bank's departamento de
estudios economicos. Supersedes its Informe semanal de café.

16. Banco de Guatemala. Informe econômico. no. 1
(1953)- monthly.
Economic survey on foreign trade, balance of payments, and international market prices on leading
commodities. Issued by the bank's departamento de
estudios econômicos. Title varies (1953-58) Informe
mensual de Mercados. vol. 1 (1953) unnumbered.

17. Bancroft, Hubert Howe. History of Central America.
San Francisco, A. L. Bancroft & Co., 1882-1887.
Three vols. in his Works, v. 6, 7, 8.
Vol. 1 (1501-1530); v. 2 (1530-1800); v. 3 (1801-
1887). The basic political history for the area, in
English. It contains excellent bibliographies and foot-
notes, with a general index in vol. 3. Many useful
reviews of the outstanding earlier histories. The
value of the work is limited only by the frequent, expressed opinions of the author in the body of the work.

18. Bandelier, Adolph Francis Alphonse. Notes on the
Bibliography of Yucatan and Central America, com-
prising Yucatan, Chiapas, Guatemala (the ruins of
Palenque, Ocosingo and Copán) and Oaxaca (ruins of
Mitla). A list of some of the writers on this subject
from the 16th century to the present time. Worces-
ter, Mass., C. Hamilton, 1881.
Arranged by area (Guatemala, p. 22-35) and sub-ar-
ranged by chronology, 16th through 19th centuries.
It has extensive commentaries for each entry, with
cross-references to earlier entries for works covering more than one area.

19. Batres Jaúregui, Antonio. Bibliografía historica guatemalteca, a la honorable municipalidad de Guatemala.
Guatemala, Tipografía nacional, 1908.
A bibliographical essay originally given as a speech,
which discusses the important histories from pre-
conquest times to the 20th century. It was later
translated into English and published by the Pan American Union in 1929. Brief but very useful for anthropologists and historians.

20. Batres Jaúregui, Antonio. Vicios del lenguaje y pro-
vincialismos de Guatemala, estudio filológico. Guatemala, Encuadernación y tipografía nacional, 1892.
A dictionary of words and phrases as used in Guatemala, spelled phonetically. Each entry gives the
proper Castilian pronunciation or definition, along

with the local usage. Many interesting colloquialisms are defined, but no effort is made to estimate how widely the expressions or mispronunciations are used. The dictionary is preceded by a brief philological introduction to the Spanish language.

21. Beristaín y Souza, José Mariano de. "Escritores del antiguo reino de Guatemala, extracto de su Biblioteca Hispanoamericana (1816)." Sociedad de geografía e historia de Guatemala, Anales. vol. IV, no. 3 (1928), p. 290-300; and vol. V, no. 2, 3, 4 (1929), p. 211-241; 336-350; 454-468.
Alphabetical arrangement of authors, giving short biographies with works of each and commentary, or locations of manuscripts. This separate group of Guatemalan writers is taken from Beristain's basic three-volume work.

22. Bernal, Ignacio. Bibliografía de arqueología y etnografía: mesoamérica y Norte de Mexico, 1514-1960. Mexico, Instituto Nacional de Antropología e Historia, Memorias VII, 1962.
Arranged by geographical areas, taking in all of Mexico and Central America. (Zona Maya, Centro, p. 385-412, includes lowland Guatemala, and Zona Maya, Sur., p. 413-440, includes highland and west coast Guatemala). Lists monographs and articles in English, Spanish, German and French.

23. Bernal, Ignacio. Mesoamérica, periodo indígena. Mexico, Instituto Panamericano de geografía e historia, 1953. With suplemento, 1953.
An outline of pre-Columbian Yucatan-Guatemala, with a lengthy bibliography for each subject period covered. Of interest to anthropologists and archaeologists.

24. Besso, Henry V., comp. A Guide to the Official Publications of the Other American Republics. Vol. XI, Guatemala. Washington, D.C., Library of Congress Latin American Series, no. 30, 1947.
A bibliography of the series and of the regular publications of the various agencies of the Guatemalan government. This includes a brief outline of the ministries and their agencies. The guide is an expansion of the briefer works by J.B. Childs.

25. Bibliografía de Centroamérica y del Caribe, 1956-1959. Madrid, Dirección general de archivos y bibliotecas de España, 1958-1961. Four volumes only.
An annual bibliography compiled in Havana, which includes books, pamphlets and articles published by

presses, academies, universities and societies. Arranged by subject, each volume carries its own author index. Much on Guatemala, but no breakdown
by geographic area.

26. Bibliografía geológica de Guatemala, América Central
     (hasta 1965). 1st ed. Guatemala, Instituto geográf-
     ico nacional, 1966.
     An extensive bibliography of monographs and articles
     in western languages that are concerned with or touch
     on Guatemala. Alphabetically arranged, there are
     many unpublished dissertations included.
27. "Bibliografía y cartografía Centro-Americanas." Centro
     América, órgano de publicidad de la oficina interna-
     cional Centro Americana. Vol. 5, no. 2 (1913), p.
     182-196.
     An excellent bibliography of history and geography,
     published in English, German, French and Spanish.
     A listing of maps, 1818 through 1898, arranged by
     date of publication, gives map size, compiler. Each
     entry carries a location symbol, most in the U.S. Li-
     brary of Congress.
28. Biografías ilustres, compilación de los veintidos,Batones
     de oro conferidos por la municipalidad de la ciudad
     de Quezaltenango, 1961-66. Edición coordinada por
     Julio César de la Roca. Quezaltenango, Editorial
     Casa de la cultura, 1967.
     Outstanding living persons and organizations (22) which
     have contributed to the cultural heritage of Guatemala.
     Included are sketches, portraits, and cultural activi-
     ties.
29. Brasseur de Bourbourg, Charles Etienne. Bibliotheque
     Mexico-Guatemalienne. Paris, Maisonneuve, 1871.
     An annotated bibliography of manuscripts and printed
     works on the history and language of pre-Columbian
     America, especially strong in the Yucatan-Guatemalan
     area. An index by language appears in the back.
30. Calendario de la aurora para 1845. Guatemala, 1844?
     Calendar of events for each month, containing bio-
     graphical sketches of noted Guatemalans.
31. California. University. Berkeley. Libraries. Ban-
     croft Library Catalog of Printed Books. Boston, G.K.
     Hall, 1964. 22 vols.
     Arranged by author, title and subject, a good source
     for older material on the history of Guatemala (see
     vols. 8-9). There is also considerable material under
     Central America; an important guide for the historian.
32. Castañeda, Carlos E. Guide to the Latin American

Manuscripts in the University of Texas Library.
Cambridge, Harvard University Press, American
Council of Learned Societies, Miscellaneous publications, no. 1, 1939.
Arranged by country (Guatemala, p. 15-25). Deals
primarily with pre-19th century commerce and religion. Most items are found in Medina.

33. Castillo Cordero, Clemento. Atlas político-adminis-
trativo de la república de Guatemala. Guatemala,
Ministerio de Educación pública, 1953.
Arranged by department, under which is listed:
municipios, their population statistics, and brief topographic descriptions.

34. Chamberlain, Robert S. "A Report on the Colonial Material in the Governmental Archives in Guatemala
City." Handbook of Latin American Studies, vol. 2
(1937), p. 387-432.
Arranged by issuing agency of the colonial government: Superior gobierno, Capitania general, and Real
haciendia (subarranged by geographic area, including
Chiapas). Each category includes a general description of the material. The listing is a shelf list of
documents with full titles given. The Archivo municipal is arranged by physical type of material. The
revolutionary period (up to 1839) is included in a
separate section. The index to the Guatemalan Archivo General contains the more extensive listing.

35. Chávez Zelaya, Enrique. Índice de libros escolares
autores Guatemaltecos. Guatemala, Impreso por el
Instituto de investigaciones y mejoramiento educativo,
1963.
A listing of textbooks and curriculum guides arranged
by subjects (aritmetica elemental through zoologia).
Also form entries as lectura, leyes, memorias, etc.
Useful to the teacher as a selection guide.

36. Chávez Zelaya, Enrique. 105 [cientocinco] titles de
obras escritas por militares de ejército de Guatemala.
Guatemala, 1960-1962. Nine parts.
Each part is arranged by author and lists the works
of each. Of limited value except as a publication list
by author.

37. Childs, James Bennett. The Memorias of the Republics of Central America and the Antilles. Washington, D.C., Government Printing Office, 1932.
A guide to the official non-periodic governmental publications, arranged by country (Guatemala, p. 70-95),
and subdivided by agencies. Each agency is outlined

for historical development with a listing of memorias
annotated and signing official.

38. Ciruti, Joan Estelle. The Guatemalan Novel, A Critical Bibliography. Tulane University, Ph.D. dissertation, 1959.
Part one contains a historical bibliography of the development of the Guatemalan novel. Part two is arranged by author, subdivided by novel, with a synop-
sis and critical articles on each novel. This is an
excellent study in English of the novel and its critics
in Guatemala.

39. Comercio. Guatemala. Año 1 (1963)-   monthly.
News on Guatemalan trade regulations and the inter-
American markets. Published by the Camara de
Comercio de Guatemala, 11 Calle 10-32, zona 1,
Guatemala City.

40. Commercial Directory of Costa Rica, Guatemala, Honduras, Nicaragua and Salvador. Washington, D.C.,
Bureau of the American Republicas, Bulletin no. 28,
1891.
Arranged by country (Guatemala, p. 11-19) and subdivided by city, it contains a listing of commercial
firms and persons.

41. Cosío Villegas, Daniel. "Mexico-Guatemala, 1867-1911.
Una bibliografía para el estudio de sus relacciones."
Mexico. Colegio nacional, Memorias. vol. 4, no.
2 (1959), p. 55-93.
A critical bibliography for the study of Mexican-Guate-
malan relations, with a discussion of the development
of historiography of the period. Later reprinted as
part of volume five of his Historia Moderna de Mexico.

42. Dardón Córdova, Gonzalo. Identificación de autores
guatemaltecos. 2d. ed. Guatemala, Instituto Guatemalteco-Americano, 1963.
A listing of authors with their dates; includes most
presidents between 1823 and 1962.

43. Dardón Córdova, Gonzalo. Series guatemaltecas en el
campo de las humanidades, 1886-1962. Guatemala,
Instituto Guatemalteco-Americano, Cooperación Inter-
bibliotecaria, III, 1962.
A listing of 63 Guatemalan literary series, giving the
author, title, date, pagination and series number of
each, with an extensive author index. Author dates
are included whenever available. An excellent source
for literary material.

44. Descampe, Emilio. Nomenclator de Guatemala, dic-

cionario, geográfico y guía de comunicaciones. Guatemala, Tallares San Antonio, 1937.
A directory of place names and locations. Part 1:
alphabetical listing of ciudades, villas, pueblos,
aldeas and caserios. Part 2: listing by departments,
with all communities in each. Part 3: listing of
communities having market days and when held. Part
4: a section of laws affecting travel.

45. Diario de Centro América, no. 1 (1931)-   .
Government paper, daily evening, Guatemala City.
Edited by Benjamin Paniagua. From 1931 to 1950,
the "seccion official" contained legislative acts and
other documents of official nature. See El Guatemalteca.

46. Diccionario de Comercio e industria de Guatemala.
6th ed., 1966-67. Guatemala, 1966.
A classified phone directory giving names, addresses
and phone numbers by sections as follows: indice;
cuerpo diplomatico y consular; alfabetica general; guia
classificada comercial y profesional; Amatitlán; Antigua; abogados y notarios; dentistas; economistas y
auditores publicados; and other professional groupings.

47. Diccionario de la literatura latinoamerica. América
Central, vol. 1, Costa Rica, El Salvador y Guatemala. Washington, D.C., Union Panoamericana,
1963.
Contains a brief bio-bibliographical description of 23
leading Guatemalan authors, past and present. Each
entry has a critical bibliography and a listing of critical articles about the authors.

48. Directory of Labor Organizations: Western Hemisphere,
Vol. 2 Guatemala. Washington, D.C., U.S. Dept. of
Labor, 1964.
A listing of labor unions, their affiliates, officers,
addresses, phone numbers, and whatever other miscellaneous information was available. Although not a
complete listing, it contains all the unions recognized
by the government and most extra-legal unions not
recognized by the government.

49. "Dos siglos de periodismo en Guatemala, un brillante
exposición que permitira apreciar los progresos de la
prensa nacional." Sociedad de geografía e historia
de Guatemala, Anales, vol. 17 (1942), p. 446-457.
A discussion of newspapers for the 1942 national exposition of printing in Guatemala, giving the newspapers printed, publication dates, significant facts since
the first paper issued in 1729. The arrangement is

by official journals, private newspapers, and administration papers. There are frequent reproductions,
in miniature, of front pages.

50. Doyle, Henry Grattan. A Tentative Bibliography of the
Belles-Lettres of Central America. Cambridge, Harvard University Press, 1935.
Arranged by country (Guatemala, p. 60-90), with a
section on general works at the beginning. Primarily
an index to anthologies of poetry, but includes biographical information when available. A listing of
current newspapers appears at the end.

51. Ewald, Robert H. Bibliografía comentada sobre antropologia social Guatemalteca, 1900-1955. Guatemala,
Tipografía Nacional, 1956.
A listing of books and articles on cultural anthropology
in the Mayan area, preceded by a commentary on the
development of scholarship in the subject area. Reprinted in 1960 as part of the series from the Seminario de Integracion social Guatemalteca.

52. Fernandez, León. Documentos relativios a los movi-
mientos de independencia en el Reino de Guatemala.
San Salvador, Ministerio de instrucción pública, 1929.
A collection of 12 letters to and from the official
government, issued between 1810 and 1816, concerned
with the various movements in Nicaragua and San Salvador, that led to independence.

53. Gallardo, Ricardo, ed. Las constituciones de la República Federal de Centro América. Madrid, Instituto de estudios políticos, Las constituciones hispanoamericanas, no. 10, 1958.
A general discussion of the development of Central
American constitutions, including the Spanish Cortez.
Unification efforts which failed are also included. The
constitutions of Central America are given in full.

54. García Icagbalceta, Joaquín. Apuntes para una catálogo
de escritores en lenguas indígenas de América. Mexico, 1866.
Arranged by author and by collector, consists mainly
of books and articles concerned with languages of
Mexico and Yucatan. Brief annotations, with a language index at the end. Later reprinted as vol. 8 of
his Obras (1898).

55. Gómez Naranjo, Pedro A. "Escritores de Guatemala."
Revista de América (Bogota), vol. 15, no. 43-44
(1948), p. 135-140.
A bibliographical essay on the literary works of José
Milla, Gomez Carrillo, M. Soto Hall, Arévalo Mar-

tinez, Flavio Herrera, M.A. Asturias, C. Wyld Ospina and Amalia Chevez.

56. Gómez Robles, J. A Statement of the Laws of Guatemala in Matters Affecting Business. Washington,
D.C., Pan American Union, 1951 (1st suppl., 1956;
2nd suppl., 1959).
A general guide interpreting existing laws and practices, arranged by broad subjects, such as: immi-
gration, commerce, copyright, etc. The first supplement updates the basic volume; the second updates
and adds a commentary on the labor code, treaties,
etc.

57. Goubaud Carrera, Antonio. "Del conocimiento del indio
guatemalteca." Revista de Guatemala, Año 1, no. 1
(1945), p. 86-104.
A bibliographical essay, the first part of which covers
anthropology and related subjects from 1884 through
1930, with a general discussion. The second part,
covering 1930 through 1945, is arranged by geographical area in Guatemala, with a discussion of the writings on each area. A bibliography by author appears
at the end.

58. El Grafico. Morning and evening daily newspaper,
Guatemala City. Edited by Hector Aguirre.

59. Gt. Britain. Commercial Relations and Exports Department. Guatemala, Economic and Commercial
Conditions. London, HMSO, 1922-1937; 1951-1956.
An irregular annual, published by various departments of the British government over the years and
made up of statistical analysis of the trade, including
charts with an index by country and type of trade with
that country. Much on natural resources, social conditions, foreign trade, etc. Very useful for background on commercial happenings. See also item 161.

60. Griscom, Ludlow. The Distribution of Bird-Life in
Guatemala, a contribution of a study of the origin of
Central American bird-life. New York, American
Museum of Natural History, Bulletin 64, 1932.
Gives source of first description, Latin name (ar-
ranged by species), range and a comment. The book
has an alphabetical index, two maps and several
photos of the terrain.

61. Grismer, Raymond L. A New Bibliography of the Literature of Spain and Spanish America ... vols. 1-7
(1941-1946). A through Cez, only, published.
Arranged by author, this is an extensive listing of
journal articles, pamphlets and books on anthropology,

art, economics, education, history, law, music, etc.
Published in Minneapolis (v. 1-4), St. Louis (v. 5),
and Dubuque, Iowa (v. 6-7). Although completed only through Cez, the section on Central America (p.
1782-1805) contains a considerable amount of material on Guatemala.

62. Gropp, Arthur E. Guide to Libraries and Archives in
Central America and the West Indies, Panama, Ber-
muda, and British Guiana. New Orleans, Tulane
University Press, 1941.
Arranged by country (Guatemala, p. 359-462) with
subdivision by city. A brief description is given of
the libraries in each city, type of material and pa-
trons, and budget. Archives are described by type
of manuscripts. Also included is a listing of book
binders, book dealers, and printers.

63. Guatemala. Archivo general del gobierno. Boletín.
T. 1-11 (1935-1945).
Articles from the archives illustrating the history of
Guatemala. One of the more valuable historical pub-
lications from the area.

64. Guatemala. Archivo general del gobierno. Indice de
los documentos existentes en el archivo general del
gobierno. Guatemala, vol. 1 (1936). Only vol. pub.
A preliminary shelf listing of documents, arranged
chronologically under issuing agency, made up of descriptive titles. Subject index. First published in
the Boletin del Archivo general del gobierno, vol. 1
(1935).

65. Guatemala. Archivo general del gobierno. Indice del
archivo de la enseñanza superior de Guatemala, por
E.C. Irunguray. Guatemala, Editorial Universitario
no. 45, 1962.
A shelf listing of documents, arranged chronologically under issuing agency and giving title, author, date,
with a general subject guide. Not too useful unless
the issuing agency and author of the document are
known.

66. Guatemala. Ayuntamiento. Collección de documentos
antiguos del archivo del ayuntamiento de la ciudad de
Guatemala. Guatemala, Imprenta de Luna, 1857.
A general collection of documents (1532-1782) compiled by Rafael de Arevalo, concerned with administration, treatment of the Indians, establishment of
the university, the earthquakes of 1717 and 1773 and
the move of the capital in 1776. Included also are
letters of various leaders, from Alvarado through the

19th century. There is no table of contents or general index. Later reprinted as a lengthy appendix to the third edition of Isagoge historica apologetica de las Indias Occidentales (Guatemala, 1935).

67. Guatemala. Biblioteca nacional. Boletín de la biblioteca nacional de Guatemala, año 1-9 (1932-1941). A general review of articles on history, literature and biographies, with occasional lists of items added to the Biblioteca; see año 8, nos. 2, 3, and 4 for "Bibliografia Guatemalteca." Continued as: Bolletin de museos y bibliotecas. Series 2, año 1-4 (1941-45). Less history than the above, more on fine arts. Continued as: Boletín de la biblioteca nacional, series 3, año 1 (1945). Only volume published, primarily literary reviews.

68. Guatemala. Biblioteca nacional. Catálogo de la biblioteca nacional. Guatemala, 1932. Section one arranged by general subjects; section two, by countries of Central America (Guatemala, p. 179-226). A general catalog, not extensive; no manuscripts.

69. Guatemala. Biblioteca nacional. "Lista de la prensa del pais existente en la biblioteca nacional de Guatemala." Boletín de la Biblioteca nacional, año 1, no. 2 (1932), p. 37-39. A listing by title of newspaper holdings of the national library, giving the place of publication and issues held in 1932.

70. Guatemala. Biblioteca nacional. Revista. Vol. 1 (1962)- quarterly. General review of the publishing and literary activities in Guatemala, scholarly articles, many lists and bibliographies.

71. Guatemala. Constitutions. Las constituciones de Guatemala, por Luis Mariñas Otero. Madrid, Instituto de estudios politícos. Las constituciones Hispanoamericanas, no. 11, 1958. The texts of constitutions and their revisions from 1823 through 1956, with an extensive discussion of the influences on constitutional development.

72. Guatemala. Dirección general de caminos. Guia kilometrica de la república de Guatemala. 2d. ed. Guatemala, Tipografía nacional, 1949. 2 vols. Vol. one lists national highways (nos. 1-22), and includes a description of each road, a fold-out map of each, showing towns and altitudes with smaller maps giving routes through wayside communities. An index

by place names is at the end of the volume. Vol.
two is arranged by department, giving a general description of roads, towns connected, distances between settlements, and total length of the roads. No
maps or index for vol. two.

73. Guatemala. Dirección general de cartografía. Diccionario geográfico de Guatemala. Guatemala, 1961-
62. 2 vols. and 2-vol. supplement (1968) published
by the Instituto geográfico nacional, covering 1961-
1964.
A gazeteer of place names, giving size or political
designations (aldea, ciudad, etc.), population and distance from nearest urban center. Usually includes
altitude, longitude and latitude. Excellent geographical tool. The supplement contains more historical
data on the various significant place names.

74. Guatemala. Dirección general de estadística. De-
partamentios, municipios, ciudades, villas, pueblos,
aldeas, y caserios de la república de Guatemala.
Guatemala, 1953.
A general list of the various political divisions and
communities, with an index by departamento and
municipio. No statistical data; gives only the political unit to which each community belongs.

75. Guatemala. Dirección general de estadística. Estadística, nos. 1-13 (Sept. 1950-Dec. 1956).
See its Trimestre estadística, 1957-

76. Guatemala. Dirección general de estadística. Sexto
censo de población, Abril 18 de 1950. Guatemala,
1957.
Includes a breakdown by urban/rural, families, age,
marital status, ethnic group, place of birth, citizenship, residence, religion, language spoken at home,
education, profession, and income. Most complete
census to date: first in 1776; second in 1880; third
in 1893; fourth, 1921, fifth, 1940. There was an
earlier attempt by the Spanish crown in 1740; see the
survey below by G. Martinez de Perada. In 1964, a
population census was made but no published report
has been issued to date, beyond a tabulation for Guatemala City and a 5 per cent sampling from the nation
as a whole. In 1969, a hand tabulation was published
which gives population breakdown at municipio level.

77. Guatemala. Dirección general de estadística. Trimestre estadística, no. 1 (1957)-   quarterly.
Statistical data on income and living costs, industrial
activity, and productivity, basically price indexes.

Earlier (1950-1956) entitled, Estadística; later published as a monthly Boletín estadística and changed to a quarterly in 1965.

78. Guatemala. Dirección general de mineria e hidrocarburos. Análisis de muestras minerales de Guatemala. Guatemala, Serie de divulgación técnica, no. 5, 1966. A sampling of minerals arranged by department, listing the municipios and the minerals found in each, with an analysis breakdown of each mineral.

79. Guatemala. Dirección general de mineria e hidrocarburos. Nomina de muestras minerales de Guatemala. Guatemala, Serie de divulgación técnica, no. 4, 1965. A listing of mineral samples arranged alphabetically by type of mineral, giving the department and municipio in which the mineral is found. The index is arranged by department, then municipio, giving the mineral found in each.

80. Guatemala. Estado mayor del ejército. Escalafón general de los señores generales, jefes, y oficiales del ejército de la república. Guatemala, Tipografía nacional, 1934. A list of military officers by military branch; gives rank, age, marital status, residence, specialty and date entering service.

81. Guatemala. Instituto Guatemalteco-Americano. Books about Guatemala, A Bibliography of Books in English and Spanish. Guatemala, IGA, 1960. A 34-page listing, compiled by Gonzalo Dardón Córdova. Arranged by subjects, divided by language. Brief, but useful.

82. Guatemala. Ministerio de educación pública. Colección bibliográfica del III centenario de la introducción de la imprenta en Centroamericana. Guatemala, José de Piñeda Ibarra, 1960-1963. 10 vols. in 11. An excellent set of guides making up the national bibliography of Guatemala, as published by the Guatemalan government. Covers well the press output and press history from 1660 through 1960, arranged by the year of publication. A must for serious students. See under the individual authors for descriptions. Vol. 1, J. E. O'Ryan; vol. 2, J. T. Medina, vol. 3-10, G. Valenzuela.

83. Guatemala. Museo Nacional de Antropología. Bibliography of a Collection of Books pertaining to the archaeology, ethnology and anthropology of Mexico, Guatemala and Central America, with particular reference to Guatemala. Presented by Matilda Geddings Gray to

the Museo Nacional. San Francisco, Grabhorn Press,
1948.
A special printing of the private library of M. G.
Gray which was presented, as a gift, to the Museo
Nacional de Antropologia de Guatemala. It pertains
mostly to the Mayan culture of Central America,
with considerable on anthropology in general. Also
contains full page reproductions of various title pages
and maps. A useful bibliography, limited only by its
rarity in numbers, making the item difficult to find
or use.

84. Guatemala. Tipografía Nacional. Boletín de tipografía nacional. Año 1 (1951-   ).
A general house organ (monthly); little bibliographical material, except that each issue has one page devoted to listing the national press publications since
1894. Each issue covers about half of one year's
output for the earlier years.

85. Guatemala. Tipografía nacional. Catálogo general de
libros, folletos, y revistas, editados en la Tipografía
nacional de Guatemala desde 1892 hasta 1943. Guatemala, Tipografía nacional, 1944.
Arranged alphabetically by year, with a section for
journals published. Full bibliographical information.
An up-dating supplement (1944-53) was published in
1954 and a second supplement (1954-62) published in
1963.

86. Guatemala. Treaties, etc. Colección de tratados de
Guatemala, formado por Ramón A. Zalazar y Federico S. de Tejada. Guatemala, Tipografía nacional,
1892-1919. 3 vols.
A compilation of complete treaty texts without commentary, arranged by country as follows: vol. 1:
trade and navigation, arranged alphabetically with a
separate section for Central America; vol. 2: general conventions and treaties arranged alphabetically;
vol. 3: special conventions and treaties arranged
alphabetically, with Central America in a special section. Includes treaties of five Central American conferences.

87. Guatemala. Treaties, etc. Colección de tratados de
Guatemala, por José Rodríguez Cerna. Guatemala,
1939-1943. 3 vols. in 4.
Treaty texts without notes or commentaries. Vol. 1:
multilateral treaties, with a section on bilateral
treaties with Central American countries. Vol. 2:
treaties with other American countries, multilateral

and bilateral.   Vol. 3: pt. 1:   bilateral treaties with
European and Asiatic countries.   pt. 2:   treaties
from the first eight Inter-American conferences.   See
also item 140, by Rodriguez Cerna.

88.   Guatemala.   Treaties, etc.   Tratados y convenciones
internacionales vigentes para Guatemala, por José
Luis Mendoza.   Guatemala, 1958-1960.   4 vols.
Treaty texts without commentary; each volume is indexed by type of treaty, and includes a chronological
listing of the treaties.   Vol. 1:   International military treaties, 1884-1949 and 1949-1958.   Vol. 2:
Multilateral Inter-American treaties.   Vol. 3:   Multilateral Central American and regional treaties.   Vol.
4:   Bilateral treaties.

89.   Guatemala.   Universidad de San Carlos.   Editorial
Universitaria.   no. 1 (1949)-
Edited by Roberto Giron Lemus.   Irregular (ca. 10
per year) scholarly monographs, primarily on Guatemalan history and culture.   Set up to make available
in book form the thought and culture of Guatemala
from the university.

90.   Guatemala en cifras.   Guatemala, Dirección general de
Estadística, 1955-
An annual general compilation in chart form, of statistics taken from various published sources covering
the following areas: geography, demography, agriculture and livestock, industrial production and con-
sumption, transportation, international commerce,
price index, annual governmental expenses and income, banking, balance of payments, insurance, social, hospital, work and social security.

91.   Guatemala Indígena.   Guatemala.   no. 1 (1961)-
quarterly.
Published by the Instituto Indigena Nacional, edited
by J. L. Arriola, concerned with the history and culture of Mayan Guatemala.   Continues its earlier
Boletín, series 1 & 2.

92.   El Guatemalteco, diario oficial de la República de
Guatemala.   1886-1931, 1950-
A newspaper printing of the official publications and
official interpretation of events, along with legislative
acts, etc.   Published as the seccion oficial of the
Diario de Centro América (2 epoca, 1931-1950), continued as El Guatemalteco ... 1950-   .   Continues
the volume numbering of the first series (1886-1931).
Edited by Augusto Mulet Descamps.

93.   Handbook of Latin American Studies, a Guide to the

Material Published on Anthropology, Archaeology,
Economics, Geography, History, Law and Literature.
Harvard University Press, 1936-1947; University of
Florida Press, 1948-
An annual subject arrangement of articles, books and
pamphlets, annotated. Each vol. has an index of
varying detail and entries from all countries, in all
languages. A basic guide to published material.

94. Hernández de León, Federico. El libro de las efem-
erides, capítulos de la historia de la América Cen-
tral. Guatemala, Tipografía Sánchez y de Guisse,
1925-1959. 4 vols. plus addenda, 1963, in 2 vols.
A day-by-day journalistic chronology of happenings in
Guatemala from the conquest through the 19th century.
The addenda supplements only the first six months
(January through June) thus far.

95. Herrera, Marta Josefina. Semblanzas (Figuros de
Guatemala). Guatemala, 1966.
A collection of brief popular sketches, with photos:
Rodolfo Robles Valverde; Juan José Ortega; Antonio
Batres Jauregui; Jorge Ubico; Mariano Pacheco Herr-
arte; Cesar Brañas; Rafael Alvarez Ovalle; José
Joaquin Palma; Clemente Marroquin Rojas ...

96. La Hora (Diario independiente).
Daily evening conservative newspaper, Guatemala
City. Founded in 1942; directed by Clemente Morro-
quin Rojas. Weekly supplement called La Hora
Dominical.

97. Horizonte, revista interamericana. Guatemala, no. 1,
1947- irregular, usually quarterly.
Popular articles of historical and cultural interest,
formerly, Nuestra Guatemala, revista ilustrada. Edited by Victor Soto de Avila.

98. Humphreys, Robert A. Latin American History, A
Guide to the Literature in English. London, Oxford
University Press, 1958.
Arranged by country (Guatemala, p. 149-151), the
annotated bibliography covers the colonial period by
general topics. The national period is arranged as
follows: general, special aspects, nineteenth century,
twentieth century, and the Belice dispute.

99. Impacto, organo informativo de La Hora Dominical.
Daily morning conservative newspaper, Guatemala
City. Founded in 1954. Directed by Oscar Morro-
quin Rojas.

100. El Imparcial. Daily evening, conservative news-

paper, Guatemala City.   Edited by David Vela.
Founded in 1922 by Alejandro Córdova.

101.   Indice bibliográfico guatemalteco.   Guatemala, 1951-
52, 1958-60.   Four issues only.   Edited by Gonzalo
Dardón Córdova.
An author, subject index to selected periodicals and
monographs, including an address list to publishing
houses in Guatemala.   A brief but useful national
bibliography and index to material published in Guatemala.

102.   Ireland, Gordon.   Boundaries, Possessions and Conflicts in Central and North America and the Caribbean.   Cambridge, Harvard University Press, 1941.
A guide to boundary conflicts (Guatemala, p. 69-128),
giving a brief historical sketch and the situation or
settlement in map form.   A section at the end lists
treaties of arbitration, subdivided by bipartite treaties and multipartite treaties.

103.   Jones Vargas, Fernando.   Estudio bibliográfico sobre
la sociología rural en Centroamérica.   Costa Rica,
Ciudad Universitaria "Rodrigo Facio," 1964.
An annotated bibliography of books, articles, pamphlets, and theses divided by country.   Useful but not
too comprehensive.

104.   Kunze, Albert F.   Who's Who on the Postage Stamps
of Guatemala.   Washington, D.C., Pan American
Union Philatelic series, no. 11, 1955.
Biographical sketches of persons portrayed on post-
age stamps issued in Guatemala and shown at the
Inter-American exposition of 1944.   Those Guatemal-
ans included are: P. de Alvarado (1485-1541); R.
Alvarez Ovalle (1858-1946), J.R. Barrios (1835-85),
J. Batres Montufar (1809-44), P.E. de Rivera (d.
1684), M. Estrada Cabrera (1857-1924), M. Garcia
Granados (1809-78), R. Landivar (1731-93), J. Milla
(1822-82), L. Montufar (1823-1898), J.M. Orellana
(1872-1926), J.J. Palma (1844-1911), J.M. Reyna
Barrios (1845-98), J. Ubico (1878-1946).

105.   Lamadrid, Lázaro.   "A survey of the historiography
of Guatemala since 1821."   Américas, vol. 8 (Oct.
1951; Jan. 1952), p. 189-202; 305-320.
A bibliographical essay on the development of historical research, arranged by time periods: 1821-
1839; 1839-1871; 1871-1900.   The 20th century is by
general categories: societies, personalities, essay-
ists, political writers and official writers.   An ex-

cellent guide for the serious student.
106. Land, Hugh C. Birds of Guatemala. Lynnewood,
Pa., Livingston Publ. Co., 1970.
Description, with color plates and maps, of birds.
Arranged by species and popular name, indexed, a
bibliography. Each entry carries the popular name,
Latin name, range of the bird, any subspecies, its
status for Guatemala, elevation found, habitat, description and general comments. A Peterson type
guide with more detail, quite useful.
107. Lansing, Marion Florence. Liberators and Heroes
of Mexico and Central America. Boston, Page &
Co., 1942.
Popular sketches with little or no documentation; included are sketches of J. Del Valle; J. Simeon Cañas;
F. Morazán; M. Galez; and J.R. Barrios.
108. Lauerhass, Ludwig, Jr. Communism in Latin America, A Bibliography, the Postwar Years (1945-1960).
Los Angeles, University of California, 1962.
A brief listing by country (Guatemala, p. 52-63) of
articles, books and government publications relating
to the political activities of various leftwing groups.
109. El libro azul de Guatemala, 1915. Relato e historia
sobre la vida de las personas mas prominentes ....
New Orleans, Impreso por Searcy y Pfaff, 1915.
English/Spanish edition, a general directory with descriptions of commercial firms in Guatemala; includes photos, biographies, list by professions and a
general index.
110. Lines, Jorge A. Anthropological Bibliography of
Aboriginal Guatemala-British Honduras. San Jose,
C.R., Tropical Science Center, Occasional paper no.
6, 1967.
Including articles and books from Western countries
with Belice listed separately. Alphabetical arrangement with a preliminary code for each to reflect the
basic approach: A-archaeology, F-folklore (13 categories). Extensive, useful and specialized.
111. McMurtrie, Douglas C. A Preliminary Checklist of
Published Materials relating to the history of printing in Guatemala. Chicago, Club of printing house
craftsmen, 1942.
A brief list of books and articles on printing in Guatemala, taken from U.S. and Guatemalan sources.
112. Maldonado-Koerdell, Manuel. Bibliografía geológica y
paleontológica de América Central. Mexico, Instituto
Panamericano de geografía e historia, publicación no.

204, 1958.
An alphabetical listing of articles and books pertaining to the area, on the general subject of geology and paleontology, with a brief introductory history in Spanish and English. The detailed analytical index (Guatemala, p. 233-237) makes the work extremely valuable.

113. Martínez de Pereda, Guillermo. "Relación geográfica del Valle de Goathemala ... de Escuintla ... de Huehuetenango ... de Totonicapán ... de Atitlán y Tecpanatitlán." Guatemala, Archivo General del gobierno. Boletín. vol. 1, no. 1 (Oct. 1935), p. 7-29.
A general census (1740-1743) carried out by the church, which covered most of present-day Guatemala, except for Petén and Chiquimula. Useful for general information. The various areas were divided geographically and the census taken by the following persons: Valle de Guatemala (Martinez de Pereda); Escuintla (Alonso Crespo); Huehuetenango (José de Olaverreta); Totonicapán (José Antonio de Aldana); Atitlán y Tecpanatitlán (Felipe Manrique de Guzman). Also included are reports from Tegucigalpa (Baltasar Ortiz de Letona) and Costa Rica (Juan Gemmir de Lleonatt).

114. Marure, Alejandro. Efemerides de los hechos notables acaecidos en la república de Centro-América desde el año de 1821 hasta el de 1842. Guatemala, Imprenta de la Paz, 1844. Reprinted in 1895 by Tipografía Nacional.
A chronology of happenings, with presidents listed separately along with cabinet ministers, state governors, military governors, foreign ambassadors, battles and newspapers by the state.

115. Medina, José Toribio. Imprenta en Guatemala. 2d. ed. Guatemala, Tipografía nacional, 1960. 2 vols. Items published in Guatemala are arranged by the year of imprint, then alphabetically under the year. Many notes on size, pagination, material covered. Vol. one covers 1660 through 1799; vol. 2, 1800-1821, with undated items and additions compiled by Gilberto Valenzuela and A. Taracena Flores. This is a reprint of the 1910 edition published in Chile, with the addition of only the addendas.

116. Middle America. New York, Middle American information Bureau. Vol. 1 (March, 1946) only vol. pub.
A bibliography of books and articles arranged by sub-

267 Bibliography

ject, with brief annotations. Of interest to agronomists; brief.

117. Montúfar, Lorenzo. Reseña historia de Centro América. Guatemala, 1878-1888. 7 vols.
A collection of documents on the history of the area, with some historical commentary; includes portraits of leading persons. Each volume has a detailed table of contents, no indexes.

118. Moore, Richard E. "Miguel Ángel Asturias; A Bio-Bibliography," Bulletin of Bibliography, vol. 27, no. 4 (Oct./Dec. 1970), p. 85-90, 107-111.
A brief biography with an extensive listing of works, translations and criticisms.

119. Morley, Sylvanus G. The Inscriptions of Petén. 5 vols. Washington, D.C., Carnegie Institution publication no. 437, 1938.
Vol. 4, p. 423-448: bibliography of general Mayan archaeology containing books, articles and maps relative to the area, some general in nature, from German, French, Spanish and English. Arranged by author.

120. Noguera, Eduardo. "Bibliografía de los códices pre-Colombinos y documentos indígenas posteriores a la conquista." Sociedad de geografía e historia de Guatemala, Anales. Vol. 14, no. 2-3 (1938), p. 230-240; 341-351.
Arranged by the name of the codice, with a bibliography of articles and books on each codice. At the end is a list of important documents on the study of Yucatan, along with a list by Indian nation, of the various codices from each. Frequent illustrations of codice pages.

121. Obiols del Cid, Ricardo. Clasificación preliminar de climas en la República de Guatemala. Guatemala, 1966.
A classification of the climate with a colored map, presented to the Universidad de San Carlos as a thesis. It gives the rainfall, humidity, temperature and extent of the variations in temperature.

122. Okinshevich, Leo A. Latin America in Soviet Writings, 1945-1964, A Bibliography. Vol. 1, 1945-1958; vol. 2, 1959-1964. Vol. 1 published by Library of Congress, (1959); vol. 2, by Johns Hopkins Press (1966).
Arranged by broad subject headings with geographical subdivision by country, it has considerable on Guatemala in the period prior to 1954. Included is an au-

thor index, an index to Soviet reviews of books from
Latin America, and a geographical index.

123. O'Ryan, Juan Enrique. Bibliografía de la imprenta
en Guatemala en los siglos XVII y XVIII. Guatemala,
Imprenta José de Piñeda Ibarra, 1960.
Arranged alphabetically under each year, includes
books, folios, and broadsides, giving descriptions
and frequent title page reproductions, along with the
source for the entry. First published in Santiago,
Chile, in 1897.

124. Ovalle, N. K. Industrial Report on the Republic of
Guatemala. Washington, D. C. Inter-American Development Commission, 1946.
The census (1940) breakdown by department, with a
discussion of transportation facilities, main occupa-
tions, statistical outline of industry and commentary
on potential growth.

125. Pan American Union. Columbus Memorial Library.
Union List of Latin American Newspapers in Li-
braries in the United States. Compiled by Arthur
E. Gropp. Washington, D. C., Pan American Union
Bibliographic series, no. 39, 1953.
Arranged under country by cities (Guatemala, p. 89-
93), gives frequency, beginning date, libraries having
runs and years available.

126. Pan American Union. Department of Economic Affairs. Guatemala, índice anotado de los trabajos
aerofotográficos y los mapas topografías y de re-
cursos naturales. Washington, D. C., 1965.
Maps and surveys with an annotated index in English/
Spanish. Aerial photographic surveys, topographic
mapping, geologic and soil surveys, land capacity and
use, vegetation maps, and index giving area covered,
scales, date, surveyor. Does not include climatologi-
cal or hydrologic maps.

127. Pardo, José Joaquín. Efemerides para escribir la
historia de la muy noble y muy leal ciudad de Santiago de los Caballeros del reino de Guatemala.
Guatemala, Tipografía nacional, 1944.
A chronology of significant days concerned with historical Antigua, beginning August 29, 1541 and ending November 22, 1779. First printed in serial form
by the Sociedad de geografia e historia.

128. Pardo, José Joaquín. "Indice de documentos existentes en el Archivo de Indias de Sevilla, que tienen
interes para Guatemala." Anales de la Sociedad de
Geografía y historia, vol. 16 (1939/1940), p. 401-424.

A brief title list of documents arranged by the shelving order; no index. The arrangement is a loose chronology by the grouping or volume, with no other apparent arrangement.

129. Pardo, José Joaquín. Prontuario de reales cédulas, 1529-1599. Guatemala, Unión Tipografía, 1941. Index to royal decrees found in the Archivo General de Guatemala, which pertain to Central America. It is arranged by the subject of the cedula, with an index by proper names. Only the crux of the cedulas is given, not the complete document. One item may appear under several subject lists. First published in the newspaper, El Imparcial, to supplement the index, Prontuario de todas las reales cedulas, cartas acordadas y ordenes comunicadas a la audiencia del antigua reino de Guatemala desde el año 1600 hasta 1818 (Guatemala, 1857) by Miguel Larreinaga, which was not located by this compiler to inspect and use.

130. Parker, Franklin D. "The Histories and Historians of Central America to 1850." Ph.D. dissertation, University of Illinois, 1951. A critical review of all major works done on Central America, containing analysis of contents; variant editions are mentioned as well as important differences. This is an outstanding piece of historiography on the region.

131. Parra, Manuel German. Bibliografía indigenista de México y Centroamérica, 1850-1950. For M.G. Parra y W. Jiménez Moreno. México, Memoria del Instituto nacional indigenista, vol. 4, 1954. An extensive subject arrangement, primarily for anthropologists, with indexes to persons, places, and language groups. Also included is an outline development of the Indian society.

132. Phillips, Philip Lee. A List of Books, Magazine Articles and Maps Relating to Central America, Including the Republics of Costa Rica, Guatemala, Honduras, Nicaragua, and Salvador, 1800-1900. Compiled for the Bureau of the American Republics. Washington, D.C., Government Printing Office, 1902. An arrangement by country (Guatemala, p. 51-67) primarily of items in English. Many of the items were not examined by the compiler, but taken from other bibliographies. A very useful source for 19th century Guatemala, especially the section on maps.

133. Pilón, Manuel Antonio. Commerical, Industrial and Professional Directory of the Republic of Guatemala.

Guatemala, Centro Editorial, S. A., 1935.
In English/Spanish, with a detailed index by title and
subject. It contains a list of foreign consulates in
Guatemala and members of the Guatemalan consular
service. One of the more useful directories of
Guatemala.

134. Prensa Libre. Liberal daily morning newspaper, except Sunday. Guatemala City.
Founded in 1951. Edited by Pedro Julio Garcia.

135. Quien, diccionario biográfico. Guatemala (Libro de
Oro) vol. 1, 1966.
Projected as an annual publication (only one volume
thus far), contains sketches, some lengthy, of well
known persons in cultural and political activities as
well as in industry, agriculture, commerce and finance. Intended as a future guide to the current
leaders, the sketches usually give birth dates, parent
names, a listing of activities, interests and accom-
plishments. A very good guide to present-day recognized influential persons.

136. Quiñónez, José A. Directorio general de la República de Guatemala. Guatemala, Tipografía Nacional,
1929.
A general compilation of information, including a
brief geo-historical guide; leading agriculturalists, by
department; leading commercial people, by city; governmental personnel, with portraits of most presidents and intellectual leaders; social clubs and members; and a tourist guide.

137. Rey, Julio Adolfo. "Revolution and Liberation: A
Review of Recent Literature on the Guatemalan Situation." Hispanic American Historical Review, vol.
38 (May, 1958), p. 239-255.
A critical review of the political writings concerned
with the revolution of 1954. Several little known documents are discussed in detail. A brief, but useful
guide.

138. Reyes Monroy, José Luis. Bibliografía de los estudios geográficas de la república de Guatemala desde
1574 hasta nuestros dias. Guatemala, José de Piñeda
Ibarra, 1960.
Alphabetical arrangement of travelogues, archaeological explorations, and geo-historical accounts, with a
chronological listing at the end for maps published
prior to 1947.

139. Rodríguez Beteta, Virgilio. "Nuestra bibliografía
colonial." Sociedad de geografía e historia de Guate-

mala. Anales. vol. 2 (1925), p. 83-98; 227-238.
A bibliographical essay on the development of printing, with frequent illustrations of title pages, etc.
The first part relates to the 17th and 18th centuries;
the second part concerns various subjects, as: geography, history, linguistics, poetry, travel, and science.

140. Rodríguez Cerna, José. Nuestro derecho internacional, sinopsis de tratados y anotaciones historicas,
1821-1937. Guatemala, Tipografía nacional, 1938.
Arranged by historical period (Mexican federation,
Central American federation), with the republican
period arranged by type of treaty. Bilateral treaties
are in a separate section. Indexes by type of treaty
and proper names. Only the crux of the treaty is
given, with a running commentary on the important
issues. See also item 87, Colección de tratados.

141. Rodríguez Herrera, Juan Humberto. Guía geográfica
postal. Guatemala, José de Piñeda Ibarra, 1961.
An alphabetical list of settlements and a separate list
for municipios, cabeceras and departamentos, with
fold-out maps of major roads. Departamento charts
give municipios and distance to each cabecera, mail
services, telegraph, telephone and radio services.

142. Sáenz de Santa María, Carmelo. "Una ojeada a la
bibliográfica lingüística guatemalteca." Revista de
Indias, Madrid, vol. 19, no. 76 (1959), p. 255-271.
Arranged by language and subdivided by documents,
dictionaries, grammars, and religious items, with a
commentary on the various editions of the more important items. Also included is a brief linguistic
historiography of the area in general.

143. Salazar, Ramón A. Los hombres de la independencia.
Guatemala, Tipografía nacional, 1899.
Rambling biographical sketches of various leaders, including Arce, Aycinena and Molina. Others were
projected but were never published.

144. Salón 13. Guatemala. Vols. 1-3 (1960-62).
In English and Spanish, published by the Instituto
Guatemalteco-Americano. Articles included poetry,
short stories, drama and essays; good for contemporary literature.

145. Sánchez O., Víctor. Primer directorio de la capital
y guía general de la República de Guatemala, con
anuncios y referencias al comercio, agricultura e industria nacionales. Guatemala. Tipografía Sánchez
y de Guise, 1894.

A brief description of the cultural activities of the
capital city with a listing of public office holders,
tradesmen and professional people. Included is a
large folded map of Guatemala City, with proposed
areas of development, scale 1:10,000 (1894).

146. Sandoval, Lisandro. Semantica guatemalense, o diccionario de Guatemaltequismos. Guatemala, Tipografía nacional, 1941-42. 2 vols.
Vol. 1, A-K, vol. 2, L-Z. A dictionary of words
and idioms peculiar to Guatemala, including mispronunciations.

147. Saville, Marshall Howard. Bibliographic Notes on
Quirigua. New York, Heye Foundation Indian Notes
and Monographs, vol. 1, no. 1, 1919.
An extensive listing by date (1840's through 1917) of
publication of books and articles related to the study
or description of Quirigua, with brief annotations.

148. Schuster, Edward. Guide to the Laws and Legal Literature of Central American Republics. New York,
American Foreign Law Association, Bibliographies of
Foreign Law series, no. 11, 1937.
Arranged by country (Guatemala, p. 43-63) and subdivided by type of law (constitutional, commercial,
military, etc.). A separate section surveys material
relating to the various federations of 1824-38; 1896-
98; and 1921-22. Included is an extensive index with
subject listings by type of law.

149. Silvert, Kalman H. A Study in Government, Guatemala. New Orleans, Tulane University Press, 1954.
A penetrating study of the structure of government in
the municipio, the departamento, and the nation, including a section which reproduces in English the
various constitutions and amendments between 1823
and 1945.

150. Simmons, Charles Shaffer. Clasificación de recono-
cimiento de los suelos de la República de Guatemala.
Guatemala, José de Piñeda Ibarra, 1959.
A guide to soils, arranged by department. For each,
there are charts giving the geographic characteristics,
climate, water sources (with rain tables), crops,
population, transportation system, markets, the
amount of land under cultivation and soil type by
municipio. Besides maps of each department, there
is a pocket containing three folded maps of the republic.

151. Skinner-Klee, Jorge. Legislación indigenista de
Guatemala. Mexico, Instituto indigenista inter-amer-

icano, 1954.
Laws affecting the Indians (the complete article is
given), taken from the constitution of 1945 and arranged by subject, as follows: administrative (founding municipios), alcohol, political rights, education,
official alphabets of the various languages, judicial
rights and procedures, labor laws, land ownership,
and military service.

152. Sociedad de geografía e historia, Guatemala. Anales,
no. 1, 1924+ irregular, usually quarterly.
Much on cultural history, many signed articles.
Colonial history, art and folklore, with some biography. Annual index since 1935, cumulative index vol.
1-22 (1924-47). Edited by Ricardo Castañeda Paganini.

153. Soto de Avila, J. V. Quien es quien en Centro-América y Panamá. 2d. ed. Guatemala, 1954.
Arranged by country (Guatemala, p. 46-173).
Sketches with portraits of leading governmental officials, intellectuals, and businessmen, including non-
citizens of importance. First published in 1944, up-
dated and revised extensively for 1954 publication.

154. Spain. Archivo general de Indias, Seville. Relación
descriptiva de los mapas, planos, etc. de la Audiencia y capitania general de Guatemala existentes en
el Archivo General de Indias, por Pedro Torres
Lanzas. Madrid, Tipografía de la Revista de Archivo,
1903.
Arranged by year (1590-1892). Covers Guatemala,
Salvador, Honduras, Nicaragua, and Costa Rica. Includes frequent illustrations of the city maps and
plans, with map description, including names of the
cartographers. The index includes geographic names
and cartographers.

155. Squier, Ephraim George. Catalogue of the Library of
E. G Squier. Edited by Joseph Sabin to be sold by
auction on Monday, April 24, 1876. New York, C. C.
Shelley, 1876.
This annotated sale catalogue is made up of 2034
items, primarily on Central and South America. In-
cluded is a list of 102 pamphlets and books written by
Squier.

156. Squier, Ephraim George. Monograph of Authors Who
Have Written on the Languages of Central America
and collected vocabularies on composed works in the
native dialects of that country. New York, Richard-
son, 1861. Published in London by Truebner.

Arranged by author, with annotations. Made up
mostly of dictionaries, this bibliography contains a
general discussion of the scholarship of the period.

157. Stoll, Otto. "Nota bibliográfica, obras sobre Guatemala escritas por Otto Stoll, Universidad de Zurich."
Sociedad de geografía e historia de Guatemala, Anales,
vol. XII (1935), pp. 78-79.
German language items on the ethnography of Guatemala, 15 in all.

158. Stuart, L. C. A Checklist of the Herpetofauna of
Guatemala. Ann Arbor, Michigan. Museum of
Zoology publications, no. 122, 1963.
This list of reptiles and amphibians is arranged by
class and order, families, etc., with each entry
carrying the source of the first description, the type,
where found and its range. Indexed, with a map.

159. Taracena Flores, Arturo. "Nuevas adiciones a la imprenta en Guatemala de José Toribio Medina." An-
thropología e historia de Guatemala. Año 2 (Enero,
1950), p. 68-81.
A listing by year of 94 items, mostly manuscripts,
with full bibliographical descriptions, which were
later added to the 2d. edition (1960) of Medina's work.

160. Thompson, Nora B. "Algunos manuscritos guatemaltecos en Filadelfia." Anales de la Sociedad de Geografía e Historia, Guatemala, vol. 23 (1948), p. 3-10.
A bibliographical essay about manuscripts located in
the American Philosophical Society. Included are
copies of the title pages of selected items. Most of
the manuscripts are Spanish to native language dictionaries (11 items).

161. Three-Monthly Economic Review of Central America.
London, Economist Intelligence Unit Ltd., no. 1
(1953)-
A detailed newsletter and economic report (by country)
concerning economics, population, employment, national accounts, finance, mining, fuel, power, agriculture, manufacturing, transport and foreign trade.
Annual supplement since 1955 with appendix covering
Central America as a whole, with trade among the
Central American republics. Formerly called Quarterly Economic Review of Central America; see also
item 59.

162. Tozzer, Alfred M. A Maya Grammar with Bibliography and Appraisement of the Works Noted. Cambridge, Harvard University. Peabody Museum.
Papers, vol. 1, 1921.

Part one consists of a general grammar.   Part two
presents a discussion of existing texts.   Part three
is a bibliographical essay on linguistic studies and
authorities.   Part four is an exhaustive bibliography
of works relating to the Mayan language.   An excellent historical survey of Mayan linguistic studies.

163.   Tristan, José M.   Bibliografia maya yucateca.   Ro-
chester, N. Y.   (mimeographed), 1949.   125 p.
An annotated bibliography for the anthropologist or
archaeologist in Middle America.   Much on pre-conquest Mayas.

164.   Tulane University.   Middle American Research Insti-
tutue.   Library.   An Inventory of the Manuscript Collection of the Department of Middle American Research.   New Orleans, 1937-1944.   4 vols.
Each vol. covers a subject area (v. 1, William Walker papers; v. 2, unpublished letters; v. 3, maps in
the F. D. Hoffman collection; and v. 4, maps) and is
subarranged by physical type (manuscripts, maps,
printed).   Each vol. is well indexed.

165.   United Nations.   Population Division.   The Population
of Central America, Including Mexico, 1950-1980.
Future population estimates by sex and age.   Report
no. 1.   New York, United Nations, 1954.
Charts with three estimates (high, medium and low)
of various aspects of the population, projected through
1980.

166.   U. S. Bureau of the Census.   Guatemala, Summary of
Biostatistics.   Maps and charts, population, natality
and mortality statistics.   Washington, D. C., U. S. Department of Commerce, 1944.
A graphic breakdown by department of the growth of
population between 1900 and 1940, using whatever published accounts that were available.

167.   U. S. Library of Congress.   Latin American Periodicals Currently Received in the Library of Congress
and in the Library of the Department of Agriculture.
Edited by Charmion Shelby.   Washington, D. C., Library of Congress, 1944.
Arranged alphabetically by title, with an index by
country.   Each entry is annotated and signed.

168.   U. S. Office of Geography.   Guatemala, Official Standard Names approved by the United States Board of
Geographic Names.   Washington, D. C., Office of Geography, Gazetteer no. 94, 1965.
An alphabetical listing of place names, giving longi-
tude/latitude, department, and type of settlement.

169. Universidad de San Carlos. no. 1, 1945+ quarterly.
      Edited by Carlos Martinez Duran. Articles and items
      on the culture and criticism of the society through
      creative writing, published by the Facultad de Humani-
      dades of the Universidad de San Carlos.
170. Uriarte, Ramon. Galería poética Centro-Américana,
      colección de poesías de los mejores poetas de la
      América del Centro precedidas de los ligeros apuntes
      biográficos y breves juicios críticos sobre cada uno
      de los autores que la formen. Guatemala, Tipografía
      La Unión, 1888. 3 vols.
      An anthology of poets, mostly Guatemalan, with bio-
      graphical introductions to each.
171. Valázquez Bringas, Esperanza. Indice de escritores,
      por E. Velázquez y R. Heliodoro Valle. Mexico,
      Herrero Hermanos, 1928.
      A general "who's who," giving offices held, place and
      date of birth, and bibliographies. It includes the fol-
      lowing Guatemalans: G. Aleman Belaños (1884-   ),
      R. Arevalo Martinez (1884-   ), J.A. Beteta (1861-
      1930), A. Cordova (1889-1944), J.V. Mejia (1877-
      1945), A. Recinos (1886-1962), A. Rey Soto (1879-
          ), V. Rodriguez Beteta (1885-   ), J.A. Villa-
      corta (1879-   ), C. Wyld Ospina (1881-1956), P.
      Zamos Castellaños (1879-1954).
172. Valenzuela, Gilberto. Bibliografía guatemalteca, cata-
      logo de obras, folletos, etc., publicados en Guate-
      mala desde la independencia hasta el año de 1850.
      Guatemala, 1933. Vol. 1, 1821-1839, only pub-
      lished.
      Arranged by year between 1821 and 1830 only. En-
      tries are annotated. Author index with a 72-page
      addenda to Medina's Imprenta en Guatemala (later
      reprinted as part of the 1960 edition of Medina).
173. Valenzuela, Gilberto. Bibliografia guatemalteca y
      catálogo general de libros, folletos, periódicos,
      revistas, etc., 1821-1860. Guatemala, Imprenta
      José de Piñeda Ibarra, 1961-1962. 3 vols.
      Arranged alphabetically under the year of publica-
      tion, as follows: vol. 1 (1821-30); vol. 2 (1831-40);
      vol. 3 (1841-60). Each entry carries extensive con-
      tent notes in an effort to continue the work of Medina.
      Also included is an annual calendar of events in the
      National Assembly and a list of the presidents and
      ministers. Vols. 4-8 (1861-1960) were compiled by
      G. Valenzuela Reyna.
174. Valenzuela, Gilberto. La imprenta en Guatemala,

algunas adiciones a la obra que con este título público en Santiago de Chile el ilustre literato Don José Toribio Medina. Guatemala, 1933.
Alphabetically arranged under date of imprint (1676 through 1821) with a general index of proper names and presses. Later republished with the 2d. edition of Medina in 1961.

175. Valenzuela Reyna, Gilberto. Bibliografía guatemalteca y catalogo general de libros, folletos, periódicos, revistas, etc., 1861-1960. Guatemala, Imprenta José de Piñeda Ibarra, 1962-1964.
Vol. 4 (1861-1900), vol. 5 (1901-1930), vol. 6 (1931-1940), vol. 7 (1941-1950), vol. 8 (1951-1960). Five vols. of the ten-vol. series Bibliografía guatemalteca (see items 115, 123 and 174).

176. Valenzuela Reyna, Gilberto. Guatemala y sus gobernantes, 1821-1958, recopilación. Guatemala, Ministerio de Educación pública, Biblioteca guatemalteca de cultural popular, vol. 28, 1959.
Arranged chronologically, giving dates of office and usually the first designate (Vice-President) and those filling in while the President was out of the country on business. Includes many portraits, no biographical information.

177. Valle, Rafael Heliodoro. La anexión de Centroamérica a Mexico, documentos y escritos de 1821, 1821-22, 1822, 1823, 1823 a 1828. Mexico, Secretaría de Relaciones exteriores, 1924-1949. 6 vols.
A general collection of documents relative to the federation. Vol. six has a general index of names found in the set. The set appears as a sub-series in the publication, Archivo historico diplomatico Mexicano.

178. Valle, Rafael Heliodoro. "Bibliografia Centro Americana de 1921." Libro y el Pueblo (Mexico), vol. 1 (1922/23), p. 145-147.
A general commentary on publications from and about Central America, arranged by type of publication. A translation of this essay appears in the Hispanic American Historical Review (vol. 8, 1928, p. 125-130) under the title "Central American Bibliographical Output for 1922."

179. Valle, Rafael Heliodoro. Bibliografia de Don José Cecilio del Valle. Mexico, Ediciones de "Número," 1934.
Contains: a brief biography, a bibliography of items written by del Valle (68 items), most with descriptive notes, a listing of pictures of del Valle (11 items),

and a listing of books and articles about him (137 items).

180. Valle, Rafael Heliodoro. Bibliografia maya. Mexico, Instituto Panamericano de geografía e historia, 1938-41.
An alphabetical arrangement of books and articles relating to all aspects of the Mayan life and history, annotated. Following entries for basic works, such as Popol Vuh, are listings of commentaries. Issued as appendix to vols. 1-5 (1937-41) of the Boletín bibliográfico de antropología e historia.

181. Valle, Rafael Heliodoro. "El folklore en la literatura de Centro America." Journal of American Folklore, vol. 36, no. 140 (April-June, 1923), p. 105-134.
An annotated bibliography of journal articles and monographs.

182. Valle Matheu, Jorge del. Guía sociogeografía de Guatemala, con referencia a las condiciones de vida. Guatemala, Tipografía nacional, 1956.
A guide to the municipios, arranged by departamento; describes: crops, population, industries, roads, and community facilities available.

183. Vela, David. "Bibliografía guatemalteca, compilaciones hechos hasta el presente y servicios que presten al lector curioso y al estudioso." Guatemala Biblioteca nacional, Boletín. Año 8 (1940), p. 161-166.
A discussion of the development of scholarship, based on a commentary of standard works.

184. Villacorta Calderón, José Antonio. "Bibliografía de la lengua maya y de los mayances guatemaltecas." In Primer centenario de la sociedad mexicana de geografía y estadística. Mexico, 1933, p. 71-104.
After a lengthy bibliographical essay on the outstanding early language studies, the main bibliography is arranged by language studied and further broken down into general subjects. The languages studied are: Cakchiquel, Quiché, miscellaneous native dialects, and Pokoman.

185. Villacorta Calderón, José Antonio. Bibliografía guatemalteca. Exposiciones abiertas en el salón de historia y bellas artes del Museo Nacional en los meses de noviembre de 1939, 1940, 1941 y 1942. Guatemala, Tipografía nacional, 1944.
A catalog of a national exposition, containing title pages of important works and portraits of intellectual leaders. This work is an outstanding example of fine

press printing. The four parts of the catalog are arranged as follows: (1) Monographs, by year from 1660 through 1860; (2) Engravings, by subject, published between 1660 and 1860; (3) Periodicals from 1729 through 1929, arranged by period; and (4) Books since 1860 (through 1940), arranged by author. An addenda was published in the Revista de Museo Nacional de Guatemala in 1946.

186. Villacorta Calderón, José Antonio. "Ensayo sobre una bibliografía geográfico-histórica de Guatemala." Sociedad de geografía e historia de Guatemala. Anales. vol. 2 (1925), p. 99-111.
A discussion of books written before 1773, arranged chronologically. Extensive notes and criticisms on each.

187. Villacorta Calderón, José Antonio. "Nuestras exposiciones bibliográficas y la obra publicada." Revista de Museo nacional de Guatemala. Epoca 3, no. 3 (July-Sept., 1946) p. 75-102.
An addenda of additions and corrections to the author's Bibliografía guatemalteca ...

188. Viñaza, Cipriano Muñoz y Manzano, Conde de La. Bibliografía española de lenguas indigenas de America. Madrid, Sucesores de Rivadeneyra, 1892.
A list of dictionaries, grammars, and other books translated into one of the Indian languages of America from Spanish or Latin. The first part is arranged by year of publication, 16th, 17th, 18th, and 19th centuries; the second part, alphabetically by author, under the century. Indices by language, author, translator, and titles of anonymous works. Pages xix through xxv list the bibliographies from which the above bibliography is taken.

189. Wauchope, Robert. Ten Years of Middle American Archaeology, annotated bibliography and news summary, 1948-1957. Tulane University, Middle American Research Institute, publication no. 28, 1961.
Arranged by author; includes books and articles mostly in English and Spanish. Brief subject index.

190. Who's Who in Latin America, a biographical dictionary of notable living men and women of Latin America. 3d. edition, edited by Ronald Hilton. Stanford University Press, 1945-1951. 7 vols.
Arranged by geographical area (vol. 2, Central America and Panama), it contains brief, factual sketches of political and intellectual leaders on the contemporary scene, with cross-references from pseudonyms.

There are 189 sketches covering Guatemala.   The
1st (1935) and 2d (1941) editions were one-vol. works,
edited by P.M. Martin.   Many sketches from the 1st
and 2d editions do not appear in the 3d.

191.   Williams, Mary Wilhelmine.   Cartographical and Geographical Report Bearing Upon the Honduran-Guatemalan Boundary Questions [with] Reply by Dr. Mary
W. Williams to remarks by counsel for Guatemala in
his memorandum on the economic survey report of
December, 1919, regarding cartographical evidence
submitted by Honduras.   Washington, D.C., 1918-
1920.
"Anexo informe cartografico" to accompany 99 maps
on the boundary question, in Spanish/English: an extensive list and discussion of maps relating to Central
American boundaries.

192.   Wilson, Charles Morrow.   Books About Middle Amer-
ica, A Selected Bibliography.   New York, Middle
American Information Bureau conducted by the United
Fruit Company, 1943.
Arranged by country, an annotated guide to publica-
tions in English, with the emphasis on travelogues.
Quite brief.

193.   Woodbridge, Hensley C.   "Central American Spanish,
A Bibliography (1940-1953)," Revista Interamericana
de Bibliografía, vol. 6, no. 2 (1956), p. 103-115.
Guatemala (p. 107-110), a supplement to Nichols' general study (see item 119).   Eleven articles and books
concerned with linguistics in Guatemala are briefly
annotated.

194.   Woolrich B., M.A. Bibliografía sobre Belice.   Mexico,
Vargas Rea, 1957.
A general bibliography of books and articles with por-
tions on Belice.   Some maps and travelogues.   Considerable on the boundary question.

195.   Zimmerman, Irene.   "Central America, Bibliography,
Indexes, Guides." The Caribbean: the Central American area.   Series 1, vol. XI (1960), p. 345-378.
Guatemala, p. 373-375.   An annotated bibliography of
general reference books on the area, most useful for
contemporary literature.

SUBJECT INDEX TO THE BIBLIOGRAPHY

This index does not include material from the dictionary portion.   Citations to the essay preceding the item-

numbered bibliography are shown by a dagger (†). The re-
maining items are indexed by the item number. No entries
appear under the article (el, la, los, las) unless a part of
the person's surname.